A Basic Guide To
Exporting

U.S. D E P A R T M E N T O F C O M M E R C E

WORLD
TRADE
PRESS®

Resources for International Trade

1505 Fifth Avenue
San Rafael, California 94901

Library of Congress Cataloging-in-Publication Data

A Basic guide to exporting.
        p.   cm.
   Includes bibliographical references.
   ISBN 0-9631864-9-3 : $16.50
    1. Export marketing- -United States- -Handbooks, manuals, etc.
  2. Export sales- -United States- -Handbooks, manuals, etc.
  HF1416.5.B37   1994
  658.8'48- -dc20
                                         93-50658
                                             CIP

Acknowledgments

In addition to the numerous trade-related offices of the Department of Commerce, a wide range of other U.S. government agencies provide information to U.S. companies in their efforts to export both products and services. They include the following:

Department of State
Department of the Treasury
Department of Defense
Department of Agriculture
Department of Labor
Department of Transportation
Department of Energy
Office of Management and Budget
Office of the U.S. Trade Representative
Council of Economic Advisors
Environmental Protection Agency
Small Business Administration
Agency for International Development
Export-Import Bank of the United States
Overseas Private Investment Corporation
U.S. Trade and Development Program
U.S. Information Agency

Various state agencies, associations, private sector organizations, and individual companies, as well as many of the above-mentioned U.S. government agencies, have reviewed sections of *A Basic Guide to Exporting* and contributed their specialized knowledge. These include the following:

American Bankers Association, Washington, D.C.
California Export Finance Office, Los Angeles, California
Colorado International Capital Corporation, Denver, Colorado
C&S Sovran Corporation, Atlanta, Georgia
Federal Express Corporation, Memphis, Tennessee
Hatteras International, High Point, North Carolina
Hosford International, Erie, Pennsylvania
International Trade Development, Inc., Fairfax, Virginia
KSK Communications, Ltd., Tysons Corner, Virginia
Minnesota Trade Office, St. Paul, Minnesota
National Association of State Development Agencies, Washington, D.C.
National Customs Brokers & Forwarders Association of America, Inc., New York City, New York
Seattle Trade International, Seattle, Washington
South Carolina Jobs & Economic Development Authority, Columbia, South Carolina
Wells International, Pearblossom, California

Table of contents

Part B. Making the sale

Part C. After the sale

Appendices

Introduction

U.S. exports and the economy

Exports have become an engine of growth for the U.S. economy. Between 1986 and 1990, U.S. merchandise exports contributed more than 40 percent to the rise in Gross National Product (GNP). In 1990 alone, nearly 84 percent of U.S. GNP growth was due to exports, which totaled a record high of $394 billion.

The result of the increase of U.S. exports in the late 1980s is a significantly lower trade deficit and, more important, 2 million new jobs attributed to exports. The U.S. Department of Commerce estimates that for every $45,000 in export sales one job is created – more than double the rate of jobs created by domestic sales.

Today, many firms export occasionally but want exporting fully integrated into their marketing plans. Others export regularly to one or two markets and want to expand into additional countries.

There is tremendous potential for U.S. business to become more active in exporting. Just 15 percent of U.S. exporters account for 85 percent of the value of U.S.-manufactured exports. One-half of all exporters sell in only one foreign market. Fewer than 20 percent of exporters – less than 3 percent of U.S. companies overall – export to more than five markets.

Ten keys to export success

There is profit to be made by U.S. firms in exports. The international market is more than four times larger than the U.S. market. Growth rates in many overseas markets far outpace domestic market growth. And meeting and beating innovative competitors abroad can help companies keep the edge they need at home.

There are also real costs and risks associated with exporting. It is up to each company to weigh the necessary commitment against the potential benefit.

Ten important recommendations for successful exporting should be kept in mind:

1. Obtain qualified export counseling and develop a master international marketing plan before starting an export business. The plan should clearly define goals, objectives, and problems encountered.

2. Secure a commitment from top management to overcome the initial difficulties and financial requirements of exporting. Although the early delays and costs involved in exporting may seem difficult to justify in comparison with established domestic sales, the exporter should take a long-range view of this process and carefully monitor international marketing efforts.

3. Take sufficient care in selecting overseas distributors. The complications involved in overseas communications and transportation require international distributors to act more independently than their domestic counterparts.

4. Establish a basis for profitable operations and orderly growth. Although no overseas inquiry should be ignored, the firm that acts mainly in response to unsolicited trade leads is trusting success to the element of chance.

5. Devote continuing attention to export business when the U.S. market booms. Too many companies turn to exporting when business falls off in the United States. When domestic business starts to boom again, they neglect their export trade or relegate it to a secondary position.

6. Treat international distributors on an equal basis with domestic counterparts. Companies often carry out institutional advertising campaigns, special discount offers, sales incentive programs, special credit term programs, warranty offers, and so on in the U.S. market but fail to make similar offers to their international distributors.

7. Do not assume that a given market technique and product will automatically be successful in all countries. What works in Japan may fall flat in Saudi Arabia. Each market has to be treated separately to ensure maximum success.

8. Be willing to modify products to meet regulations or cultural preferences of other countries. Local safety and security codes as well as import restrictions cannot be ignored by foreign distributors.

9. Print service, sale, and warranty messages in locally understood languages. Although a distributor's top management may speak English, it is unlikely that all sales and service personnel have this capability.

10. Provide readily available servicing for the product. A product without the necessary service support can acquire a bad reputation quickly.

Using *A Basic Guide to Exporting*

A Basic Guide to Exporting is designed to help U.S. firms learn the costs and risks associated with exporting and develop a strategy for exporting. The 10 keys to export success that have been mentioned will be explored, along with ways to avoid the pitfalls and roadblocks that may be encountered. Five appendixes are provided for reference: I, Export Glossary; II, Directory of Federal Export Assistance; III, State and Local Sources of Assistance; IV, U.S. and Overseas Contacts for Major Foreign Markets; and V, Selected Bibliography.

This guide discusses what decisions need to be made and where to get the knowledge to make those decisions. Although it is a publication of the U.S. Department of Commerce, it directs readers to sources of assistance throughout the federal and state governments as well as the private sector.

Before the sale

Part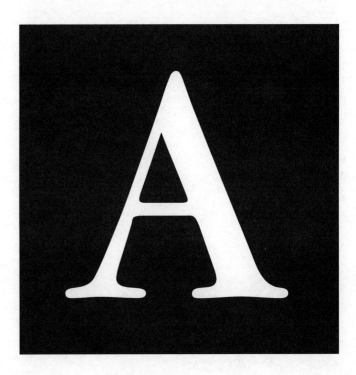

Export strategy

1

Assessing a product's export potential

There are several ways to gauge the overseas market potential of products and services. (For ease of reading, products are mentioned more than services in this guide, but much of the discussion applies to both.) One of the most important ways is to assess the product's success in domestic markets. If a company succeeds at selling in the U.S. market, there is a good chance that it will also be successful in markets abroad, wherever similar needs and conditions exist.

In markets that differ significantly from the U.S. market, some products may have limited potential. Those differences may be climate and environmental factors, social and cultural factors, local availability of raw materials or product alternatives, lower wage costs, lower purchasing power, the availability of foreign exchange (hard currencies like the dollar, the British pound, and the Japanese yen), government import controls, and many other factors. If a product is successful in the United States, one strategy for export success may be a careful analysis of why it sells here, followed by a selection of similar markets abroad. In this way, little or no product modification is required.

If a product is not new or unique, low-cost market research may already be available to help assess its overseas market potential (see chapter 3 for more information on market research techniques and resources). In addition, international trade statistics (available in many local libraries) can give a preliminary indication of overseas markets for a particular product by showing where similar or related products are already being sold in significant quantities. One of the best sources for U.S. export-import statistics is the National Trade Data Bank (NTDB), which can be accessed at many U.S. Department of Commerce district offices across the country.

If a product is unique or has important features that are hard to duplicate abroad, chances are good for finding an export market. For a unique product, competition may be nonexistent or very slight, while demand may be quite high.

Finally, even if U.S. sales of a product are now declining, sizeable export markets may exist, especially if the product once did well in the United States but is now losing market share to more technically advanced products. Countries that are less developed than the United States may not need state-of-the-art technology and may be unable to afford the most sophisticated and expensive products. Such markets may instead have a surprisingly healthy demand for U.S. products that are older or that are considered obsolete by U.S. market standards.

Making the export decision

Once a company determines it has exportable products, it must still consider other factors, such as the following:

- What does the company want to gain from exporting?

- Is exporting consistent with other company goals?

- What demands will exporting place on the company's key resources – management and personnel, production capacity, and finance – and how will these demands be met?

- Are the expected benefits worth the costs, or would company resources be better used for developing new domestic business?

A more detailed list of questions is shown in table 1-1. Answers to these questions can help a company not only decide whether or not to export but also determine what methods of exporting should be initially used.

The value of planning

Many companies begin export activities haphazardly, without carefully screening markets or options for market entry. While these companies may or may not have a measure of success, they may overlook better export opportunities. In the event that early export efforts are unsuccessful because of poor planning, the company may even be misled into abandoning exporting altogether. Formulating an export strategy based on good information and proper assessment increases the chances that the best options will be chosen, that resources will be used effectively, and that efforts will consequently be carried through to completion.

The purposes of the export plan are, first, to assemble facts, constraints, and goals and, second, to create an action statement that takes all of these into account. The statement includes specific objectives; it sets forth time schedules for implementation; and it marks milestones so that the degree of success can be measured and help motivate personnel.

The first draft of the export plan may be quite short and simple, but it should become more detailed and complete as the planners learn more about exporting and their company's competitive position. At least the following ten questions should ultimately be addressed:

1. What products are selected for export development? What modifications, if any, must be made to adapt them for overseas markets?

2. What countries are targeted for sales development?

3. In each country, what is the basic customer profile? What marketing and distribution channels should be used to reach customers?

4. What special challenges pertain to each market (competition, cultural differences, import controls, etc.), and what strategy will be used to address them?

5. How will the product's export sales price be determined?

6. What specific operational steps must be taken and when?

7. What will be the time frame for implementing each element of the plan?

8. What personnel and company resources will be dedicated to exporting?

9. What will be the cost in time and money for each element?

10. How will results be evaluated and used to modify the plan?

One key to developing a successful plan is the participation of all personnel who will be involved in the exporting process. All aspects of an export plan should be agreed upon by those who will ultimately execute them.

A clearly written marketing strategy offers six immediate benefits:

1. Because written plans display their strengths and weaknesses more readily, they are of great help in formulating and polishing an export strategy.

2. Written plans are not as easily forgotten, overlooked, or ignored by those charged with executing them. If deviation from the original plan occurs, it is likely to be due to a deliberate choice to do so.

3. Written plans are easier to communicate to others and are less likely to be misunderstood.

4. Written plans allocate responsibilities and provide for an evaluation of results.

5. Written plans can be of help in seeking financing. They indicate to lenders a serious approach to the export venture.

6. Written plans give management a clear understanding of what will be required and thus help to ensure a commitment to exporting. In fact, a written plan signals that the decision to export has already been made.

This last advantage is especially noteworthy. Building an international business takes time; it is usually months, sometimes even several years, before an exporting company begins to see a return on its investment of time and money. By committing to the specifics of a written plan, top management can make sure that the firm will finish what it begins and that the hopes that prompted its export efforts will be fulfilled.

The planning process and the result

A crucial first step in planning is to develop broad consensus among key management on the company's goals, objectives, capabilities, and constraints. Answering the questions listed in table 1-1 is one way to start.

The first time an export plan is developed, it should be kept simple. It need be only a few pages long, since important market data and planning elements may not yet be available. The initial planning effort itself gradually generates more information and insight that can be incorporated into more sophisticated planning documents later.

From the start, the plan should be viewed and written as a management tool, not as a static document. For instance, objectives in the plan should be compared with actual results as a measure of the success of different strategies. Furthermore, the company should not hesitate to modify the plan and make it more specific as new information and experience are gained.

A detailed plan is recommended for companies that intend to export directly. Companies choosing indirect export methods may require much simpler plans. An outline of an export plan is presented in table 1-2.

Approaches to exporting

The way a company chooses to export its products can have a significant effect on its export plan and specific marketing strategies. The basic distinction among approaches to exporting relates to a company's level of involvement in the export process. There are at least four approaches, which may be used alone or in combination:

1. *Passively filling orders from domestic buyers who then export the product.* These sales are indistinguishable from other domestic sales as far as the original seller is concerned. Someone else has decided that the product in question meets foreign demand. That party takes all the risk and handles all of the exporting details, in some cases without even the awareness of the original seller. (Many companies take a stronger interest in exporting when they discover that their product is already being sold overseas.)

2. *Seeking out domestic buyers who represent foreign end users or customers.* Many U.S. and foreign corporations, general contractors, foreign trading companies, foreign government agencies, foreign distributors and retailers, and others in the United States purchase for export. These buyers are a large market for a wide variety of goods and services. In this case a company may know its product is being exported, but it is still the buyer who assumes the risk and handles the details of exporting.

3. *Exporting indirectly through intermediaries.* With this approach, a company engages the services of an

intermediary firm capable of finding foreign markets and buyers for its products. Export management companies (EMCs), export trading companies (ETCs), international trade consultants, and other intermediaries can give the exporter access to well-established expertise and trade contacts. Yet, the exporter can still retain considerable control over the process and can realize some of the other benefits of exporting, such as learning more about foreign competitors, new technologies, and other market opportunities.

4. *Exporting directly.* This approach is the most ambitious and difficult, since the exporter personally handles every aspect of the exporting process from market research and planning to foreign distribution and collections. Consequently, a significant commitment of management time and attention is required to achieve good results. However, this approach may also be the best way to achieve maximum profits and long-term growth. With appropriate help and guidance from the Department of Commerce, state trade offices, freight forwarders, international banks, and other service groups, even small or medium-sized firms, can export directly if they are able to commit enough staff time to the effort. For those who cannot make that commitment, the services of an EMC, ETC, trade consultant, or other qualified intermediary are indispensable.

Approaches number 1 and 2 represent a substantial proportion of total U.S. sales, perhaps as much as 30 percent of U.S. exports. They do not, however, involve the firm in the export process. Consequently, this guide concentrates on approaches 3 and 4. (There is no single source or special channel for identifying domestic buyers for overseas markets. In general, they may be found through the same means that U.S. buyers are found, for example, trade shows, mailing lists, industry directories, and trade associations.)

If the nature of the company's goals and resources makes an indirect method of exporting the best choice, little further planning may be needed. In such a case, the main task is to find a suitable intermediary firm that can then handle most export details. Firms that are new to exporting or are unable to commit staff and funds to more complex export activities may find indirect methods of exporting more appropriate.

Using an EMC or other intermediary, however, does not exclude all possibility of direct exporting for the firm. For example, a U.S. company may try exporting directly to such "easy" nearby markets as Canada, Mexico, or the Bahamas while letting its EMC handle more ambitious sales to Egypt or Japan. An exporter may also choose to gradually increase its level of direct exporting later, after experience has been gained and sales volume appears to justify added investment.

For more information on different approaches to exporting and their advantages and disadvantages, see chapter 4. Consulting advisers before making these decisions can be helpful. The next chapter presents information on a variety of organizations that can provide this type of help – in many cases, at no cost.

Table 1-1.
Management Issues Involved in the Export Decision

Management objectives

- What are the company's reasons for pursuing export markets? Are they solid objectives (e.g., increasing sales volume or developing a broader, more stable customer base) or are they frivolous (e.g., the owner wants an excuse to travel)?

- How committed is top management to an export effort? Is exporting viewed as a quick fix for a slump in domestic sales? Will the company neglect its export customers if domestic sales pick up?

- What are management's expectations for the export effort? How quickly does management expect export operations to become self-sustaining? What level of return on investment is expected from the export program?

Experience

- With what countries has business already been conducted, or from what countries have inquiries already been received?

- Which product lines are mentioned most often?

- Are any domestic customers buying the product for sale or shipment overseas? If so, to what countries?

- Is the trend of sales and inquiries up or down?

- Who are the main domestic and foreign competitors?

- What general and specific lessons have been learned from past export attempts or experiences?

Management and personnel

- What in-house international expertise does the firm have (international sales experience, language capabilities, etc.)?

- Who will be responsible for the export department's organization and staff?

- How much senior management time (a) should be allocated and (b) could be allocated?

- What organizational structure is required to ensure that export sales are adequately serviced?

- Who will follow through after the planning is done?

Production capacity

- How is the present capacity being used?

- Will filling export orders hurt domestic sales?

- What will be the cost of additional production?

- Are there fluctuations in the annual work load? When? Why?

- What minimum order quantity is required?

- What would be required to design and package products specifically for export?

Financial capacity

- What amount of capital can be committed to export production and marketing?

- What level of export department operating costs can be supported?

- How are the initial expenses of export efforts to be allocated?

- What other new development plans are in the works that may compete with export plans?

- By what date must an export effort pay for itself?

Table 1-2.
Sample Outline for an Export Plan

Table of Contents

Executive Summary (one or two pages maximum)

Introduction: Why This Company Should Export

Part I – Export Policy Commitment Statement

Part II – Situation/Background Analysis

- Product or Service
- Operations
- Personnel and Export Organization
- Resources of the Firm
- Industry Structure, Competition, and Demand

Part III – Marketing Component

- Identifying, Evaluating, and Selecting Target Markets
- Product Selection and Pricing
- Distribution Methods
- Terms and Conditions
- Internal Organization and Procedures
- Sales Goals: Profit and Loss Forecasts

Part IV – Tactics: Action Steps

- Primary Target Countries
- Secondary Target Countries
- Indirect Marketing Efforts

Part V – Export Budget

- Pro Forma Financial Statements

Part VI – Implementation Schedule

- Follow-up
- Periodic Operational and Management Review (Measuring Results Against Plan)

Addenda: Background Data on Target Countries and Market

- Basic Market Statistics: Historical and Projected
- Background Facts
- Competitive Environment

Export advice

For companies making initial plans to export or to export in new areas, considerable advice and assistance are available at little or no cost. It is easy, through lack of experience, to overestimate the problems involved in exporting or to get embroiled in difficulties that can be avoided. For these and other good reasons, it is important to get expert counseling and assistance from the beginning.

This chapter gives a brief overview of sources of assistance available through federal, state, and local government agencies and in the private sector. Other chapters in this guide give more information on the specialized services of these organizations and how to use them. Information on where to find these organizations can be found in the appendixes.

Some readers may feel overwhelmed at first by the number of sources of advice available. Although it is not necessary to go to all of these resources, it is valuable to know at least a little about each of them and to get to know several personally. Each individual or organization contacted can contribute different perspectives based on different experience and skills.

While having many sources to choose from can be advantageous, deciding where to begin can also be difficult. Some advice from experienced exporters may be helpful in this regard. Recognizing this point, President George Bush created the Trade Promotion Coordinating Committee (TPCC) and charged it with harnessing all the resources of the federal government to serve American exporting business. The TPCC conducts export conferences, coordinates trade events and missions that cross-cut federal agencies, and operates an export information center that can help exporters find the right federal program to suit their needs (telephone 1-800-USA-TRADE).

In general, however, the best place to start is the nearest U.S. Department of Commerce district office, which can not only provide export counseling in its own right but also direct companies toward other government and private sector export services.

Department of Commerce

The scope of services provided by the Department of Commerce to exporters is vast, but it is often overlooked by many companies. Most of the information and programs of interest to U.S. exporters are concentrated in the department's International Trade Administration (ITA), of which the subdivision called the U.S. and Foreign Commercial Service (US&FCS) maintains a network of international trade specialists in the United States and commercial officers in foreign cities to help American companies do business abroad. By contacting the nearest Department of Commerce district office, the U.S. exporter can tap into all assistance programs available from ITA and all trade information gathered by U.S. embassies and consulates worldwide. Addresses and phone numbers for all district offices, listed by state, are given in appendix III. The following sections detail the kinds of assistance offered.

Export assistance available in the United States

Department of Commerce District Offices

Sixty-eight Department of Commerce district and branch offices in cities throughout the United States and Puerto Rico provide information and professional export counseling to business people. Each district office is headed by a director and supported by trade specialists and other staff. Branch offices usually consist of one trade specialist. These professionals can counsel companies on the steps involved in exporting, help them assess the export potential of their products, target markets, and locate and check out potential overseas partners. In fact, because Commerce has a worldwide network of international business experts, district offices can answer almost any question exporters are likely to ask – or put them in touch with someone who can.

Each district office can offer information about

- international trade opportunities abroad,
- foreign markets for U.S. products and services,
- services to locate and evaluate overseas buyers and representatives,
- financial aid to exporters,
- international trade exhibitions,
- export documentation requirements,
- foreign economic statistics,
- U.S. export licensing and foreign nation import requirements, and
- export seminars and conferences.

Most district offices also maintain business libraries containing Commerce's latest reports as well as other publications of interest to U.S. exporters. Important data bases, such as the NTDB, are also available through many district offices that provide trade leads, foreign business contacts, in-depth country market research, export-import trade statistics, and other valuable information.

District Export Councils

Besides the immediate services of its district offices, the Department of Commerce gives the exporter direct contact with seasoned exporters experienced in all phases of export trade. The district offices work closely with 51 district export councils (DECs) comprising nearly 1,800 business and trade experts who volunteer to help U.S. firms develop solid export strategies.

These DECs assist in many of the workshops and seminars on exporting arranged by the district offices (see below) or sponsor their own. DEC members may also provide direct, personal counseling to less experienced exporters, suggesting marketing strategies, trade contacts, and ways to maximize success in overseas markets.

Assistance from DECs may be obtained through the Department of Commerce district offices with which they are affiliated.

Export Seminars and Educational Programming

In addition to individual counseling sessions, an effective method of informing local business communities of the various aspects of international trade is through the conference and seminar program. Each year, Commerce district offices conduct approximately 5,000 conferences, seminars, and workshops on topics such as export documentation and licensing procedures, country-specific market opportunities, export trading companies, and U.S. trade promotion and trade policy initiatives. The seminars are usually held in conjunction with DECs, local chambers of commerce, state agencies, and world trade clubs. For information on scheduled seminars across the country, or for educational programming assistance, contact the nearest district office.

Assistance Available From Department of Commerce Specialists in Washington, D.C.

Among the most valuable resources available to U.S. exporters are the hundreds of trade specialists, expert in various areas of international business, that the Department of Commerce has assembled in its Washington headquarters.

Country counseling. Every country in the world is assigned a *country desk officer.* These desk officers (see appendix II for a list), in Commerce's International Economic Policy (IEP) area, look at the needs of an individual U.S. firm wishing to sell in a particular country, taking into account that country's overall economy, trade policies, political situation, and other relevant factors. Each desk officer collects up-to-date information on the country's trade regulations, tariffs and value-added taxes, business practices, economic and political developments, trade data and trends, market size and growth, and so on. Desk officers also participate in preparing Commerce's country-specific market research reports, such as *Foreign Economic Trends* and *Overseas Business Reports* (see appendix V), available from the U.S. Government Printing Office and through the NTDB. The value of IEP's market data

may be gauged from the fact that this agency develops much of the country-specific background for negotiating positions of the U.S. trade representative.

Product and service sector counseling. Complementing IEP's country desks are the *industry desk officers* of Commerce's Trade Development area. They are grouped in units (with telephone numbers):

- Aerospace, 202-377-2835.
- Automotive Affairs and Consumer Goods, 202-377-0823.
- Basic Industries, 202-377-0614.
- Capital Goods and International Construction, 202-377-5023.
- Science and Electronics, 202-377-3548.
- Services, 202-377-5261.
- Textiles and Apparel, 202-377-3737.

The industry desk officers (see appendix II for a list) participate in preparing reports on the competitive strength of selected U.S. industries in domestic and international markets for the publication *U.S. Industrial Outlook* (available from the U.S. Government Printing Office). They also promote exports for their industry sectors through marketing seminars, trade missions and trade fairs, foreign buyer groups, business counseling, and information on market opportunities.

Export counseling and international market analysis. The Market Analysis Division provides U.S. firms with assistance in market research efforts and export counseling on market research. Many of the research reports described in this chapter are planned and prepared by the Office of Product Development and Distribution, Market Analysis Division (202-377-5037).

Major projects. For major projects abroad, the International Construction unit works with American planning, engineering, and construction firms to win bid contracts. The Major Projects Reference Room in Commerce's Washington headquarters keeps detailed project documents on multilateral development bank and U.S. foreign assistance projects. Companies able to bid on major overseas projects can reach the Major Projects Reference Room on 202-377-4876.

The Office of Telecommunications (202-377-4466) has major projects information exclusively for that sector.

Other assistance. Rounding out the Trade Development area is a unit that cuts across industry sector issues. Trade Information and Analysis gathers, analyzes, and disseminates trade and investment data for use in trade promotion and policy formulation. It also includes specialists in technical areas of international trade finance, such as countertrade and barter, foreign sales corporations, export financing, and the activities of multilateral development banks. For more information, contact the nearest Department of Commerce district office.

Export marketing information and assistance available overseas

US&FCS Overseas Posts

Much of the information about trends and actual trade leads in foreign countries is gathered on site by the commercial officers of the US&FCS. About half of the approximately 186 US&FCS American officers working in 67 countries (with 127 offices) have been hired from the private sector, many with international trade experience. All understand firsthand the problems encountered by U.S. companies in their efforts to trade abroad. U.S.-based regional directors for the US&FCS can be contacted at the following telephone numbers:

- Africa, Near East and South Asia, 202-377-4836.

- East Asia and Pacific, 202-377-8422.

- Europe, 202-377-1599.

- Western Hemisphere, 202-377-2736.

- Fax (Europe and Western Hemisphere), 202-377-3159.

- Fax (all others), 202-377-5179.

In addition, a valued asset of the US&FCS is a group of about 525 foreign nationals, usually natives of the foreign country, who are employed in the U.S. embassy or consulate and bring with them a wealth of personal understanding of local market conditions and business practices. The US&FCS staff overseas provides a range of services to help companies sell abroad: background information on foreign companies, agency-finding services, market research, business counseling, assistance in making appointments with key buyers and government officials, and representations on behalf of companies adversely affected by trade barriers. (Some of the more important services are described fully in chapter 7.)

U.S. exporters usually tap into these services by contacting the Department of Commerce district office in their state. While exporters are strongly urged to contact their district office *before* going overseas, U.S. business travelers abroad can also contact U.S. embassies and consulates directly for help during their trips. District offices can provide business travel facilitation assistance before departure by arranging advance appointments with embassy personnel, market briefings, and other assistance in cities to be visited.

US&FCS posts also cooperate with overseas representatives of individual states. Almost all 50 states have such representation in overseas markets, and their efforts are closely coordinated with the resources of the US&FCS.

Other Commerce export services

Besides ITA, a number of other Department of Commerce agencies offer export services.

Export Administration

The under secretary for export administration is responsible for U.S. export controls (see chapter 11). Assistance in complying with export controls can be obtained directly from local district offices or from the Exporter Counseling Division within the Bureau of Export Administration (BXA) Office of Export Licensing in Washington, DC (202-377-4811). BXA also has four field offices that specialize in counseling on export controls and regulations: the Western Regional Office (714-660-0144), the Northern California Branch Office (408-748-7450), the Portland Branch Office (503-326-5159), and the Eastern Regional Office (603-834-6300).

Trade Adjustment Assistance

Trade Adjustment Assistance, part of Commerce's Economic Development Administration, helps firms that have been adversely affected by imported products to adjust to international competition. Companies eligible for trade adjustment assistance may receive technical consulting to upgrade operations such as product engineering, marketing, information systems, export promotion, and energy management. The federal government may assume up to 75 percent of the cost of these services. For more information call 202-377-3373.

Travel and Tourism

The U.S. Travel and Tourism Administration (USTTA) promotes U.S. export earnings through trade in tourism. USTTA stimulates foreign demand, helps to remove barriers, increases the number of small and medium-sized travel businesses participating in the export market, provides timely data, and forms marketing partnerships with private industry and with state and local governments.

To maintain its programs in international markets, USTTA has offices in Toronto, Montreal, Vancouver, Mexico City, Tokyo, London, Paris, Amsterdam, Milan, Frankfurt, Sydney, and (serving South America) Miami.

Travel development activities in countries without direct USTTA representation are carried out under the direction of USTTA regional directors, who cooperate with Visit USA committees composed of representatives from the U.S. and foreign travel industry in those countries, and also with the US&FCS. For more information, U.S. destinations and suppliers of tourism services interested in the overseas promotion of travel to the United States should call 202-377-4003.

Foreign Requirements for U.S. Products and Services

For information about foreign standards and certification systems, write National Center for Standards and Certificates Information, National Institute for Standards and Technology (NIST), Administration Building, A629, Gaithersburg, MD 20899; telephone 301-975-4040, 4038, or 4036. NIST maintains a General Agreement on Tariffs and Trade (GATT) hotline (301-975-4041) with a recording that reports on the latest notifications of proposed foreign regulations that may affect trade. Exporters can also get information from the nongovernmental American National Standards Institute (212-354-3300).

Minority Business Development Agency (MBDA)

The MBDA identifies minority business enterprises (MBEs) in selected industries to increase their awareness of their relative size and product advantages and to aggressively take them through the advanced stages of market development.

Through an interagency agreement with the ITA, MBDA provides information on market and product needs worldwide. MBDA and ITA coordinate MBE participation in Matchmaker and other trade delegations.

MBDA provides counseling through the Minority Business Development Center network to help MBEs prepare international marketing plans and promotional materials and to identify financial resources.

For general export information, the field organizations of both MBDA and ITA provide information kits and information on local seminars. Contact Minority Business Development Agency, Office of Program Development, U.S. Department of Commerce, Washington, DC 20230; telephone 202-377-3237.

Foreign Metric Regulations

The Office of Metric Programs (202-377-0944) provides exporters with guidance and assistance on matters relating to U.S. transition to the metric system. It can also give referrals to metric contacts in state governments.

Fishery Products Exports

The National Oceanic and Atmospheric Administration (NOAA) assists seafood exporters by facilitating access to foreign markets. NOAA's National Marine Fisheries Service provides inspection services for fishery exports and issues official U.S. government certification attesting to the findings. Contact Office of Trade and Industry Services, National Marine Fisheries Service, Room 6490, 1335 East-West Highway, Silver Spring, MD 20910. Telephone numbers are as follows: Trade Matters, 301-427-2379 or 2383; Export Inspection, 301-427-2355; and Fisheries Promotion, 301-427-2379.

Bureau of the Census

The Bureau of the Census is the primary source of trade statistics that break down the quantity and dollar value of U.S. exports and imports by commodity (product) and country. Commerce district offices can help retrieve Census export statistics for exporters who want to identify potential export markets for their products. Firms interested in more extensive statistical data can contact the Bureau of the Census at 301-763-5140.

Census can also provide authoritative guidance on questions concerning shippers' export declarations (see chapter 12). Call 301-763-5310.

Department of State

The Department of State has a diverse staff capable of providing U.S. exporters with trade contacts. These staff members include bureau commercial coordinators, country desk officers, policy officers in the functional bureaus (such as the Bureau of Economic and Business Affairs), and all U.S. embassies and consular posts abroad. While the Department of Commerce's US&FCS is present in 67 countries, the Department of State provides commercial services in 84 embassies and numerous consular posts. Their addresses and telephone numbers are published in the directory titled *Key Officers of Foreign Service Posts,* available from the U.S. Government Printing Office (202-783-3238).

The ambassador takes the lead in promoting U.S. trade and investment interests in every U.S. embassy. All members of U.S. diplomatic missions abroad have the following continuing obligations:

- To ascertain the views of the American business sector on foreign policy issues that affect its interests, in order to ensure that those views are fully considered in the development of policy.

- To seek to ensure that the ground rules for conducting international trade are fair and nondiscriminatory.

- To be responsive when U.S. firms seek assistance, providing them with professional advice and analysis as well as assistance in making and developing contacts abroad.

- To vigorously encourage and promote the export of U.S. goods, services, and agricultural commodities and represent the interests of U.S. business to foreign governments where appropriate.

- To assist U.S. business in settling investment disputes with foreign governments amicably and, in cases of expropriation or similar action, to obtain prompt, adequate, and effective compensation.

Bureau of Economic and Business Affairs

The Bureau of Economic and Business Affairs has primary responsibility within the Department of State for (1) formulating and implementing policies regarding foreign economic matters, trade promotion, and business services of an international nature and (2) coordinating regional economic policy with other bureaus. The bureau is divided functionally as follows: Planning and Economic Analysis Staff; Office of Commercial, Legislative, and Public Affairs; Trade and Commercial Affairs (including textiles and food policy); International Finance and Development (including investment and business practices); Transportation (including aviation and maritime affairs); International Energy and Resources Policy; and International Trade Controls. For more information, contact Commercial Coordinator, Bureau of Economic and Business Affairs; telephone 202-647-1942.

Regional bureaus

Regional bureaus, each under the direction of an assistant secretary of state, are responsible for U.S. foreign affairs activities in specific major regions of the world. Bureau commercial coordinators can be reached on the following telephone numbers:

- Bureau of African Affairs, 202-647-3503.

- Bureau of East Asian and Pacific Affairs, 202-647-2006.

- Bureau of Near Eastern and South Asian Affairs, 202-647-4835.

- Bureau of European and Canadian Affairs, 202-647-2395.

- Bureau of International Communications and Information Policy, 202-647-5832.

Country desk officers maintain day-to-day contact with overseas diplomatic posts and provide country-specific economic and political analysis and commercial counseling to U.S. business.

Cooperation between state and commerce

The Departments of State and Commerce provide many services to U.S. business jointly. Firms interested in establishing a market for their products or expanding sales abroad should first seek assistance from their nearest Department of Commerce district office, which can tap into the worldwide network of State and Commerce officials serving in U.S. missions abroad and in Washington.

Small Business Administration

Through its 107 field offices in cities throughout the United States (see appendix III for addresses and telephone numbers), the U.S. Small Business Administration (SBA) provides counseling to potential and current small business exporters. These no-cost services include the following:

- *Legal advice.* Through an arrangement with the Federal Bar Association (FBA), exporters may receive initial export legal assistance. Under this program, qualified attorneys from the International Law Council of the FBA, working through SBA field offices, provide free initial consultations to small companies on the legal aspects of exporting.

- *Export training.* SBA field offices cosponsor export training programs with the Department of Commerce, other federal agencies, and various private sector international trade organizations. These programs are conducted by experienced international traders.

- *Small Business Institute and small business development centers.* Through the Small Business Institute, advanced business students from more than 500 colleges and universities provide in-depth, long-term counseling under faculty supervision to small businesses. Additional export counseling and assistance are offered through small business development centers, which are located in some colleges and universities. Students in these two programs provide technical help by developing an export marketing feasibility study and analysis for their client firms.

- *Export counseling.* Export counseling services are also furnished to potential and current small business exporters by executives and professional consultants. Members of the Service Corps of Retired Executives, with practical experience in international trade, help small firms evaluate their export potential and strengthen their domestic operations by identifying financial, managerial, or technical problems. These advisers also can help small firms develop and implement basic export marketing plans, which show where and how to sell goods abroad.

For information on any of the programs funded by SBA, contact the nearest SBA field office (see appendix III).

Department of Agriculture

The U.S. Department of Agriculture (USDA) export promotion efforts are centered in the Foreign Agricultural Service (FAS), whose marketing programs are discussed in chapter 7. However, other USDA agencies also offer services to U.S. exporters of agricultural products: the Economic Research Service, the Office of Transportation, the Animal and Plant Health Inspection Service, the Food Safety and Inspection Service, and the Federal Grain Inspection Service. A wide variety of other valuable programs is offered, such as promotion of U.S. farm products in foreign markets; services of commodity and marketing specialists in Washington, D.C.; trade fair exhibits; publications and information services; and financing programs. For more information on programs contact the director of the High-Value Product Services Division, Foreign Agricultural Service, U.S. Department of Agriculture, Washington, DC 20250; telephone 202-447-6343.

State governments

State economic development agencies, departments of commerce, and other departments of state governments often provide valuable assistance to exporters. State export development programs are growing rapidly. In many areas, county and city economic development agencies also have export assistance programs. The aid offered by these groups typically includes the following:

- *Export education* – helping exporters analyze export potential and orienting them to export techniques and strategies. This help may take the form of group seminars or individual counseling sessions.

- *Trade missions* – organizing trips abroad enabling exporters to call on potential foreign customers. (For more information on trade missions, see chapter 7.)

- *Trade shows* – organizing and sponsoring exhibitions of state-produced goods and services in overseas markets.

Appendix III lists the agencies in each state responsible for export assistance to local firms. Also included are the names of other government and private organizations, with their telephone numbers and addresses. Readers interested in the role played by state development agencies in promoting and supporting exports may also wish to contact the National Association of State Development Agencies, 444 North Capitol Street, Suite 611, Washington, DC 20001; telephone 202-624-5411.

To determine if a particular county or city has local export assistance programs, contact the appropriate economic development agency. Appendix III includes contact information for several major cities.

Commercial banks

More than 300 U.S. banks have international banking departments with specialists familiar with specific foreign countries and various types of commodities and transactions. These large banks, located in major U.S. cities, maintain correspondent relationships with smaller banks throughout the country. Larger banks also maintain correspondent relationships with banks in most foreign countries or operate their own overseas branches, providing a direct channel to foreign customers.

International banking specialists are generally well informed about export matters, even in areas that fall outside the usual limits of international banking. If they are unable to provide direct guidance or assistance, they may be able to refer inquirers to other specialists who can. Banks frequently provide consultation and guidance free of charge to their clients, since they derive income primarily from loans to the exporter and from fees for special services. Many banks also have publications available to help exporters. These materials often cover particular countries and their business practices and can be a valuable tool for initial familiarization with foreign industry. Finally, large banks frequently conduct seminars and workshops on letters of credit, documentary collections, and other banking subjects of concern to exporters.

Among the many services a commercial bank may perform for its clients are the following:

- Exchange of currencies.

- Assistance in financing exports.

- Collection of foreign invoices, drafts, letters of credit, and other foreign receivables.

- Transfer of funds to other countries.

- Letters of introduction and letters of credit for travelers.

- Credit information on potential representatives or buyers overseas.

- Credit assistance to the exporter's foreign buyers.

Export intermediaries

Export intermediaries are of many different types, ranging from giant international companies, many foreign owned, to highly specialized, small operations. They provide a multitude of services, such as performing market research, appointing overseas distributors or commission representatives, exhibiting a client's products at international trade shows, advertising, shipping, and arranging documentation. In short, the intermediary can often take full responsibility for the export end of the business, relieving the manufacturer of all the details except filling orders.

Intermediaries may work simultaneously for a number of exporters on the basis of commissions, salary, or retainer plus commission. Some take title to the goods they handle, buying and selling in their own right. Products of a trading company's clients are often related, although the items usually are noncompetitive. One advantage of using an intermediary is that it can immediately make available

marketing resources that a smaller firm would need years to develop on its own. Many export intermediaries also finance sales and extend credit, facilitating prompt payment to the exporter. For more information on using export intermediaries see chapter 4.

World trade centers and international trade clubs

Local or regional world trade centers and international trade clubs are composed of area business people who represent firms engaged in international trade and shipping, banks, forwarders, customs brokers, government agencies, and other service organizations involved in world trade. These organizations conduct educational programs on international business and organize promotional events to stimulate interest in world trade. Some 80 world trade centers or affiliated associations are located in major trading cities throughout the world.

By participating in a local association, a company can receive valuable and timely advice on world markets and opportunities from business people who are already knowledgeable on virtually any facet of international business. Another important advantage of membership in a local world trade club is the availability of benefits – such as services, discounts, and contacts – in affiliated clubs from foreign countries.

Chambers of commerce and trade associations

Many local chambers of commerce and major trade associations in the United States provide sophisticated and extensive services for members interested in exporting. Among these services are the following:

- Conducting export seminars, workshops, and round-tables.

- Providing certificates of origin.

- Developing trade promotion programs, including overseas missions, mailings, and event planning.

- Organizing U.S. pavilions in foreign trade shows.

- Providing contacts with foreign companies and distributors.

- Relaying export sales leads and other opportunities to members.

- Organizing transportation routings and shipment consolidations.

- Hosting visiting trade missions from other countries.

- Conducting international activities at domestic trade shows.

In addition, some industry associations can supply detailed information on market demand for products in selected countries or refer members to export management companies. Most trade associations play an active role in lobbying for U.S. trade policies beneficial to their industries.

Industry trade associations typically collect and maintain files on international trade news and trends affecting manufacturers. Often they publish articles and newsletters that include government research.

American chambers of commerce abroad

A valuable and reliable source of market information in any foreign country is the local chapter of the American chamber of commerce. These organizations are knowledgeable about local trade opportunities, actual and potential competition, periods of maximum trade activity, and similar considerations.

American chambers of commerce abroad usually handle inquiries from any U.S. business. Detailed service, however, is ordinarily provided free of charge only for members of affiliated organizations. Some chambers have a set schedule of charges for services rendered to nonmembers. For contact information on American chambers in major foreign markets, see appendix IV.

International trade consultants and other advisers

International trade consultants can advise and assist a manufacturer on all aspects of foreign marketing. Trade consultants do not normally deal specifically with one product, although they may advise on product adaptation to a foreign market. They research domestic and foreign regulations and also assess commercial and political risk. They conduct foreign market research and establish contacts with foreign government agencies and other necessary resources, such as advertising companies, product service facilities, and local attorneys.

These consultants can locate and qualify foreign joint venture partners as well as conduct feasibility studies for the sale of manufacturing rights, the location and construction of manufacturing facilities, and the establishment of foreign branches. After sales agreements are completed, trade consultants can also ensure that follow-through is smooth and that any problems that arise are dealt with effectively.

Trade consultants usually specialize by subject matter and by global area or country. For example, firms may specialize in high-technology exports to the Far East. Their consultants can advise on which agents or distributors are likely to be successful, what kinds of promotion are needed, who the competitors are, and how to deal with them. They are also knowledgeable about foreign government regulations, contract laws, and taxation. Some firms may be more specialized than others; for example, some may be thoroughly knowledgeable on legal aspects and taxation and less knowledgeable on marketing strategies.

Many large accounting firms, law firms, and specialized marketing firms provide international trade consulting services. When selecting a consulting firm, the exporter should pay particular attention to the experience and knowledge of the consultant who is in charge of its project. To find an appropriate firm, advice should be sought from other exporters and some of the other resources listed in this chapter, such as the Department of Commerce district office or local chamber of commerce.

Consultants are of greatest value to a firm that knows exactly what it wants. For this reason, and because private consultants are expensive, it pays to take full advantage of publicly funded sources of advice before hiring a consultant.

Market research

3

To be successful, exporters must assess their markets through market research. Exporters engage in market research primarily to identify their marketing opportunities and constraints within individual foreign markets and also to identify and find prospective buyers and customers.

Market research includes all methods that a company uses to determine which foreign markets have the best potential for its products. Results of this research inform the firm of

- the largest markets for its product,
- the fastest growing markets,
- market trends and outlook,
- market conditions and practices, and
- competitive firms and products.

A firm may begin to export without conducting any market research if it receives unsolicited orders from abroad. Although this type of selling is valuable, the firm may discover even more promising markets by conducting a systematic search. A firm that opts to export indirectly (see chapter 4) by using an intermediary such as an EMC or ETC may wish to select markets to enter before selecting the intermediary, since many EMCs and ETCs have strengths in some markets but not in others.

A firm may research a market by using either primary or secondary data resources. In conducting primary market research, a company collects data directly from the foreign marketplace through interviews, surveys, and other direct contact with representatives and potential buyers. Primary market research has the advantage of being tailored to the company's needs and provides answers to specific questions, but the collection of such data is time-consuming and expensive.

When conducting secondary market research, a company collects data from compiled sources, such as trade statistics for a country or a product. Working with secondary sources is less expensive and helps the company focus its marketing efforts. Although secondary data sources are critical to market research, they do have limitations. The most recent statistics for some countries may be more than two years old. Product breakdowns may be too broad to be of much value to a company. Statistics on services are often unavailable. Finally, statistics may be distorted by incomplete data-gathering techniques. Yet, even with these limitations, secondary research is a valuable and relatively easy first step for a company to take. It may be the only step needed if the company decides to export indirectly through an intermediary, since the other firm may have advanced research capabilities.

Methods of market research

Because of the expense of primary market research, most firms rely on secondary data sources. Secondary market research is conducted in three basic ways:

1. By keeping abreast of world events that influence the international marketplace, watching for announcements of specific projects, or simply visiting likely markets. For example, a thawing of political hostilities often leads to the opening of economic channels between countries.

2. By analyzing trade and economic statistics. Trade statistics are generally compiled by product category and by country. These statistics provide the U.S. firm with information concerning shipments of products over specified periods of time. Demographic and general economic statistics such as population size and makeup, per capita income, and production levels by industry can be important indicators of the market potential for a company's products.

3. By obtaining the advice of experts. There are several ways of obtaining expert advice:

   - Contacting experts at the U.S. Department of Commerce and other government agencies.
   - Attending seminars, workshops, and international trade shows.
   - Hiring an international trade and marketing consultant.
   - Talking with successful exporters of similar products.
   - Contacting trade and industry association staff.

Gathering and evaluating secondary market research can be complex and tedious. However, several publications are available that can help simplify the process. The following approach to market research refers to these publications and resources described later in this chapter.

A step-by-step approach to market research

The U.S. company may find the following approach useful.

1. **Screen potential markets.**

- **Step 1.** Obtain export statistics that indicate product exports to various countries. *Foreign Trade Report: Monthly Exports and Imports – SITC Commodity by Country,* FT 925 (Department of Commerce) provides statistics on all U.S. exports and imports. Firms should also consult the NTDB, available through many Commerce district offices, the Export Information System (XIS) Data Reports (SBA), or U.S. Industrial Outlook (Commerce).

- **Step 2.** Identify 5 to 10 large and fast-growing markets for the firm's product. Look at them over the past three to five years. Has market growth been consistent year to year? Did import growth occur even during periods of economic recession? If not, did growth resume with economic recovery?

- **Step 3.** Identify some smaller but fast-emerging markets that may provide ground-floor opportunities. If the market is just beginning to open up, there may be fewer competitors than in established markets. Growth rates should be substantially higher in these countries to qualify as up-and-coming markets, given the lower starting point.

- **Step 4.** Target three to five of the most statistically promising markets for further assessment. Consult with Commerce district offices, business associates, freight forwarders, and others to help refine targeted markets.

2. **Assess targeted markets.**

- **Step 1.** Examine trends for company products as well as related products that could influence demand. Calculate overall consumption of the product and the amount accounted for by imports. *Industry sector analyses* (ISAs), *alert reports,* and *country marketing plans,* all from Commerce, give economic backgrounds and market trends for each country. Demographic information (population, age, etc.) can be obtained from *World Population* (Census) and *Statistical Yearbook* (United Nations).

- **Step 2.** Ascertain the sources of competition, including the extent of domestic industry production and the major foreign countries the firm is competing against in each targeted market, by using ISAs and *competitive assessments* (all from Commerce). Look at each competitor's U.S. market share.

- **Step 3.** Analyze factors affecting marketing and use of the product in each market, such as end user sectors, channels of distribution, cultural idiosyncrasies, and business practices. Again, ISAs are useful, as is the *Comparison Shopping Service* (CSS) offered by Commerce.

- **Step 4.** Identify any foreign barriers (tariff or nontariff) for the product being imported into the country (see chapter 11 for an analysis of tariff and nontariff barriers). Identify any U.S. barriers (such as export controls) affecting exports to the country. *Country information kits* produced by the Overseas Private Investment Corporation (OPIC) can be helpful.

- **Step 5.** Identify any U.S. or foreign government incentives to promote exporting of the product or service.

3. **Draw conclusions.**

After analyzing the data, the company may conclude that its marketing resources would be applied more effectively to a few countries. In general, efforts should be directed to fewer than 10 markets if the company is new to exporting; one or two countries may be enough to start with. The company's internal resources should help determine its level of effort.

The following section describes the publications that have been mentioned and includes additional sources. Because there are many research sources, the firm may wish to seek advice from a Department of Commerce district office (see appendix III).

Sources of market research

There are many domestic, foreign, and international sources of information concerning foreign markets. Several of these sources are given here, and others may be found in the bibliography (appendix V). Available information ranges from simple trade statistics to in-depth market surveys.

Trade statistics indicate total exports or imports by country and by product and allow an exporter to compare the size of the market for a product among various countries. Some statistics also reflect the U.S. share of the total country market in order to gauge the overall competitiveness of U.S. producers. By looking at statistics over several years, an exporter can determine which markets are growing and which are shrinking.

Market surveys provide a narrative description and assessment of particular markets along with relevant statistics. The reports are often based on original research conducted in the countries studied and may include specific information on both buyers and competitors.

Potential exporters may find many of the reports referred to in this section at a Department of Commerce district office (see appendix III) or at a business or university library. In addition, the Foreign Trade Reference Room in the Department of Commerce (Room 2233) offers extensive trade statistics. The NTDB is a source for much of the following information. Call 202-377-1986 for more information on the NTDB.

The following sources fall into two broad categories – general information resources and industry- or country-specific information resources. Each category is divided into several subgroups.

General information resources

One of the best sources of information is personal interviews with private and government officials and experts. A surprisingly large number of people in both the public and private sectors are available to assist exporters interested in any aspect of international market research. Either in face-to-face interviews or by telephone, these individuals can provide a wealth of market research information.

In the private sector, sources of market research expertise include local chambers of commerce, world trade centers or clubs, and trade associations. In the federal government, industry and commodity experts are available through the Department of Commerce, USDA, and SBA. In addition, these agencies provide the following publications, many of which can be found in local libraries.

Sources of General Information

- **Business America.** This biweekly publication of the Department of Commerce contains country-by-country marketing reports, incisive economic analyses, worldwide trade leads, advance notice of planned exhibitions of U.S. products worldwide, and success stories of export marketing. Annual subscriptions cost $49 (GPO:703-011-00000-4). Contact Superintendent of Documents, U.S. Government Printing Office, Washington, DC 20402; telephone 202-783-3238.

- **Commerce Business Daily (CBD).** Published daily, Monday through Friday (except holidays), by the Department of Commerce, CBD lists government procurement invitations, contract awards, subcontracting leads, sales of surplus property, and foreign business opportunities as well as certain foreign government procurements. It is available by subscription and on line (electronically). A first-class mail subscription is $260 per year or $130 for six months; second-class, $208 per year or $104 for six months (GPO:703-013-00000-7.) Contact Superintendent of Documents, U.S. Government Printing Office, Washington, DC 20402; telephone 202-783-3238.

- **Trade Information Center.** This information center was established as a comprehensive source for U.S. companies seeking information on federal programs and activities that support U.S. exports, including information on overseas markets and industry trends. The center maintains a computerized calendar of U.S. government-sponsored domestic and overseas trade events. Telephone 1-800-USA-TRADE.

- **Economic Bulletin Board (EBB).** The PC-based EBB is an on-line source for trade leads as well as the latest statistical releases from the Bureau of the Census, the Bureau of Economic Analysis, the Bureau of Labor Statistics, the Federal Reserve Board, and other federal agencies. Subscribers pay an annual fee of $35 (for 300-2400 baud service) or $100 (for 9600 baud service), which allows two hours of free access. Additional access at 300-2400 baud is billed quarterly at between 20 cents and 50 cents per minute depending on the time of day. Additional access at 9600 baud is 50 cents per minute at any time of day.

Telephone 202-377-1986 or fax 202-377-2164, or try the EBB as a guest by dialing 202-377-3870 with a personal computer and modem (eight bits, no parity, one stop bit). Enter "GUEST" when prompted for a User ID.

- **National Trade Data Bank.** The NTDB contains export promotion and international trade data collected by 15 U.S. government agencies. Updated each month and released on CD-ROM, the data bank enables access to more than 100,000 documents. The NTDB contains the latest census data on U.S. imports and exports by commodity and country; the complete Central Intelligence Agency (CIA) *World Factbook;* current market research reports compiled by US&FCS; the complete *Foreign Traders Index,* which contains more than 50,000 names and addresses of individuals and firms abroad interested in importing U.S. products; and many other data sources. The NTDB is available at more than 600 federal depository libraries nationwide and can be purchased for $35 per single disc or $360 for a 12-month subscription. Telephone 202-377-1986 or fax 202-377-2164 or contact the nearest Department of Commerce district office.

- **Selected SBA market research-related general resources.** Each of the following general resources is published by the SBA: *Marketing for Small Business: An Overview* (MT2, $1); *Researching Your Market* (MT8, 50 cents); *Export Indicators* (free); *Exporter's Guide to Federal Resources for Small Business* (GPO:045-000-00250-1, $4); *Market Overseas with Government Help* (MT10, $1); and the video *Marketing: Winning Customers with a Workable Plan* (VT1, $30). Contact the local SBA field office or telephone the Small Business Answer Desk, 800-368-5855 or 202-653-7561.

Worldwide General Information

- **International Financial Statistics (IFS).** Published by the International Monetary Fund, IFS presents statistics on exchange rates, money and banking, production, government finance, interest rates, and other subjects. It is available by monthly subscription for $188 yearly (yearbook, $50 alone, included in the price); single copy, $20. Contact International Financial Statistics, Publication Services, Room C100, 700 19th Street, N.W., Washington, DC 20431; telephone 202-623-7430.

- **UN Statistical Yearbook.** Published by the United Nations (UN), this yearbook is one of the most complete statistical reference books available. It provides international trade information on products, including information on importing countries useful in assessing import competition. The yearbook contains data for 220 countries and territories on economic and social subjects including population, agriculture, manufacturing, commodity, export-import trade, and many other areas. The latest edition available (1987) is about 900 pages and costs $100. Contact United Nations Publications, Room DC2-0853, New York, NY 10017; telephone 212-963-8302.

- **World Bank Atlas.** The *World Bank Atlas* provides demographics, gross domestic product, and average growth rates for every country. The latest edition, 1990, covers data for 1980 to 1989 and costs $6.95. Contact

World Bank Publications, 1818 H Street, N.W., Washington, DC 20433; telephone 202-473-1154.

- **World Factbook.** Produced annually by the CIA, this publication provides country-by-country data on demographics, economy, communications, and defense. The cost is $23 (GPO:041-015-00169-8). Contact Superintendent of Documents, U.S. Government Printing Office, Washington, DC 20402; telephone 202-783-3238.

- **World Population.** The U.S. Bureau of the Census collects and analyzes worldwide demographic data that can help exporters identify potential markets for their products. Information on each country – total population, fertility, mortality, urban population, growth rate, and life expectancy – is updated every two years. It also contains detailed demographic profiles of individual countries, including analysis of labor force structure, infant mortality, and so on. The cost of the latest edition, 1989, is $7.50 (GPO:031-024-07074-0). Contact Superintendent of Documents, U.S. Government Printing Office, Washington, DC 20402; telephone 202-783-3238.

- **Worldcasts.** This eight-volume annual series presents 60,000 abstracted forecasts for products and markets outside the United States (150 countries). Forecasts are arranged by modified standard industrial classification (SIC) codes and are typically one-line entries providing short- and long-range projections for consumption, employment, production, and capacity. A product volume and a regional volume are published each quarter. The complete annual set of four product volumes and four regional volumes costs $1,300; the product set and the regional set, $900 each; single volumes, $450 each. Contact Predicasts, 11001 Cedar Avenue, Cleveland, OH 44106; telephone 800-321-6388 or 216-795-3000.

General industry and agriculture information

Industry Information

- **Foreign Trade Report: Monthly Exports and Imports – SITC Commodity by Country,** FT 925. This monthly publication by the Department of Commerce provides statistics on all export and import trade engaged in by the United States. Annual subscription cost is $139 (GPO:703-091-00000-8). Contact Superintendent of Documents, U.S. Government Printing Office, Washington, DC 20402; telephone 202-783-3238.

- **U.S. Industrial Outlook.** This annual publication of the Department of Commerce provides economic and commercial assessments and forecasts on U.S. industry, including statistics on trade, investment, and finance. The cost for the 1991 edition is $28 (GPO:003-009-00586-8). Contact Superintendent of Documents, U.S. Government Printing Office, Washington, DC 20402; telephone 202-783-3238.

- **Export Information System Data Reports.** Produced by the SBA, each data report covers approximately 2,700 product categories. XIS helps small businesses

determine which export markets to pursue. Upon request, SBA provides a small business with a list of the 25 largest importing markets for its product, the 10 best markets for U.S. exporters of that product, the trends in those markets, and the major sources of foreign and UN data. This service is available free to small business. Contact the local SBA field office or telephone the Small Business Answer Desk, 800-368-5855 or 202-653-7561.

Agriculture Information

- **AgExporter.** This monthly magazine is published by the USDA's FAS. Appealing to the farm exporter, the articles analyze conditions affecting U.S. agricultural trade. *AgExporter* highlights market development and export activity. The annual subscription cost is $14. Contact Trade Assistance and Planning Office, Foreign Agricultural Service, U.S. Department of Agriculture, Washington, DC 20250; telephone 703-756-6001.

- **Export Briefs.** This weekly bulletin produced by the FAS presents current news and statistics on world production and trade of agricultural commodities and highlights upcoming trade shows. Available free and on line (electronically). Contact High-Value Products Division, Foreign Agricultural Service, U.S. Department of Agriculture, Washington, DC 20250; telephone 202-447-3031.

- **Trade Policies and Opportunities for U.S. Farm Products.** Published by the FAS, these reports document the policies other governments use to help their agricultural exporters compete against U.S. suppliers. Also identified are import barriers to U.S. farm products and marketing opportunities for U.S. agricultural exporters. Fifty countries and the trading blocs of the European Community (EC) and the Gulf Cooperative Council are covered. Available free. Contact Trade Assistance and Planning Office, FAS, U.S. Department of Agriculture, Washington, DC 20250; telephone 703-756-6001.

Country and Area Information

- **Country marketing plans (CMPs).** CMPs are prepared annually by the commercial sections of U.S. embassies for the US&FCS, covering 67 countries. Each CMP is a planning tool that analyzes an individual country's business and economic climate, emphasizing the marketing and trade statistics, development, and issues. CMPs are available at $10 per report through the Commercial Information Management System (CIMS) and also through the NTDB, electronic data bases operated and managed by the Department of Commerce. Contact the local Department of Commerce district office or telephone 202-377-4767.

- **Foreign Economic Trends (FETs).** Published by the Department of Commerce, each FET covers a single country and provides in-depth assessment of political, commercial, economic, and investment conditions and developments. Special emphasis is given to implications for U.S. business opportunities. Annual subscription cost is $50 (GPO: 803-006-00000-8). Contact Superintendent of Documents, U.S. Government

Printing Office, Washington, DC 20402; telephone 202-783-3238.

- **Overseas Business Reports (OBRs).** Published by the Department of Commerce, the OBRs provide background statistics and information on specific countries useful to exporters, current economic and commercial profiles, and information on U.S. foreign trade with the country. Annual subscription is $14 (GPO:803-007-00000-4). Contact Superintendent of Documents, U.S. Government Printing Office, Washington, DC 20402; telephone 202-783-3238.

- **EC 1992: A Commerce Department Analysis of European Community Directives.** This three-volume publication contains an analysis of the likely impact on U.S. industry of 282 directives of the EC to harmonize practices within the EC countries. The three volumes cover transportation services, telecommunications, broadcasting, food, government procurement, standards, and many other issues. Volume 1, $10, stock no. 003-009-00557-4; volume 2, $9.50, stock no. 003-009-00564-7; volume 3, $13, stock no. 003-009-00572-8. Contact Superintendent of Documents, U.S. Government Printing Office, Washington, DC 20402.

- **Background Notes.** This series surveys a country's people, geography, economy, government, and foreign policy. Prepared by the Department of State, it includes important national economic and trade information, including major trading partners. Available by set or by subscription. Price of the set is $58 (GPO:844-000-914-7); with binder, add $4.75. Annual subscription cost is $18 (GPO:844-002-00000-9). Contact Superintendent of Documents, U.S. Government Printing Office, Washington, DC 20402; telephone 202-783-3238.

- **Commercial Activities Report (CAR).** The CAR is prepared annually by the economic and commercial sections of the U.S. embassies, covering 67 countries where the Department of Commerce is not represented. Designed as a planning tool, each CAR provides the basis for an ongoing evaluation of a particular country's political, economic, and business activities. Special emphasis is given to identifying U.S. marketing opportunities, particularly to assessing market potential and strategies for increasing U.S. sales. Topics include the commercial setting and trends, import data, best prospects, major projects, and trade information and event activity. CARs are available at $10 per report through CIMS and NTDB. Contact the local Commerce district office or telephone 202-377-4767.

- **Congressional Presentations of the State Department's Trade and Development Program.** This annual document reports Department of State dollar expenditures by industry in specific countries around the world for the past several years. (For a description of U.S. Trade and Development Program [TDP] activities to stimulate U.S. exports, see chapter 7.) Contact U.S. Department of State, Information Office, Trade and Development Program, Room 301, SA-16, Washington, DC 20523; telephone 703-875-4357.

- **Congressional Presentations of the U.S. Agency for International Development (AID).** Published by AID's Office of Small and Disadvantaged Business Utilization, this document provides country-by-country data on nations to which AID will provide funds in the coming year, as well as detailed information on past funding activities in each country. It also lists projects the agency desires to fund in the upcoming year, for example, a hydroelectrical project in Egypt. Since these projects require U.S. goods and services, these presentations give U.S. exporters an early look at potential projects and, therefore, an opportunity to plan ahead. (See chapter 7 for more details on AID's programs.) Available through the National Technical Information Service (NTIS) by the set or as separate volumes (hard copy price/microfiche price). Set of six volumes (PB:91-155-549), $145.50/$54.50. Basic document (PB:91-155-556), $60/$17. Statistical annex (PB:91-155-564), $45/$15. Summary tables (PB:91-155-572), $17/$8. International organizations and programs (PB:91-155-580), $17/$8. U.S. trade and development programs (PB:91-155-598), $17/$8. Part 2, mostly statistics (PB:91-155-606), $15/$8. Contact National Technical Information Service, 5285 Port Royal Road, Springfield, VA 22161; telephone 703-487-4650.

- **Country information kits.** Covering developing countries and 16 regions worldwide, the kits are put together by OPIC. Each kit includes most of the background information considered necessary when a business is considering entry into a specific foreign market. Available free. Contact Overseas Private Investment Corporation, 1615 M Street, N.W., Washington, DC 20527; telephone 800-424-OPIC or 202-457-7128.

- **Exporters Encyclopedia.** This extensive handbook on exporting is updated annually and contains exhaustive, in-depth shipping and marketing information. More than 220 world markets are covered country by country. Topics include country profile, communications, trade regulations, documentation, marketing data, health and safety regulations, transportation, and business travel. The annual price is $535. Contact Dun's Marketing Services, 3 Sylvan Way, Parsippany, NJ 07054-3896; telephone 800-526-0651 or 201-605-6749.

- **Foreign Agriculture.** This annual factbook published by the FAS presents agricultural profiles of 65 countries, focusing on production, marketing, and trade, and it includes a full atlas of world agriculture with maps and graphics. The cost is $12. Contact Trade Assistance and Planning Office, Foreign Agricultural Service, U.S. Department of Agriculture, Washington, DC 20250; telephone 703-756-6001.

- **Investment climate statements (ICSs).** ICSs are prepared annually by the commercial sections of the U.S. embassies for the US&FCS, covering 67 individual countries and designed as a planning tool. Through statistics, policies, issues, and analyses, each ICS comprehensively assesses a particular country's environment for direct investment, particularly foreign direct investment. Available at $10 per report through CIMS and NTDB. Contact the local Commerce district office or telephone 202-377-4767.

- **Organization for Economic Cooperation and Development (OECD) surveys.** These economic development surveys produced by OECD cover each of the 24-

member OECD countries individually. Each survey presents a detailed analysis of recent developments in market demand, production, employment, and prices and wages. Short-term forecasts and analyses of medium-term problems relevant to economic policies are provided. The surveys are shipped from France. The complete set costs $180 ($203, airmail); a single copy, $13. Contact Organization for Economic Cooperation and Development, Publications and Information Center, 2001 L Street, Suite 700, Washington, DC 20036; telephone 202-785-6323.

- **OECD publications.** OECD publishes widely on a broad range of social and economic issues, concerns, and developments, including reports on international market information country by country, such as import data useful in assessing import competition. The chartered mission of OECD is to promote within and among its 24-member countries policies designed to support high economic growth, employment, and standard of living and to contribute to sound economic expansion in development and in trade. For information and prices on these publications, contact Organization of Economic Cooperation and Development, Publications and Information Center, 2001 L Street, Suite 700, Washington, DC 20036; telephone 202-785-6323.

Detailed product- and industry-specific data resources

U.S. Government Product and Industry Resources

- **Comparison Shopping Service.** CSS is a custom market survey service produced by US&FCS. On request, CSS provides a U.S. firm with detailed market information on a selected single product in a selected market worldwide. CSS answers basic questions about the marketability of the product, key competitors, comparative prices, customary distribution and promotion practices, trade barriers, and other factors. Available at fees ranging from $500 to $4,000 depending on the particular country market chosen. Contact the local Commerce district office or telephone 202-377-4767.

- **Industry sector analyses.** Prepared by the commercial sections of the U.S. embassies for US&FCS, ISAs provide the basis for quickly sizing up one particular commercial or industrial market in a particular country. ISAs present market demand, market size, competitive analysis, end user analysis, and market access criteria as well as marketing opportunities. Available at $10 per report through CIMS and NTDB. Contact the local Commerce district office or telephone 202-377-4767.

- **Alert reports.** Prepared on an ad hoc basis by the economic and commercial sections of U.S. embassies and consulates for US&FCS, alert reports help to identify unique market situations and marketing opportunities for U.S. business. Available at $10 per report through CIMS, NTDB, and EBB. Contact the local Commerce district office or telephone 202-377-4767.

- **Agricultural Trade Highlights.** The *Highlights*, published by FAS, provide economic analyses of major overseas markets and demand trends. They also provide in-depth monthly summaries of major activities and events affecting U.S. agriculture exports and imports, and year-to-date summaries of commodity performance. Available as a single free copy or by subscription. For a single free copy, contact Information Division, Foreign Agricultural Service, U.S. Department of Agriculture, Washington, DC 20250; telephone 202-447-7937. For the annual subscription, contact Trade Assistance and Planning Office, Foreign Agricultural Service, U.S. Department of Agriculture, Washington, DC 20250; telephone 703-756-6001.

- **Staff papers on best prospects.** These reports, produced by FAS, offer the best overall prospects for expansion of U.S. agricultural products over the next three to five years. They cover about 15 countries and are available free. Contact Trade Assistance and Planning Office, Foreign Agricultural Service, U.S. Department of Agriculture, Washington, DC 20250; telephone 703-756-6001.

Private Sector Product and Industry Resources

- **American Export Register.** This two-volume directory of 38,000 U.S. exporters and the materials, products, or services they sell internationally is published annually. Advertising is accepted. The cost is $120. Contact Thomas International Publishing Company, Inc., One Penn Plaza, New York, NY 10119; telephone 212-290-7343.

- **Export Shipping Manual.** Published annually and updated weekly, the manual is a three-volume looseleaf reference service containing up-to-date, country-by-country shipping and market research information. Social, political, economic, and commercial conditions of each country are profiled. Detail is given to policies, regulations, issues, development, and laws pertaining to commerce, especially foreign trade. The cost is $524. Contact Bureau of National Affairs, Inc., Distribution Center, Keywest Avenue, Rockville, MD 20850; telephone 800-372-1033 or 202-452-4200.

- **FINDEX: The Directory of Market Research Reports, Studies and Surveys.** This reference guide to commercially available market and business research, including international market research, contains more than 10,000 listings of reports, studies, and surveys. The 1991 edition (900 pages) costs $325 (ISBN:0-942189-03-5). Contact Cambridge Information Group, 7200 Wisconsin Avenue, Bethesda, MD 20814; telephone 800-227-3052 or 301-961-6750.

- **Inside Washington: The International Business Executive's Guide to Government Money and Resources.** This publication is a complete source book on government assistance programs and services. It is organized the way executives think about international business and includes comprehensive contact information. The latest edition, 1988 (ISBN:0-8191-6934-X), is 295 pages long and costs $49.95. *Inside Washington* publications are now available for specific industry sectors and have a special emphasis on financial support programs. Each book contains case studies and a comprehensive exporters telephone directory. The following editions are available at $24.95 each: Environment-Money, High Technology, and Food-Business. Contact Delphos International, 600 Watergate N.W., Suite 960, Washington, DC 20037; telephone 800-288-2582 or 202-337-6300; fax 202-333-1158.

- *Electronic data bases.* A number of private sector data bases are available to provide specific marketing information for firms interested in doing business internationally, such as the PIER service of the *Journal of Commerce* and DIALOG. Many of these data bases are accessible both at local public libraries and universities and directly by personal computer.

Methods of exporting and channels of distribution

The most common methods of exporting are indirect selling and direct selling (see chapter 1). In indirect selling, an export intermediary such as an EMC or an ETC normally assumes responsibility for finding overseas buyers, shipping products, and getting paid. In direct selling, the U.S. producer deals directly with a foreign buyer.

The paramount consideration in determining whether to market indirectly or directly is the level of resources a company is willing to devote to its international marketing effort. These are some other factors to consider when deciding whether to market indirectly or directly:

- The size of the firm.
- The nature of its products.
- Previous export experience and expertise.
- Business conditions in the selected overseas markets.

Distribution considerations

- Which channels of distribution should the firm use to market its products abroad?
- Where should the firm produce its products and how should it distribute them in the foreign market?
- What types of representatives, brokers, wholesalers, dealers, distributors, retailers, and so on should the firm use?
- What are the characteristics and capabilities of the available intermediaries?
- Should the assistance of an EMC or ETC be obtained?

Indirect exporting

The principal advantage of indirect marketing for a smaller U.S. company is that it provides a way to penetrate foreign markets without the complexities and risks of direct exporting. Several kinds of intermediary firms provide a range of export services. Each type of firm offers distinct advantages for the U.S. company.

Commission agents

Commission or buying agents are finders for foreign firms that want to purchase U.S. products. They seek to obtain the desired items at the lowest possible price and are paid a commission by their foreign clients. In some cases, they may be foreign government agencies or quasi-governmental firms empowered to locate and purchase desired goods. Foreign government purchasing missions are one example.

Export management companies

An EMC acts as the export department for one or several producers of goods or services. It solicits and transacts business in the names of the producers it represents or in its own name for a commission, salary, or retainer plus commission. Some EMCs provide immediate payment for the producer's products by either arranging financing or directly purchasing products for resale. Typically, only larger EMCs can afford to purchase or finance exports.

EMCs usually specialize either by product or by foreign market or both. Because of their specialization, the best EMCs know their products and the markets they serve very well and usually have well-established networks of foreign distributors already in place. This immediate access to foreign markets is one of the principal reasons for using an EMC, since establishing a productive relationship with a foreign representative may be a costly and lengthy process.

One disadvantage in using an EMC is that a manufacturer may lose control over foreign sales. Most manufacturers are properly concerned that their product and company image be well maintained in foreign markets. An important way for a company to retain sufficient control in such an arrangement is to carefully select an EMC that can meet the company's needs and maintain close communication with it. For example, a company may ask for regular reports on efforts to market its products and may require approval of certain types of efforts, such as advertising programs or service arrangements. If a company wants to maintain this type of relationship with an EMC, it should negotiate points of concern before entering an agreement, since not all EMCs are willing to comply with the company's concerns.

Export trading companies

An ETC facilitates the export of U.S. goods and services. Like an EMC, an ETC can either act as the export department for producers or take title to the product and export for its own account. Therefore, the terms ETC and EMC are often used interchangeably. A special kind of ETC is a group organized and operated by producers. These ETCs can be organized along multiple- or single-industry lines and can represent producers of competing products.

Export Trading Company Act of 1982

The goal of the Export Trading Company Act of 1982 is to stimulate U.S. exports by (1) promoting and encouraging the formation of export management and export trading companies; (2) expanding the options available for export financing by permitting bank holding companies to invest in ETCs and reducing restrictions on trade finance provided by financial institutions; and (3) reducing uncertainty about applying U.S. antitrust law to export operations. This legislation allows banks, for the first time in recent history, to make equity investments in commercial ventures that qualify as ETCs. In addition, for the first time, the Export-Import Bank (Eximbank) of the United States is allowed to make working capital guarantees to U.S. exporters. Through the Office of Export Trading Company Affairs (OETCA) within the ITA, the U.S. Department of Commerce promotes the formation and use of U.S. export intermediaries and issues export trade certificates of review providing limited immunity from U.S. antitrust laws.

OETCA informs the business community of the benefits of export intermediaries through conferences, presentations before trade associations and civic organizations, and publications. The major publication on this subject is the *Export Trading Company Guidebook,* available for purchase through the U.S. Government Printing Office. OETCA provides counseling to businesses seeking to take advantage of the act.

OETCA also maintains the Contact Facilitation Service (CFS) data base, a listing of U.S. producers of goods and services and of organizations that provide trade facilitation services. Under a public-private sector arrangement, the CFS data base is published annually in a directory entitled *The Export Yellow Pages,* which is available free from local Department of Commerce district offices. The directory provides users with the names and addresses of banks, EMCs, ETCs, freight forwarders, manufacturers, and service organizations and names the export products or export-related services that these firms supply. By obtaining CFS registration forms from Commerce district offices, firms can register in the data base free of charge and be listed in subsequent editions of *The Export Yellow Pages.*

The certificates of review are issued by the Secretary of Commerce with the concurrence of the U.S. Department of Justice. Any U.S. corporation or partnership, any resident individual, or any state or local entity may apply for a certificate of review. A certificate can be issued to an applicant if it is determined that the proposed "export trade activities and methods of operation" will not result in a substantial lessening of domestic competition or restraint of trade within the United States. For the conduct covered by the certificate, its holder and any other individuals or firms named as members are given immunity from government suits under U.S. federal and state antitrust laws. In private party actions, liability is reduced from treble to single damages, greatly reducing the probability of nuisance suits. Moreover, in the event of private litigation involving conduct covered by the certificate of review, a prevailing certificate holder recovers the costs of defending the suit, including reasonable attorney's fees.

The certificate of review program provides exporters with an antitrust "insurance policy" intended to foster joint activities where economies of scale and risk diversification can be achieved. The act also amends the Sherman Antitrust Act and the Federal Trade Commission Act to clarify the jurisdictional reach of these statutes to export trade. Both acts now apply to export trade only if there is a "direct substantial and reasonably foreseeable" effect on domestic or import commerce of the United States or the export commerce of a U.S. competitor.

Firms and individuals interested in additional information should contact the Office of Export Trading Company Affairs, Room 1800, U.S. Department of Commerce, Washington, DC 20230; telephone 202-377-5131. For a copy of *The Export Yellow Pages,* contact the nearest Commerce district office.

Export agents, merchants, or remarketers

Export agents, merchants, or remarketers purchase products directly from the manufacturer, packing and marking the products according to their own specifications. They then sell overseas through their contacts in their own names and assume all risks for accounts.

In transactions with export agents, merchants, or remarketers, a U.S. firm relinquishes control over the marketing and promotion of its product, which could have an adverse effect on future sales efforts abroad. For example, the product could be underpriced or incorrectly positioned in the market, or after-sales service could be neglected. On the other hand, the effort required by the manufacturer to market the product overseas is very small and may lead to sales that otherwise would take a great deal of effort to obtain.

Piggyback marketing

Piggyback marketing is an arrangement in which one manufacturer or service firm distributes a second firm's product or service. The most common piggybacking situation is when a U.S. company has a contract with an overseas buyer to provide a wide range of products or services. Often, this first company does not produce all of the products it is under contract to provide, and it turns to other U.S. companies to provide the remaining products. The second U.S. company thus piggybacks its products to the international market, generally without incurring the marketing and distribution costs associated with exporting. Successful arrangements usually require that the product lines be complementary and appeal to the same customers.

Direct exporting

The advantages of direct exporting for a U.S. company include more control over the export process, potentially higher profits, and a closer relationship to the overseas buyer and marketplace. These advantages do not come easily, however, since the U.S. company needs to devote more time, personnel, and corporate resources than are needed with indirect exporting.

When a company chooses to export directly to foreign markets, it usually makes internal organizational changes to support more complex functions. A direct exporter normally selects the markets it wishes to penetrate, chooses the best channels of distribution for each market, and then makes specific foreign business connections in order to sell its product. The rest of this chapter discusses these aspects of direct exporting in more detail.

Organizing for exporting

A company new to exporting generally treats its export sales no differently from domestic sales, using existing personnel and organizational structures. As international sales and inquiries increase, however, the company may separate the management of its exports from that of its domestic sales.

The advantages of separating international from domestic business include the centralization of specialized skills needed to deal with international markets and the benefits of a focused marketing effort that is more likely to lead to increased export sales. A possible disadvantage of such a separation is the less efficient use of corporate resources due to segmentation.

When a company separates international from domestic business, it may do so at different levels in the organization. For example, when a company first begins to export, it may create an export department with a full- or part-time manager who reports to the head of domestic sales and marketing. At later stages a company may choose to increase the autonomy of the export department to the point of creating an international division that reports directly to the president.

Larger companies at advanced stages of exporting may choose to retain the international division or to organize along product or geographic lines. A company with distinct product lines may create an international department in each product division. A company with products that have common end users may organize geographically; for example, it may form a division for Europe, another for the Far East, and so on. A small company's initial needs may be satisfied by a single export manager who has responsibility for the full range of international activities. Regardless of how a company organizes for exporting, it should ensure that the organization facilitates the marketer's job. Good marketing skills can help the firm overcome the handicap of operating in an unfamiliar market. Experience has shown that a company's success in foreign markets depends less on the unique attributes of its products than on its marketing methods.

Once a company has been organized to handle exporting, the proper channel of distribution needs to be selected in each market. These channels include sales representatives, agents, distributors, retailers, and end users.

Sales representatives

Overseas, a sales representative is the equivalent of a manufacturer's representative in the United States. The representative uses the company's product literature and samples to present the product to potential buyers. A representative usually handles many complementary lines that do not compete. The sales representative usually works on a commission basis, assumes no risk or responsibility, and is under contract for a definite period of time (renewable by mutual agreement). The contract defines territory, terms of sale, method of compensation, reasons and procedures for terminating the agreement, and other details. The sales representative may operate on either an exclusive or a nonexclusive basis.

Agents

The widely misunderstood term *agent* means a representative who normally has authority, perhaps even power of attorney, to make commitments on behalf of the firm he or she represents. Firms in the United States and other developed countries have stopped using the term and instead rely on the term *representative,* since *agent* can imply more than intended. Any contract should state whether the representative or agent does or does not have legal authority to obligate the firm.

Distributors

The foreign distributor is a merchant who purchases merchandise from a U.S. exporter (often at substantial discount) and resells it at a profit. The foreign distributor generally provides support and service for the product, relieving the U.S. company of these responsibilities. The distributor usually carries an inventory of products and a sufficient supply of spare parts and maintains adequate facilities and personnel for normal servicing operations. The distributor typically carries a range of noncompetitive but complementary products. End users do not usually buy from a distributor; they buy from retailers or dealers.

The payment terms and length of association between the U.S. company and the foreign distributor are established by contract. Some U.S. companies prefer to begin with a relatively short trial period and then extend the contract if the relationship proves satisfactory to both parties.

Foreign retailers

A company may also sell directly to a foreign retailer, although in such transactions, products are generally limited to consumer lines. The growth of major retail chains in markets such as Canada and Japan has created new opportunities for this type of direct sale. The method relies mainly on traveling sales representatives who directly contact foreign retailers, although results may be accomplished by mailing catalogs, brochures, or other literature. The direct mail approach has the benefits of eliminating commissions, reducing traveling expenses, and reaching a broader audience. For best results, however, a firm that uses direct mail to reach foreign retailers should support it with other marketing activities.

American manufacturers with ties to major domestic retailers may also be able to use them to sell abroad. Many large American retailers maintain overseas buying offices and use these offices to sell abroad when practicable.

Direct sales to end users

A U.S. business may sell its products or services directly to end users in foreign countries. These buyers can be foreign governments; institutions such as hospitals, banks, and schools; or businesses. Buyers can be identified at trade shows, through international publications, or through U.S. government contact programs, such as the Department of Commerce's Export Contact List Service (ECLS). Chapter 7 details these and other buyer contact activities and programs.

The U.S. company should be aware that if a product is sold in such a direct fashion, the exporter is responsible for shipping, payment collection, and product servicing unless other arrangements are made. Unless the cost of providing these services is built into the export price, a company could end up making far less than originally intended.

Locating foreign representatives and buyers

A company that chooses to use foreign representatives may meet them during overseas business trips or at domestic or international trade shows. There are other effective methods, too, that can be employed without leaving the United States. Ultimately, the exporter may need to travel abroad to identify, evaluate, and sign overseas representatives; however, a company can save time by first doing homework in the United States. Methods include use of US&FCS contact programs, banks and service organizations, and publications. For more information on these methods, see chapter 7.

Contacting and evaluating foreign representatives

Once the U.S. company has identified a number of potential representatives or distributors in the selected market, it should write directly to each. Just as the U.S. firm is seeking information on the foreign representative, the representative is interested in corporate and product information on the U.S. firm. The prospective representative may want more information than the company normally provides to a casual buyer. Therefore, the firm should provide full information on its history, resources, personnel, the product line, previous export activity, and all other pertinent matters. The firm may wish to include a photograph or two of plant facilities and products or possibly product samples, when practical. (Whenever the danger of piracy is significant, the exporter should guard against sending product samples that could be easily copied.) For more information on correspondence with foreign firms see chapter 9.

A U.S. firm should investigate potential representatives of distributors carefully before entering into an agreement. See table 4-1 for an extensive checklist of factors to consider in such evaluations. In brief, the U.S. firm needs to know the following points about the representative or distributor's firm:

- Current status and history, including background on principal officers.

- Personnel and other resources (salespeople, warehouse and service facilities, etc.).

- Sales territory covered.

- Current sales volume.

- Typical customer profiles.

- Methods of introducing new products into the sales territory.

- Names and addresses of U.S. firms currently represented.

- Trade and bank references.

- Data on whether the U.S. firm's special requirements can be met.

- View of the in-country market potential for the U.S. firm's products. This information is not only useful in gauging how much the representative knows about the exporter's industry, it is also valuable market research in its own right.

A U.S. company may obtain much of this information from business associates who currently work with foreign representatives. However, U.S. exporters should not hesitate to ask potential representatives or distributors detailed and specific questions; exporters have the right to explore the qualifications of those who propose to represent them overseas. Well-qualified representatives will gladly answer questions that help distinguish them from less-qualified competitors.

In addition, the U.S. company may wish to obtain at least two supporting business and credit reports to ensure that the distributor or representative is reputable. By using a second credit report from another source, the U.S. firm may gain new or more complete information. Reports are available from commercial firms and from the Department of Commerce's World Traders Data Report (WTDR) program.

The WTDR service (see chapter 7) provides background reports on specific foreign firms prepared by the US&FCS posts overseas. In addition to information on size, product lines, and financial stability, each WTDR also contains a general narrative statement by the commercial officer who conducted the investigation.

Commercial firms and banks are also sources of credit information on overseas representatives. They can provide information directly or from their correspondent banks or branches overseas. Directories of international companies may also provide credit information on foreign firms.

If the U.S. company has the necessary information, it may wish to contact a few of the foreign firm's U.S. clients to obtain an evaluation of their representative's character, reliability, efficiency, and past performance. To protect itself against possible conflicts of interest, it is also important for the U.S. firm to learn about other product lines that the foreign firm represents.

Once the company has qualified some foreign representatives, it may wish to travel to the foreign country to observe the size, condition, and location of offices and warehouses. In addition, the U.S. company should meet the sales force and try to assess its strength in the marketplace. If traveling to each distributor or representative is difficult, the company may decide to meet with them at U.S. and worldwide trade shows.

Negotiating an agreement with a foreign representative

When the U.S. company has found a prospective representative that meets its requirements, the next step is to negotiate a foreign sales agreement. The Department of Commerce district offices can provide counseling to firms planning to negotiate foreign sales agreements with representatives and distributors.

The potential representative is interested in the company's pricing structure and profit potential. Representatives are also concerned with the terms of payment, product regulation, competitors and their market shares, the amount of support provided by the U.S. firm (sales aids, promotional material, advertising, etc.), training for sales and service staff, and the company's ability to deliver on schedule.

The agreement may contain provisions that the foreign representative

- not have business dealings with competitive firms (this provision may cause problems in some European countries and may also cause problems under U.S. antitrust laws);

- not reveal any confidential information in a way that would prove injurious, detrimental, or competitive to the U.S. firm;

- not enter into agreements binding to the U.S. firm; and

- refer all inquiries received from outside the designated sales territory to the U.S. firm for action.

To ensure a conscientious sales effort from the foreign representative, the agreement should include a requirement that the foreign representative apply the utmost skill and ability to the sale of the product for the compensation named in the contract. It may be appropriate to include performance requirements such as a minimum sales volume and an expected rate of increase.

In the drafting of the agreement, special attention must be paid to safeguarding the exporter's interests in cases in which the representative proves less than satisfactory. (See chapter 11 for recommendations on specifying terms of law and arbitration.) It is vital to include an escape clause in the agreement, allowing the exporter to end the relationship safely and cleanly if the representative does not work out. Some contracts specify that either party may terminate the agreement with written notice 30, 60, or 90 days in advance. The contract may also spell out exactly what constitutes just cause for ending the agreement (e.g., failure to meet specified performance levels). Other contracts specify a certain term for the agreement (usually one year) but arrange for automatic annual renewal unless either party gives notice in writing of its intention not to renew.

In all cases, escape clauses and other provisions to safeguard the exporter may be limited by the laws of the country in which the representative is located. For this reason, the U.S. firm should learn as much as it can about the legal requirements of the representative's country and obtain qualified legal counsel in preparing the contract. These are some of the legal questions to consider:

- How far in advance must the representative be notified of the exporter's intention to terminate the agreement? Three months satisfy the requirements of most countries, but a verifiable means of conveyance (e.g., registered mail) may be needed to establish when the notice was served.

- What is just cause for terminating a representative? Specifying causes for termination in the written contract usually strengthens the exporter's position.

- Which country's laws (or which international convention) govern a contract dispute? Laws in the representative's country may forbid the representative from waiving its nation's legal jurisdiction.

- What compensation is due the representative on dismissal? Depending on the length of the relationship, the added value of the market the representative has created for the exporter, and whether termination is for just cause as defined by the foreign country, the U.S. exporter may be required to compensate the representative for losses.

- What must the representative give up if dismissed? The contract should specify the return of patents, trademarks, name registrations, customer records, and so on.

- Should the representative be referred to as an agent? In some countries, the word *agent* implies power of attorney. The contract may need to specify that the representative is not a legal agent with power of attorney.

- In what language should the contract be drafted? An English-language text should be the official language of the contract in most cases.

The exporter should also be aware of U.S. laws that govern such contracts. For instance, the U.S. company should seek to avoid provisions that could be contrary to U.S. antitrust laws. The Export Trading Company Act provides a means to obtain antitrust protection when two or more companies combine for exporting. In any case, the U.S. firm should obtain legal advice when preparing and entering into any foreign agreement.

Table 4-1.
Factors to Consider When Choosing a Foreign Representative or Distributor

The following checklist should be tailored by each company to its own needs. Key factors vary significantly with the products and countries involved.

Size of sales force

- How many field sales personnel does the representative or distributor have?
- What are its short- and long-range expansion plans, if any?
- Would it need to expand to accommodate your account properly? If so, would it be willing to do so?

Sales record

- Has its sales growth been consistent? If not, why not? Try to determine sales volume for the past five years.
- What is its sales volume per outside salesperson?
- What are its sales objectives for next year? How were they determined?

Territorial analysis

- What territory does it now cover?
- Is it consistent with the coverage you desire? If not, is it able and willing to expand?
- Does it have any branch offices in the territory to be covered?
- If so, are they located where your sales prospects are greatest?
- Does it have any plans to open additional offices?

Product mix

- How many product lines does it represent?
- Are these product lines compatible with yours?
- Would there be any conflict of interest?
- Does it represent any other U.S. firms? If so, which ones?
- If necessary, would it be willing to alter its present product mix to accommodate yours?
- What would be the minimum sales volume needed to justify its handling your lines? Do its sales projections reflect this minimum figure? From what you know of the territory and the prospective representative or distributor, is its projection realistic?

Facilities and equipment

- Does it have adequate warehouse facilities?
- What is its method of stock control?
- Does it use computers? Are they compatible with yours?
- What communications facilities does it have (fax, modem, telex, etc.)?
- If your product requires servicing, is it equipped and qualified to do so? If not, is it willing to acquire the needed equipment and arrange for necessary training? To what extent will you have to share the training cost?
- If necessary and customary, is it willing to inventory repair parts and replacement items?

Table 4-1. (continued)

Marketing policies

- How is its sales staff compensated?
- Does it have special incentive or motivation programs?
- Does it use product managers to coordinate sales efforts for specific product lines?
- How does it monitor sales performance?
- How does it train its sales staff?
- Would it share expenses for sales personnel to attend factory-sponsored seminars?

Customer profile

- What kinds of customers is it currently contacting?
- Are its interests compatible with your product line?
- Who are its key accounts?
- What percentage of its total gross receipts do these key accounts represent?

Principals represented

- How many principals is it currently representing?
- Would you be its primary supplier?
- If not, what percentage of its total business would you represent? How does this percentage compare with other suppliers?

Promotional thrust

- Can it help you compile market research information to be used in making forecasts?
- What media does it use, if any, to promote sales?
- How much of its budget is allocated to advertising? How is it distributed among various principals?
- Will you be expected to contribute funds for promotional purposes? How will the amount be determined?
- If it uses direct mail, how many prospects are on its mailing list?
- What type of brochure does it use to describe its company and the products that it represents?
- If necessary, can it translate your advertising copy?

Preparing products for export

Selecting and preparing a product for export requires not only product knowledge but also knowledge of the unique characteristics of each market being targeted. The market research conducted (chapter 3) and the contacts made with foreign representatives (chapter 4) should give the U.S. company an idea of what products can be sold where. Before the sale can occur, however, the company may need to modify a particular product to satisfy buyer tastes or needs in foreign markets.

The extent to which the company will modify products sold in export markets is a key policy issue to be addressed by management. Some exporters believe the domestic product can be exported without significant changes. Others seek to consciously develop uniform products that are acceptable in all export markets.

If the company manufactures more than one product or offers many models of a single product, it should start with the one best suited to the targeted market. Ideally, the firm chooses one or two products that fit the market without major design or engineering modifications. Doing so is possible when the U.S. company

- deals with international customers with the same demographic characteristics or with the same specifications for manufactured goods,

- supplies parts for U.S. goods that are exported to foreign countries without modifications,

- produces a unique product that is sold on the basis of its status or foreign appeal, or

- produces a product that has few or no distinguishing features and that is sold almost exclusively on a commodity or price basis.

Product preparation considerations

- What foreign needs does the product satisfy?

- Should the firm modify its domestic-market product for sale abroad? Should it develop a new product for the foreign market?

- What product should the firm offer abroad?

- What specific features – design, color, size, packaging, brand, warranty, and so on – should the product have?

- What specific services are necessary abroad at the presale and postsale stages?

- Are the firm's service and repair facilities adequate?

Product adaptation

To enter a foreign market successfully, a U.S. company may have to modify its product to conform to government regulations, geographic and climatic conditions, buyer preferences, or standard of living. The company may also need to modify its product to facilitate shipment or to compensate for possible differences in engineering or design standards.

Foreign government product regulations are common in international trade and are expected to expand in the future. These regulations can take the form of high tariffs or of nontariff barriers, such as regulations or product specifications. Governments impose these regulations to

- protect domestic industries from foreign competition,

- protect the health of their citizens,

- force importers to comply with environmental controls,

- ensure that importers meet local requirements for electrical or measurement systems,

- restrict the flow of goods originating in or having components from certain countries, and

- protect their citizens from cultural influences deemed inappropriate.

Detailed information on regulations imposed by foreign countries is available from the country desk officers (see appendix II) of the Department of Commerce's IEP unit. Where particularly onerous or discriminatory barriers are imposed by a foreign government, a U.S. company may be able to get help from the U.S. government to press for their removal. The firm should contact a Department of Commerce district office (see appendix III) or the Office of the U.S. Trade Representative in Washington, D.C. (see appendix II) for further information.

It is often necessary for a company to adapt its product to account for geographic and climatic conditions as well as for availability of resources. Factors such as topography, humidity, and energy costs can affect the performance of a product or even define its use. The cost of petroleum products along with a country's infrastructure, for example, may indicate the demand for a company's energy-consuming products.

Buyer preferences in a foreign market may also lead a U.S. manufacturer to modify its product. Local customs, such as religion or the use of leisure time, often determine whether a product will sell. The sensory impact of a product, such as taste or visual impact, may also be a critical factor. The Japanese desire for beautiful packaging, for example, has led many U.S. companies to redesign cartons and packages specifically for this market.

A country's standard of living can also determine whether a company needs to modify a product. The level of income, the level of education, and the availability of energy are all factors that help predict the acceptance of a product in a foreign market. If a country's standard of living is lower than that of the United States, a manufacturer may find a market for less sophisticated product models that have become obsolete in the United States. Certain high-technology products are inappropriate in some countries not only because of their cost, but also because of their function. For example, a computerized industrial washing machine might replace workers in a country where employment is a high priority. In addition, these products may need a level of servicing that is unavailable in some countries.

Market potential must be large enough to justify the direct and indirect costs involved in product adaptation. The firm should assess the costs to be incurred and the increased revenues expected from adaptation (they may be difficult to determine). The decision to adapt a product is based in part on the degree of commitment to the specific foreign market; two firms, one with short-term goals and the other with long-term goals, may have different perspectives.

Engineering and redesign

In addition to adaptations related to cultural and consumer preference, the exporter should be aware that even fundamental aspects of its products may require changing. For example, electrical standards in many foreign countries differ from U.S. electrical standards. It is not unusual to find phases, cycles, or voltages (both in home and commercial use) that would damage or impair the operating efficiency of equipment designed for use in the United States. These electrical standards sometimes vary even in the same country. Knowing this requirement, the manufacturer can determine whether a special motor must be substituted or arrange for a different drive ratio to achieve the desired operating revolutions per minute.

Similarly, many kinds of equipment must be engineered in the metric system for integration with other pieces of equipment or for compliance with the standards of a given country. The United States is virtually alone in its adherence to a nonmetric system, and U.S. firms that compete successfully in the global market have found metric measurement to be an important detail in selling to overseas customers. Even instruction or maintenance manuals should take care to give dimensions in centimeters, weights in grams or kilos, and temperatures in degrees Celsius. Information on foreign standards and certification systems is available from the National Center for Standards and Certificates Information, National Institute for Standards and Technology, Administration Building, A629, Gaithersburg, MD 20899; telephone 301-975-4040.

Since freight charges are usually assessed by weight or volume (whichever provides the greater revenue for the carrier), a company should give some consideration to shipping an item unassembled to reduce delivery costs. Shipping unassembled also facilitates movement on narrow roads or through doorways and elevators.

Branding, labeling, and packaging

Consumers are concerned with both the product itself and the product's supplementary features, such as packaging, warranties, and service.

Branding and labeling of products in foreign markets raise new considerations for the U.S. company:

- Are international brand names important to promote and distinguish a product? Conversely, should local brands or private labels be employed to heighten local interest?

- Are the colors used on labels and packages offensive or attractive to the foreign buyer? In some countries, certain colors are associated with death, national flags, or other cultural factors.

- Can labels be produced in official or customary languages if required by law or practice?

- Does information on product content and country of origin have to be provided?

- Are weights and measures stated in the local unit?

- Must each item be labeled individually?

- Are local tastes and knowledge considered? A dry cereal box picturing a U.S. athlete may not be as attractive to overseas consumers as the picture of a local sports hero.

A company may find that building international recognition for a brand is expensive. Protection for brand names varies from one country to another, and in some developing countries, barriers to the use of foreign brands or trademarks may exist. In other countries, piracy of a company's brand names and counterfeiting of its products are widespread. To protect its products and brand names, a company must comply with local laws on patents, copyrights, and trademarks. A U.S. firm may find it useful to obtain the advice of local lawyers and consultants where appropriate.

Installation

Another element of product preparation that a company should consider is the ease of installing that product overseas. If technicians or engineers are needed overseas to assist in installation, the company should minimize their time in the field if possible. To do so, the company may wish to preassemble or pretest the product before shipping.

Disassembling the product for shipment and reassembling abroad may be considered by the company. This method can save the firm shipping costs, but it may add to delay in payment if the sale is contingent on an assembled product. Even if trained personnel do not have to be sent, the company should be careful to provide all product information, such as training manuals, installation instructions, and parts lists, in the local language.

Warranties

The company should include a warranty on the product, since the buyer expects a specific level of performance and a guarantee that it will be achieved. Levels of expectation for a warranty vary from country to country depending on its level of development, competitive practices, the activism of consumer groups, local standards of production quality, and other similar factors.

A company may use warranties for advertising purposes to distinguish its product from its competition. Strong warranties may be required to break into a new market, especially if the company is an unknown supplier. In some cases, warranties may be instrumental in making the sale and may be a major element of negotiation. In other cases, however, warranties similar to those in the United States are not expected. By providing an unnecessary

warranty, the company may raise the cost of the product higher than the competitors' costs. When considering this point, exporters should keep in mind that servicing warranties will probably be more expensive and troublesome in foreign markets. It is desirable to arrange warranty service locally with the assistance of a representative or distributor.

Servicing

Of special concern to foreign consumers is the service the U.S. company provides for its product. Service after the sale is critical for some products; generally, the more complex the product technology, the greater the demand for presale and postsale service. There is, therefore, pressure in some firms to offer simpler, more robust products overseas to reduce the need for maintenance and repairs. U.S. exporters who rely on a foreign distributor or agent to provide service backup must take steps to ensure an adequate level of service. These steps include training, periodically checking service quality, and monitoring inventories of spare parts. See chapter 15 for more on after-sales service.

Service exports

6

Service industries span a wide variety of enterprises from hamburgers to high technology. The service sector accounts for about 70 percent of the U.S. GNP and 75 percent of employment. In 1988, the service sector also accounted for slightly more than two-thirds of all self-employed persons.

Internationally, a similar change has taken place. World trade in services grew in the past decade at an average rate of 5 percent a year to constitute approximately 20 percent of overall world trade today. In some countries, the share is much higher. Spain reports a 39 percent share; Austria, 36 percent. The leading exporter of services, the United States, shows services accounting for 18 percent of all merchandise and services trade and, unlike the situation with trade in goods, has had a surplus in services trade for decades.

The income generated and the jobs created through the sale of services abroad are just as important to the U.S. economy as income and jobs resulting from the production and export of goods. In view of the shift toward services both domestically and internationally and the substantial competitive advantage of the United States in the services field, those who have services to offer can become major participants in world trade.

Typical service exports

The service sector accounts for a great share of the U.S. economy, although some services are not easily exported. It would be very difficult to export most personal services, such as the service performed by waiters in restaurants; but most business services can be exported – especially those highly innovative, specialized, or technologically advanced services that are efficiently performed in the United States. The following sectors have particularly high export potential:

- **Construction, design, and engineering.** The vast experience and technological leadership of the U.S. construction industry, as well as special skills in operations, maintenance, and management, frequently give U.S. firms a competitive edge in international projects. Some U.S. firms with expertise in specialized fields, such as electric power utilities, also export related construction, design, and engineering services, such as power plant design services.

- **Banking and financial services.** U.S. financial institutions are very competitive internationally, particularly when offering account management, credit card operations, collection management, and other services they have pioneered.

- **Insurance services.** U.S. insurers offer valuable services ranging from underwriting and risk evaluation to insurance operations and management contracts in the international marketplace.

- **Legal and accounting services.** Firms in this field typically aid other U.S. firms operating abroad through their international legal and accounting activities. They also use their experience to serve foreign firms in their business operations.

- **Computer and data services.** The U.S. computer services and data industries lead the world in marketing new technologies and enjoy a competitive advantage in computer operations, data manipulation, and data transmission.

- **Teaching services.** The vast U.S. education sector offers substantial new services for foreign purchasers, particularly in areas such as management, motivation, and the teaching of operational, managerial, and theoretical issues.

- **Management consulting services.** Organizations and business enterprises all over the world look to the United States in the field of management. U.S. management consulting firms as well as other U.S. firms that are willing to sell their particular management skills find great potential overseas for export of their services.

Exporting services versus products

There are many obvious differences between services and products. Consequently, important features differentiate exporting services from exporting products:

- Services are less tangible than products, providing little in terms of samples that can be seen by the potential foreign buyer. Consequently, communicating a service offer is much more difficult than communicating a product offer. For example, brochures or catalogs explaining services often must show a proxy for the service. A construction company, for instance, can show a picture of a construction site, but a picture of the finished building communicates the actual performance of the service more effectively. Much more attention must be paid to translating the intangibility of a service into a tangible and saleable offer.

- The intangibility of services also makes financing more difficult. Frequently, even financial institutions with international experience are less willing to provide financial support for service exports than for product exports, because the value of services is more difficult to monitor. Customer complaints and difficulties in receiving payments can also appear more troublesome to assess.

- Services are often more time dependent than products. Quite frequently, a service can be offered only at a specific time, and as time passes, the service perishes if it is not used. For example, to offer data transmission through special telephone lines may require providing an open telephone line. If this line is not heavily used, the cost of maintaining it may not be covered.

- Selling services is also more personal than selling products, because it quite often requires direct involvement with the customer. This involvement demands greater cultural sensitivity when services are being provided, since a buffer of indirect communication and interaction does not exist.

- Services are much more difficult to standardize than products. Service activities must frequently be tailored to the specific needs of the buyer. This need for adaptation often necessitates the service client's direct participation and cooperation in the service delivery.

Demand for certain services can derive from product exports. Many of our merchandise exports would not take place if they were not supported by service activities such as banking, insurance, and transportation. Services can be crucial in stimulating product export and are a critical factor in maintaining such exports. However, in such cases, services follow products rather than taking the lead over them.

Marketing services abroad

Since service exports are often delivered in the support of product exports, a sensible approach for some beginning exporters is to follow the path of relevant product exports. For years, many large accounting and banking firms have exported by following their major multinational clients abroad and continuing to assist them in their international activities. Smaller service exporters who cooperate closely with manufacturing firms can also determine where these manufacturing firms are operating internationally and aim to provide service support for these manufacturers abroad.

For service providers whose activities are independent from products, a different strategy is needed. These individuals and firms should search for market situations abroad that are similar to the domestic market.

Many opportunities derive from understanding the process and stage of development of relevant trade activities abroad. Just as U.S. society has undergone change, foreign societies are subject to changing economic trends. If, for example, new transportation services are opened up in a country, an expert in the area of containerization may offer services to improve the efficiency of the new system.

Leads for service activities can also be gathered by staying informed about international projects sponsored by organizations such as the World Bank, the Caribbean Development Bank, the Inter-American Development Bank, the UN, and the World Health Organization. Very frequently, such projects are in need of service support.

Government support for service exports

In recognition of the increasing importance of service exports, the U.S. Department of Commerce has made the Office of Service Industries responsible for analyzing and promoting services trade. The Office of Service Industries (telephone 202-377-3575) provides information on opportunities and operations of services abroad. For information about specific industry sectors, contact the following divisions: Information Industries Division (202-377-4781); Transportation, Tourism, and Marketing Division (202-377-4581); and Finance and Management Industries Division (202-377-0339).

Through the Worldwide Services Program the Department of Commerce provides the same overseas exposure in *Commercial News USA* magazine for U.S. service firms as the New Product Information Service and International Market Search do for manufacturers. A brief description of the service with the firm's name and address is listed under the appropriate category. Interested overseas parties are instructed to contact listed firms directly. Application forms are available through Department of Commerce district offices. A modest fee is charged for this service, which distributes the listed information to almost 200,000 overseas agents, distributors, and government officials.

Both AID and TDP offer opportunities for U.S. service firms. For a more complete description of their activities, see chapter 7.

The Eximbank has introduced a new program to assist U.S. design, engineering, and architectural firms with foreign contracts. For information on this program, contact the Eximbank's Engineering Division (202-566-8802).

Making contacts

After a company has identified its most promising markets and devised strategies to enter those markets, the next step is to actually locate a buyer. If that buyer is the end user of a company's product or service, a relatively simple transaction may result. In many cases, however, U.S. exporters need an in-country presence through a representative or distributor to reach the eventual buyer. Alternatively, the firm may identify customers through attendance at trade shows, trade missions, direct mail campaigns, and advertising.

Regardless of how the exporter makes contacts and develops sales leads, the exporter faces many questions:

- Specifically who are potential buyers?
- What trade shows are the most effective?
- Which marketing techniques are most successful?

In this chapter U.S. exporters will find the means to answer these questions. The marketing techniques described are by no means exhaustive. However, the chapter describes sources of assistance in locating buyers, evaluating trade missions and shows, and conducting other programs designed to make contacts.

Department of Commerce contact programs

The U.S. Department of Commerce can help exporters identify and qualify direct leads for potential buyers, distributors, joint venture partners, and licensees from both private and public sources. Along with its various product, country, and program experts, the Department of Commerce has an extensive network of commercial officers posted in countries that represent 95 percent of the market for U.S. products.

Services and publications available through the Department of Commerce are listed in this section. Exporters should contact the nearest Commerce district office (see appendix III) for more information or contact Export Promotion Services, U.S. Department of Commerce, 14th Street and Constitution Avenue, N.W., Washington, DC 20230; telephone 202-377-2505.

Export Contact List Service

The ECLS provides mailing lists of prospective overseas customers from Commerce's automated worldwide file of foreign firms. It identifies manufacturers, distributors,

retailers, service firms, and government agencies. A summary of the information on the company includes name and address, cable and telephone numbers, name and title of a key official, product and service interests, year established, and additional data. The lists are drawn from an on-line search of Commerce data on the basis of the market or company criteria specified by the exporter. The information is available either as cheshire or gummed mailing labels or as a summary printout of company data. Cost is 25 cents per name, with a minimum order of $10.

Trade Opportunities Program (TOP)

This service provides timely sales leads from overseas firms seeking to buy or represent U.S. products and services. U.S. commercial officers worldwide gather leads through local channels. Lead details such as specifications, quantities, end use, and delivery and bid deadlines are telexed daily to the computer center in Washington, D.C., reviewed, and then immediately posted on Commerce's EBB. Users can retrieve the TOP files (and all other files) from the EBB each day through a personal computer and modem. Subscribers may use, edit, or redistribute the leads in any way they wish. A subscription for all files on the EBB is $35 per year.

TOP leads are also published each day in the *Journal of Commerce*. Other trade information services such as TradeNet, Intellibanc, Commodity Developers Trade Group, state trade development agencies, and world trade centers also distribute TOP leads and leads obtained from their own services.

Agent/Distributor Service (ADS)

The ADS is used to locate foreign import agents and distributors. It provides a custom search overseas for interested and qualified foreign representatives on behalf of a U.S. exporter. Officers abroad conduct the search and prepare a report identifying up to six foreign prospects that have examined the U.S. firm's product literature and have expressed interest in representing the U.S. firm's products.

The U.S. company is given the names and addresses of the foreign firms, names and titles of persons to contact, telephone numbers, cable addresses and telex numbers, and brief comments about the agent or distributor and its stated interest in the proposal. A fee of $125 is charged for this service.

ADS application forms may be obtained from Commerce district offices. Trade specialists at these offices can help with preparing applications and can provide guidance if there are any factors barring the desired relationship.

World Traders Data Reports

The WTDR service provides a background report on a specific foreign firm, prepared by commercial officers overseas. WTDRs give such information as the type of organization, year established, relative size, number of employees, general reputation, territory covered, language preferred, product lines handled, principal owners, financial references, and trade references. Each WTDR also contains a general narrative report by the U.S. commercial officer who conducted the investigation concerning the reliability of the foreign firm. A fee of $100 is charged per report. Further information on this service is available from any Commerce district office.

Commercial News USA (CNUSA)

CNUSA provides worldwide exposure for U.S. products and services through an illustrated catalog-magazine and electronic bulletin boards. The catalog-magazine is distributed through U.S. embassies and consulates to business readers in 140 countries. Copies are also made available to international visitors at trade events around the world. Current hard-copy distribution averages 110,000 copies, with 10 issues per year. Information in *CNUSA* is further disseminated by US&FCS posts or local organizations that reprint all or part of the publication. *CNUSA*'s electronic distribution in key overseas markets reaches an additional 130,000 business readers. It operates through private sector and government electronic business bulletin boards in 15 countries.

Listings in *CNUSA* describe the major features of an export product or service. The name, address, and telephone and fax numbers of the U.S. manufacturer or distributor are included along with a photo or illustration. Several size formats are available. A standard one-sixth page lists an average of 40 to 60 words and costs $250; larger formats may contain longer descriptions. The electronic versions of *CNUSA* transmit the complete text of the magazine listings, without illustrations, to EBB subscribers.

The *CNUSA* program covers more than 30 industry categories and focuses on products that have been on the U.S. market no longer than three years. Companies may also market services and trade and technical literature through *CNUSA*. Only pharmaceuticals, raw materials, agricultural commodities, and items on the Federal Register Munitions List are excluded from *CNUSA*. All products in *CNUSA* must be at least 51 percent U.S. parts and 51 percent U.S. labor.

CNUSA also profiles up to three industries per issue with high export potential. In these special industry sections, U.S. firms may promote established products as well as new models. Participants may purchase up to three separate listings per issue, each focusing on a single product model. A new product may be listed four times per year. *CNUSA* does not feature descriptions of entire product lines or accept camera-ready advertisements.

The trade leads generated by *CNUSA* help U.S. firms identify potential export markets and make contacts leading to representation, distributorships, joint venture or licensing agreements, or direct sales. Overseas inquiries come directly to participating U.S. firms and are address coded to allow for tracking and program evaluation. Interested firms should contact the nearest Commerce district office for information.

Department of Commerce trade event programs

Some products, because of their very nature, are difficult to sell unless the potential buyer has an opportunity to examine them in person. Sales letters and printed literature can be helpful, but they are certainly no substitute for an actual presentation of products in the export market. One way for a company to actually present its products to an overseas market is by participating in trade events such as trade shows, fairs, trade missions, matchmaker delegations, and catalog exhibitions.

In today's international market, trade fairs are "shop windows" where thousands of firms from many countries display their wares. They are marketplaces where buyer and seller can meet with mutual convenience. Some fairs, especially in Europe, have a history that goes back centuries.

Attending trade fairs involves a great deal of planning. The potential exhibitor must take into account the following logistic considerations:

- Choosing the proper fair out of the hundreds that are held every year.

- Obtaining space at the fair, along with designing and constructing the exhibit.

- Shipping products to the show, along with unpacking and setup.

- Providing proper hospitality (refreshments and so on), along with maintaining the exhibit.

- Breaking down and packing the exhibit, and return shipping.

There are many excellent international trade fairs, both privately run and government sponsored. A trade magazine or association can generally provide information on major shows. Because of the many considerations facing exhibitors, a company may wish to attend a Department of Commerce-organized U.S. pavilion overseas. For additional guidance, contact the local Commerce district office (see appendix III) or US&FCS International Operations regional director (see appendix II).

Certified Trade Fair Program

The Department of Commerce Certified Trade Fair Program is designed to encourage private organizations to recruit new-to-market and new-to-export U.S. firms to exhibit in trade fairs overseas. To receive certification, the organization must demonstrate that (1) the fair is a leading international trade event for an industry and (2) the fair organizer is capable of recruiting U.S. exhibitors and assisting them with freight forwarding, customs clearance, exhibit design and setup, public relations, and overall show promotion. The fair organizer must agree to assist new-to-export exhibitors as well as small businesses interested in exporting.

In addition to the services the organizer provides, U.S. exhibitors have the facilities and services of the Department of Commerce available to them. Commerce can also

- assign a Washington contact person to coordinate Commerce assistance;

- operate a business information office, which can provide meeting space, translators, hospitality, and assistance from US&FCS personnel to U.S. exhibitors and foreign customers;

- help contact buyers, agents, distributors, and other business leads and provide marketing assistance; and

- authorize use of the certification logo and provide a press release on certification.

Foreign Buyer Program

The Department of Commerce encourages foreign buyers to attend selected U.S. trade shows. US&FCS selects leading U.S. trade shows in industries with high export potential. U.S. firms are assisted in fulfilling their international business objectives through their participation in selected U.S. trade shows where they can meet foreign buyers, distributors, potential licensees or joint venture partners.

Each show selected for the Foreign Buyer Program receives special promotion through overseas mailings, U.S. embassy and regional commercial newsletters, *CNUSA, Business America,* foreign trade association and chambers of commerce journals, and trade journals overseas. US&FCS works with U.S. companies exhibiting at these shows by helping U.S. firms match their products, marketing objectives, and geographic targets with the needs of the international business visitors.

Through the Commerce district offices, international trade specialists are ready to take exhibiting U.S. firms through the exporting process and provide counseling to them before the trade show. In addition, an international trade specialist is available at each show to provide on-the-spot export counseling. The Foreign Buyer Program is also an excellent means for experienced exporters to penetrate new markets.

For additional information contact a local Commerce district office or U.S. and Foreign Commercial Service, Export Promotion Services, Room 2118, Washington, DC 20230. For an application and additional information telephone the Foreign Buyer Program manager at 202-377-0481.

Matchmaker trade delegations

Matchmaker trade delegations, organized and led by Commerce personnel, enable new-to-export and new-to-market firms to meet prescreened prospects who are interested in their products or services in overseas markets. Matchmaker delegations usually target major markets in two countries and limit trips to a week or less. In this way, U.S. firms can interview a maximum number of prospective business partners with a minimum of time away from the office. Participants also take advantage of group-rate hotels and airfare as well as on-the-spot U.S. embassy support. Thorough briefings on market requirements and business practices and interpreters' services are also provided. Delegation members pay their own expenses and a share of the operating costs of the event.

Trade missions

Department of Commerce trade missions are planned visits to potential buyers or clients overseas. Missions can be undertaken by firms individually or in an organized group. Like trade shows, trade missions require careful planning and attention to scheduling. Much of the planning and coordination is done for participants.

Commerce-sponsored trade missions are carefully organized and planned to achieve maximum results in expanding exports of U.S.-produced goods and services. They are usually composed of fewer than 12 but more than 5 U.S. business executives. Markets to be visited and products to be promoted are carefully selected on the basis of relevant market research and consultations with US&FCS officers abroad. The primary objectives of Commerce-sponsored trade missions are to introduce U.S. firms to appropriate foreign buyers and to establish representation, joint ventures, and licensing agreements.

Several types of trade missions have been developed to help U.S. exporters penetrate overseas markets:

- *U.S. specialized trade missions.* U.S. specialized trade missions are planned around the specific needs of each participating firm. Commerce personnel carefully select a product line and an itinerary that appear to offer the best potential for export sales. They then provide detailed marketing information and arrange advance programming and publicity. Commercial officers make hour-by-hour individual appointments for participants, inviting key foreign government officials in purchasing and policy-making positions to meet with the mission. Mission members pay their own expenses and a share of the operating costs of the mission.

- *State- or industry-organized, government-approved (S/IOGA) trade missions.* S/IOGA trade missions are planned and organized by state development agencies, trade associations, chambers of commerce, and other export-oriented groups. To qualify for U.S. government sponsorship, organizers of this type of trade mission must agree to follow Commerce criteria in planning and recruiting the mission. Commerce offers guidance and assistance from the planning stages to the completion of the mission and coordinates the support of all relevant offices and the assistance of the US&FCS officers in each city on the itinerary. The overseas operations of S/IOGA trade missions are substantially the same as those of specialized missions. Mission members pay their own travel and hotel expenses and the organizers are responsible for all overseas costs incurred on the mission's behalf. For more information on S/IOGA missions, contact Cooperative Events Division, Room 2114, Export Promotion Services, US&FCS, U.S. Department of Commerce, Washington, DC 20230; telephone 202-377-4908.

- *Multistate trade missions.* Delegates of the trade promotion departments of several state economic development agencies participate on each of these missions. Each delegate represents an average of 25 companies of his or her state that want to open markets in the countries visited. The US&FCS in the host countries lines up qualified foreign sales representatives, distributors, and end users to meet with the delegates. The delegates provide information on the companies they represent and bring back the leads to the companies for follow-up.

- *U.S. seminar missions.* Like trade missions, seminar missions promote the sale of U.S. goods and services abroad and help to establish agents and other foreign representation for U.S. exporters. Unlike specialized trade missions, they are especially designed to facilitate the sale of particularly sophisticated products and technology and concentrate on concepts and systems. A U.S. seminar team consisting of representatives of a high-technology industry gives presentations and leads discussions on technological subjects. The team also addresses pertinent developmental or industrial problems of the host country. The seminar is followed by individual, private, sales-oriented appointments that are scheduled by the US&FCS posts.

These missions are also published in the Export Promotion Calendar, available at local Commerce district offices (see appendix III).

Catalog exhibitions

U.S. firms may test foreign markets, develop sales leads, and locate agents or distributors through catalog exhibitions sponsored by US&FCS, in some instances in conjunction with the Department of State's foreign service posts. These exhibitions feature displays of a large number of U.S. product catalogs, sales brochures, and other graphic sales aids at up to 10 U.S. embassies and consulates or in conjunction with trade shows in a region. Commercial staff provide each participant with sales leads and a visitors list of all foreign buyers attending the event.

Because it requires the exporter to make a much smaller investment than a trade mission or other personal visits, this program is particularly well suited for use in developing markets. For more information contact a local Commerce district office or the Marketing Programs Division, Room 2119, Export Promotion Services, U.S. Department of Commerce, Washington, DC 20230; telephone 202-377-3973.

Other Department of Commerce programs

Export Development Offices (EDOs)

EDOs in seven cities overseas provide a variety of programs and services to U.S. exporters. Staffed by US&FCS commercial officers, the EDOs are the principal U.S. export promotion facilities overseas.

The primary role played by the EDO (in conjunction with the US&FCS in the local U.S. embassy or consulate) is threefold:

1. It conducts or assists in market research in the country, helping to identify specific marketing opportunities and to determine which products have the greatest sales potential.

2. It conducts export promotion events in its region that have been organized on the basis of market research findings.

3. It helps organize participation of specific U.S. exporters in these events.

Located in Tokyo, Sydney, Seoul, Milan, London, Mexico City, and Sao Paulo, these offices organize and coordinate a range of export promotion programs, including on-site trade shows, U.S. pavilions in international trade fairs, solo U.S. exhibitions, trade seminars, trade missions, catalog exhibitions, video and catalog exhibitions, and special promotions. Each EDO performs these functions only in the country in which it is located.

When not being used to stage trade exhibitions, EDOs with exhibit and conference facilities frequently are made available to individual firms or associations. Facilities can be used for sales promotions, seminars, and sales meetings. For a nominal fee, EDOs and some commercial offices overseas also provide use of limited office space for traveling U.S. business representatives as well as local telephone use, a market briefing, use of audiovisual equipment, and assistance in making appointments.

Major projects program

This program helps U.S. firms win contracts for planning, engineering, and constructing large foreign infrastructure and industrial systems projects, including equipment and turnkey installations. Assistance is provided when requested by a U.S. embassy, a prospective foreign client, or a U.S. firm, either to encourage U.S. companies to bid on a particular project or to help them pursue overseas contracts.

Speed and flexibility in developing a strategy for each case are essential elements in the assistance given U.S. firms. As circumstances warrant, the Office of International Major Projects mobilizes and coordinates appropriate support from other U.S. government agencies, including foreign service posts abroad. For further information, contact Office of International Major Projects, Room 2015B, Trade Development, International Trade Administration, U.S. Department of Commerce, Washington, DC 20230; telephone 202-377-5225.

Textile and apparel export expansion program

In recognition of the increasing importance of textile and apparel exports, Commerce has created this program to encourage and assist U.S. manufacturers in initiating or expanding export sales, and to improve foreign market access for these products. To achieve these goals, the program does the following:

- Undertakes policy efforts to identify and negotiate away foreign trade barriers and to examine other methods by which the environment for U.S. textile and apparel exports can be improved.

- Provides vehicles such as sponsoring trade fairs and trade missions to improve exposure for U.S. textile and apparel firms and products in foreign markets.

- Provides information on overseas markets and counseling on methods of entering those markets, and facilitates the exchange of information between industry and government relevant to improving exports of U.S. textile and apparel products.

The program is administered by the Market Expansion Division, Office of Textiles and Apparel; telephone 202-377-5153.

Department of Agriculture Foreign Agricultural Service

Through a network of counselors, attaches, trade officers, commodity analysts, and marketing specialists, USDA's FAS can help arrange contacts overseas and provide promotional assistance. The programs and services offered are described in this section.

Commodity and marketing programs

The Commodity and Marketing area of FAS handles inquiries for specific commodity-related information. Each division provides support for analysis of consumption, trade, stocks, and so on, and marketing information. The six divisions and their telephone numbers are as follows.

1. Dairy, Livestock, and Poultry Division, 202-447-8031.

2. Grain and Feed Division, 202-447-6219.

3. Horticultural and Tropical Products Division, 202-447-6590.

4. Oilseed and Oilseed Products Division, 202-447-7037.

5. Tobacco, Cotton, and Seed Division, 202-382-9516.

6. Forest Products Division, 202-382-8138.

High-Value Product Services Division

The High-Value Product Services Division's purpose is to expand overseas markets for U.S. agricultural and food commodities and products through a wide range of services, which are described in this section.

AgExport Connections

AgExport Connections provides information services to help expand and promote agricultural exports. It offers the AgExport Action Kit, which describes services available from USDA to help U.S. food and agricultural exporters. Other AgExport Connections services are as follows:

- *Trade leads.* These inquiries from overseas buyers looking for U.S. products are sent daily to USDA. From 2,500 to 4,000 trade leads are disseminated domestically each year. Trade leads may be obtained in four ways:

  1. *Trade Leads Fax Service.* Exporters can receive categorized trade leads by polling the AgExport fax machines each week. The faxed information is free, but the company seeking the information must pay the cost of the call. Interested companies may obtain an information sheet and directions on how to poll the Trade Leads Fax Service units by faxing AgExport Connections at 202-472-4374.

  2. *AgExport Trade Leads.* All trade leads are published in this weekly bulletin, which also highlights upcoming trade shows and foreign trade developments throughout the world. The 1991 subscription fee is $75. To subscribe, send a check payable to USDA-FAS to AgExport Connections, Room 4939, South Building, Foreign Agricultural Service, U.S. Department of Agriculture, Washington, DC 20250-1000; telephone 202-447-7103, fax 202-472-4374.

  3. *Electronic trade leads.* With a computer, a modem, and communications software, exporters can receive trade leads electronically. Information on the different types of services and prices is available from Computer Information Delivery Systems, Office of Public Affairs, U.S. Department of Agriculture, Room 536-A, Administration Building, Washington, DC 20250-1000; telephone 202-447-5505, fax 202-475-5396.

  4. *Journal of Commerce.* Selected trade leads received by USDA are published several times each week in the "Agricultural Trade Leads" columns of the *Journal of Commerce.* For subscription information telephone 800-221-3777.

- *Buyer Alert.* This weekly newsletter and free advertising service for exporters can help introduce U.S. food and agricultural products to foreign buyers. *Buyer Alert* reaches more than 9,000 buyers overseas. Only agricultural products (no equipment or services) may be announced in *Buyer Alert.* Each announcement features a product description, an optional indicator price, and specific firm information. To take advantage of the service, contact AgExport Connections, Room 4939, South Building, Foreign Agricultural Service, U.S. Department of Agriculture, Washington, DC 20250-1000; telephone 202-447-7103, fax 202-472-4374.

- **Foreign Buyer Lists.** The AgExport Connection staff maintains a data base of approximately 17,000 foreign firms from more than 70 countries. These foreign firms have expressed interest in importing specific U.S. food and agricultural products. U.S. firms may obtain these lists to match their products with prospective foreign buyers. The Foreign Buyer Lists provide company name; contact name; address; and telephone, fax, and telex numbers. The lists may be ordered for a specific commodity for the entire world or by country for all commodities. In addition, Foreign Buyer Lists may be processed on cheshire or gummed labels. For more information or to order, contact AgExport Connections, Room 4939, South Building, Foreign Agricultural Service, U.S. Department of Agriculture, Washington, DC 20250-1000; telephone 202-447-7103, fax 202-472-4374.

Trade Shows

The High-Value Product Services Division also organizes U.S. pavilions at major international trade shows and exhibitions. These events provide a cost-effective way of testing a market, checking the competition, meeting foreign buyers and consumers, and establishing new contacts. The Trade Show Coordinators Office can assist U.S. exhibitors with obtaining a booth, advance publicity, product shipment, and customs clearance.

Trade Assistance and Planning Office (TAPO)

The USDA's TAPO provides a single point of contact in the FAS for agricultural exporters who need foreign market information, as well as for those who believe they have been injured by unfair trade practices. TAPO can help U.S. agricultural exporters contact the appropriate offices of federal agencies that administer trade remedy laws, and it may be able to provide supporting data and information. The office prepares several annual reports that may be of interest to U.S. agricultural exporters. Contact Trade Assistance and Planning Office, Foreign Agricultural Service, U.S. Department of Agriculture, 3101 Park Center Drive, Suite 1103, Alexandria, VA 22302; telephone 703-756-6001.

Agency for International Development

AID administers most of the U.S. foreign economic assistance programs. These programs offer export opportunities for U.S. suppliers of professional technical assistance services and commodities (goods, products, equipment, and material). Professional technical assistance services generally offer opportunities for consultant and expert capabilities in agriculture, nutrition, and rural development; education and human resources; health and population; and energy and environmental assessment. Opportunities to export commodities are available through the commodity import programs that AID operates in select AID recipient countries, and through AID's direct procurement of commodities. In addition, AID funds may be available to finance developmentally sound projects in certain recipient countries involving U.S. capital goods

and services. U.S. exporters are best positioned to obtain orders by making the local purchasing agencies aware of their products at an early stage. For information on available funds, projects under consideration, and contacts, exporters traveling to developing countries where an AID program is in place may wish to visit the AID mission in the U.S. embassy.

For the most part, AID advertises export opportunities for both professional technical assistance and commodities in the *Commerce Business Daily,* available through paid subscription from the Superintendent of Documents, U.S. Government Printing Office, Washington, DC 20402-9371. Notices of intended procurement of AID-financed commodities are also advertised in the AID *Procurement Information Bulletin,* available through free subscription from AID's Office of Small and Disadvantaged Business Utilization/Minority Resource Center (OSDBU/MRC), Washington, DC 20523-1414; telephone 703-875-1498.

Trade and Development Program

TDP is an independent U.S. government agency that funds feasibility studies, consultancies, training programs, and other project-planning services in middle-income and developing countries and in Eastern Europe. Contracts funded by TDP grants must be awarded to U.S. companies, thus helping position potential U.S. suppliers of goods and services for follow-on contracts when these projects are implemented.

Most TDP funding is granted for feasibility studies in sectors that are of high priority to host governments: agribusiness, educational technology, electronics, energy, minerals development, telecommunications, transportation, and waste management. To ensure a satisfactory and useful study, the host governments play an active role in awarding and managing the contract. This cooperation also engenders a cooperative relationship between the host country, TDP, and the business community.

In addition, opportunities for technical consultants also arise in connection with definitional missions to investigate the scope of a project, develop a scope of work for a feasibility study, draw up a budget estimate, and make a recommendation concerning TDP support for the study. TDP selects qualified consultants through use of a consultants data base, for which U.S. small businesses are encouraged to register.

TDP-funded activities have generated approximately $3 billion of U.S. exports through fiscal year 1990, with an additional $20 billion in direct U.S. exports projected over the next decade. More than 400 companies in 40 states and the District of Columbia have benefited from activities supported by TDP, both through direct exports and through long-term enhancement of their market position.

TDP's programs are carried out by a Washington-based staff in close coordination with the Department of Commerce, AID, and other government agencies. TDP also maintains close contact with multilateral and regional development lending institutions to ensure an ongoing exchange of important project information and to keep TDP apprised of critical opportunities for U.S. companies.

Projects evaluated for TDP funding must meet the following selection criteria:

- **Development priority.** Projects must be developmental priorities of the host country and likely to be implemented. TDP must receive a formal request from the host government, and the U.S. embassy must endorse TDP's involvement in the proposed project.

- **U.S. export potential.** Projects must present an opportunity for substantial sales of U.S. goods and services.

- **Untied financing availability.** There must be assurances that untied financing for project implementation will be available and that procurement will be open to U.S. firms.

For more information on TDP contact U.S. Trade and Development Program, SA-16, Room 309, Washington, DC 20523-1602; telephone 703-875-4357.

State and local government assistance

Most states can provide an array of services to exporters. Many states maintain international offices in major markets; the most common locations are in Western Europe and Japan. Working closely with the commercial sections of U.S. embassies in these countries, they can provide assistance in making contacts in foreign markets, providing such services as the following:

- Specific trade leads with foreign buyers.

- Assistance for trade missions, such as itinerary planning, appointment scheduling, travel, and accommodations.

- Promotional service for goods or services, including representing the state at trade shows.

- Help in qualifying potential buyers, agents, or distributors.

In addition, some international offices of state development organizations help organize and promote foreign-buyer missions to the United States, which can be effective avenues of exporting with little effort. Attracting foreign investment and developing tourism are also very important activities of state foreign offices.

Increasingly, many cities and counties are providing these same services. Appendix III lists contacts at both the state and city levels.

Business and service organization contacts

Contacts made through business colleagues and associations can often prove invaluable to U.S. exporters. A colleague with firsthand experience in an international market may give a personal recommendation for an agent, distributor, or potential buyer. Conversely, the recommendation against the use of a representative for credit or reliability reasons may save the firm a number of problems. Attending export seminars and industry trade shows is an excellent method of networking with business people who have international experience. In addition, trade associations can provide a valuable source of contacts with individuals who may wish to share their experience of identifying and selling to buyers and representatives in foreign markets.

Banks can be another source of assistance in locating overseas representation. The international departments, branches, or correspondent banks of U.S. banks may help locate reputable firms that are qualified and willing to represent U.S. exporters. In addition, freight forwarders, freight carriers, airlines, port authorities, and American chambers of commerce maintain offices throughout the world. These service firms often have contacts with qualified representatives and can make recommendations to the U.S. firm. Foreign embassy and consulate commercial offices may also be able to provide directories and assistance.

Promotion in publications and other media

A large and varied assortment of magazines covering international markets is available to exporters through U.S. publishers. They range from specialized international magazines relating to individual industries such as construction, beverages, and textiles, to worldwide industrial magazines covering many industries. Many consumer publications produced by U.S.-based publishers are also available. Several are produced in national-language editions (Spanish for Latin America, and so on) and also offer "regional buys" for specific export markets of the world. In addition, several business directories published in the United States list foreign representatives geographically or by industry specialization.

Publishers frequently supply potential exporters with helpful market information, make specific recommendations for selling in the markets they cover, help advertisers locate sales representation, and render other services to aid international advertisers. For an extensive list of these international publications see the International Section of *Business Publication Rates and Data,* a book published by Standard Rate and Data Service, 5201 Old Orchard Road, Skokie, IL 60077. Another publication, *The Gale Directory,* contains an even more complete list of foreign periodicals, but it provides less detailed information on circulation and rates. These directories may be available at libraries; Commerce district offices; or in the Department of Commerce's Reference Room, Room 7046, Washington, D.C. State departments of commerce, trade associations, business libraries, and major universities may also provide these publications.

Television, radio, and specially produced motion pictures may also be used by a U.S. business for promoting products or services, depending on the country. In areas where programs may be seen and heard in public places, television and radio promotions offer one of the few means of bringing an advertising message to great numbers of people. In many countries, particularly in Latin America, various forms of outdoor advertising (billboards, posters, electric signs, and streetcar and bus cards) are widely used to reach the mass audience.

Because of the specialized knowledge required to advertise and promote successfully in foreign markets, U.S. firms may find useful the services of a U.S. advertising agency with offices or correspondents abroad. Some U.S. agencies handle nothing but foreign advertising, and some marketing consultants specialize in the problems peculiar to selling in foreign markets. The International Advertising Association, Inc., 475 Fifth Avenue, New York, NY 10017, can provide names of domestic agencies that handle overseas accounts.

Business travel abroad

Business travel abroad can locate and cultivate new customers and improve relationships and communication with current foreign representatives and associates. As in domestic business, there is nothing like a face-to-face meeting with a client or customer.

The following suggestions can help U.S. companies prepare for a trip. By keeping in mind that even little things (such as forgetting to check foreign holiday schedules or neglecting to arrange for translator services) can cost time, opportunity, and money, a firm can get maximum value from its time spent abroad.

Planning the itinerary

A well-planned itinerary enables a traveler to make the best possible use of time abroad. Although travel time is expensive, care must be taken not to overload the schedule. Two or three definite appointments, confirmed well in advance and spaced comfortably throughout one day, are more productive and enjoyable than a crowded agenda that forces the business person to rush from one meeting to the next before business is really concluded. If possible, an extra rest day to deal with jet lag should be planned before scheduled business appointments. The following travel tips should be kept in mind:

- The travel plans should reflect what the company hopes to accomplish. The traveler should give some thought to the trip's goals and their relative priorities.

- The traveler should accomplish as much as possible before the trip begins by obtaining names of possible contacts, arranging appointments, checking transportation schedules, and so on. The most important meetings should be confirmed before the traveler leaves the United States.

- As a general rule, the business person should keep the schedule flexible enough to allow for both unexpected problems (such as transportation delays) and unexpected opportunities. For instance, accepting an unscheduled luncheon invitation from a prospective client should not make it necessary to miss the next scheduled meeting.

- The traveler should check the normal work days and business hours in the countries to be visited. In many Middle Eastern regions, for instance, the work week typically runs from Saturday to Thursday. In many countries, lunch hours of two to four hours are customary.

- Along the same lines, take foreign holidays into account. The U.S. Department of Commerce's *Business America* magazine annually publishes a list of holidays observed in countries around the world. Information from this useful schedule, entitled "World Commercial Holidays," can be obtained by contacting the local Commerce district office. The potential U.S. traveler should also contact the district office to learn what travel advisories the U.S. Department of State has issued for countries to be visited. Each district office maintains a file of current travel advisory cables, which alert travelers to potentially dangerous in-country situations. The Department of State also has a telephone number for recorded travel advisories: 202-647-5225.

- The U.S. business person should be aware that travel from one country to another may be restricted. For example, a passport containing an Israeli visa may disallow the traveler from entering certain countries in the Middle East.

Other preparations

Travel agents can frequently arrange for transportation and hotel reservations quickly and efficiently. They can also help plan the itinerary, obtain the best travel rates, explain which countries require visas, advise on hotel rates and locations, and provide other valuable services. Since travel agents' fees are paid by the hotels, airlines, and other carriers, this assistance and expertise may cost nothing.

The U.S. traveler should obtain the necessary travel documents two to three months before departure, especially if visas are needed. A travel agent can help make the arrangements. A valid U.S. passport is required for all travel outside the United States and Canada. If traveling on an old passport, the U.S. citizen should make sure that it remains valid for the entire duration of the trip.

Passports may be obtained through certain local post offices and U.S. district courts. Application may be made in person or, in some cases, by mail. A separate passport is needed for each family member who will be traveling. The applicant must provide (1) proof of citizenship, (2) proof of identity, (3) two identical passport photos, (4) a completed application form, and (5) the appropriate fees. The cost is $35 per passport ($20 for travelers under 18) plus a $7 execution fee for first-time passports or travelers applying in person. The usual processing time for a passport (including time in the mail) is three weeks, but travelers should apply as early as possible, particularly if time is needed to obtain visas, international drivers licenses, or other documents. Additional information is available from the nearest local passport office or by calling the Office of Passport Services in Washington, D.C. (202-647-0518).

Visas, which are required by many countries, cannot be obtained through the Office of Passport Services. They are provided for a small fee by the foreign country's embassy or consulate in the United States. To obtain a visa, the traveler must have a current U.S. passport. In addition, many countries require a recent photo. The traveler should allow several weeks to obtain visas, especially if traveling to Eastern Europe or developing nations (embassies and consulates in the United States are listed in appendix IV). Some countries that do not require visas for tourist travel do require them for business travel. Visa requirements may change from time to time.

Requirements for vaccinations differ from country to country. A travel agent or airline can advise the traveler on various requirements. In some cases, vaccinations against typhus, typhoid, and other diseases are advisable even though they are not required.

Business preparations for international travel

Before leaving the United States, the traveler should prepare to deal with language differences by learning whether individuals to be met are comfortable speaking English. If not, plans should be made for an interpreter. Business language is generally more technical than the conversational speech with which many travelers are familiar; mistakes can be costly.

In some countries, exchanging business cards at any first meeting is considered a basic part of good business manners. As a matter of courtesy, it is best to carry business cards printed both in English and in the language of the country being visited. Some international airlines arrange this service.

The following travel checklist covers a number of considerations that apply equally to business travelers and vacationers. A travel agent or various travel publications can help take these considerations into account:

- Seasonal weather conditions in the countries being visited.

- Health care (e.g., what to eat abroad, special medical problems, and prescription drugs).

- Electrical current (a transformer or plug adapter may be needed to use electrical appliances).

- Money (e.g., exchanging currency and using credit cards and travelers' checks).

- Transportation and communication abroad.

- Cultural differences.

- Tipping (who is tipped and how much is appropriate).

- U.S. Customs regulations on what can be brought home.

Assistance from U.S. embassies and consulates

Economic and commercial officers in U.S. embassies and consulates abroad can provide assistance to U.S. exporters, both through in-depth briefings and by arranging introductions to appropriate firms, individuals, or foreign government officials. Because of the value and low cost of these services, it is recommended that the exporter visit the U.S. embassy soon after arriving in a foreign country.

When planning a trip, business travelers can discuss their needs and the services available at particular embassies with the staff of the local Commerce district office. It is also advisable to write directly to the U.S. embassy or consulate in the countries to be visited at least two weeks before leaving the United States and to address any communication to the commercial section. The U.S. business traveler should identify his or her business affiliation and complete address and indicate the objective of the trip and the type of assistance required from the post. Also, a description of the firm and the extent of its international experience would be helpful to the post. Addresses of U.S. embassies and consulates are provided in *Key Officers of Foreign Service Posts,* a publication available from the Superintendent of Documents, U.S. Government Printing Office, Washington, DC 20402-9371; telephone 202-783-3238. The cost for this publication is $5 for one year, and it is issued three times per year.

A program of special value to U.S. business travelers is the Department of Commerce's Gold Key Service, which is custom tailored to U.S. firms visiting overseas markets. This service combines several forms of Commerce assistance, including agent and distributor location, one-on-one business counseling, prescheduled appointments with key contacts, and U.S. embassy assistance with interpreters and translators, clerical support, office services, and so on. The service is not available in all markets and may be known under a different name in some countries (e.g., RepFind in Mexico). Further information and assistance are available from any Commerce district office.

Carnets

Foreign customs regulations vary widely from place to place, and the traveler is wise to learn in advance the regulations that apply to each country to be visited. If allowances for cigarettes, liquor, currency, and certain other items are not taken into account, they can be impounded at national borders. Business travelers who plan to carry product samples with them should be alert to import duties they may be required to pay. In some countries, duties and extensive customs procedures on sample products may be avoided by obtaining an ATA (Admission Temporoire) Carnet.

The ATA Carnet is a standardized international customs document used to obtain duty-free temporary admission of certain goods into the countries that are signatories to the ATA Convention. Under the ATA Convention, commercial and professional travelers may take commercial samples; tools of the trade; advertising material; and cinematographic, audiovisual, medical, scientific, or other professional equipment into member countries temporarily without paying customs duties and taxes or posting a bond at the border of each country to be visited.

The following countries currently participate in the ATA Carnet system: Australia, Austria, Belgium, Bulgaria, Canada (certain professional equipment is not accepted), Cyprus, Czechoslovakia, Denmark, Finland, France, Gibraltar, Greece, Hong Kong, Hungary, Iceland, India (commercial samples only), Iran, Ireland, Israel, Italy, Ivory Coast, Japan, Luxembourg, Mauritius, Netherlands, New Zealand, Norway, Poland, Portugal, Romania, Senegal, Singapore, Sri Lanka (certain professional equipment not accepted), South Africa, South Korea, Spain, Sweden, Switzerland, Turkey, United Kingdom, United States, Germany, and Yugoslavia.

Since other countries are continuously added to the ATA Carnet system, the traveler should contact the U.S. Council for International Business if the country to be visited is not included in this list. Applications for carnets should be made to the same organization. A fee is charged, depending on the value of the goods to be covered. A bond, letter of credit, or bank guaranty of 40 percent of the value of the goods is also required to cover duties and taxes that would be due if goods imported into a foreign country by carnet were not reexported and the duties were not paid by the carnet holder. The carnets generally are valid for 12 months. Contact U.S. Council for International Business, 1212 Avenue of the Americas, New York, NY 10036; telephone 212-354-4480. Council offices are also located in Boston; Timonium, Md.; Miami; Schaumburg, Ill.; Houston; Los Angeles; and San Francisco. Further information on the ATA Carnet system can be found in *Carnet: Move Goods Duty-free Through Customs,* an informative free brochure published by the council.

Cultural factors

Business executives who hope to profit from their travel should learn about the history, culture, and customs of the countries to be visited. Flexibility and cultural adaptation should be the guiding principles for traveling abroad on business. Business manners and methods, religious customs, dietary practices, humor, and acceptable dress vary widely from country to country. For example, consider the following:

- Never touch the head of a Thai or pass an object over it; the head is considered sacred in Thailand.

- Avoid using triangular shapes in Hong Kong, Korea, and Taiwan; the triangle is considered a negative shape.

- The number 7 is considered bad luck in Kenya and good luck in Czechoslovakia, and it has magical connotations in Benin. The number 10 is bad luck in Korea, and 4 means death in Japan.

- Red is a positive color in Denmark, but it represents witchcraft and death in many African countries.

- A nod means no in Bulgaria, and shaking the head from side to side means yes.

- The "okay" sign commonly used in the United States (thumb and index finger forming a circle and the other fingers raised) means zero in France, is a symbol for money in Japan, and carries a vulgar connotation in Brazil.

- The use of a palm-up hand and moving index finger signals "come here" in the United States and in some other countries, but it is considered vulgar in others.

- In Ethiopia, repeatedly opening and closing the palm-down hand means "come here."

Understanding and heeding cultural variables such as these is critical to success in international business travel and in international business itself. Lack of familiarity with the business practices, social customs, and etiquette of a country can weaken a company's position in the market, prevent it from accomplishing its objectives, and ultimately lead to failure.

Some of the cultural distinctions that U.S. firms most often face include differences in business styles, attitudes toward development of business relationships, attitudes toward punctuality, negotiating styles, gift-giving customs, greetings, significance of gestures, meanings of colors and numbers, and customs regarding titles.

American firms must pay close attention to different styles of doing business and the degree of importance placed on developing business relationships. In some countries, business people have a very direct style, while in others they are much more subtle in style and value the personal relationship more than most Americans do in business. For example, in the Middle East, engaging in small talk before engaging in business is standard practice.

Attitudes toward punctuality vary greatly from one culture to another and, if misunderstood, can cause confusion and misunderstanding. Romanians, Japanese, and Germans are very punctual, whereas people in many of the Latin countries have a more relaxed attitude toward time. The Japanese consider it rude to be late for a business meeting, but acceptable, even fashionable, to be late for a social occasion. In Guatemala, on the other hand, one might arrive anytime from 10 minutes early to 45 minutes late for a luncheon appointment.

When cultural lines are being crossed, something as simple as a greeting can be misunderstood. Traditional greetings may be a handshake, a hug, a nose rub, a kiss, placing the hands in praying position, or various other gestures. Lack of awareness concerning the country's accepted form of greeting can lead to awkward encounters.

People around the world use body movements and gestures to convey specific messages. Sometimes the same gestures have very different meanings, however. Misunderstanding over gestures is a common occurrence in cross-cultural communication, and misinterpretation along these lines can lead to business complications and social embarrassment.

Proper use of names and titles is often a source of confusion in international business relations. In many countries (including the United Kingdom, France, and Denmark) it is appropriate to use titles until use of first names is suggested. First names are seldom used when doing business in Germany. Visiting business people should use the surname preceded by the title. Titles such as "Herr Direktor" are sometimes used to indicate prestige, status, and rank. Thais, on the other hand, address one other by first names and reserve last names for very formal occasions and written communications. In Belgium it is important to address French-speaking business contacts as "Monsieur" or "Madame," while Dutch-speaking contacts should be addressed as "Mr." or "Mrs." To confuse the two is a great insult.

Customs concerning gift giving are extremely important to understand. In some cultures gifts are expected and failure to present them is considered an insult, whereas in other countries offering a gift is considered offensive. Business executives also need to know when to present gifts – on the initial visit or afterwards; where to present gifts – in public or private; what type of gift to present; what color it should be; and how many to present.

Gift giving is an important part of doing business in Japan, where gifts are usually exchanged at the first meeting. In sharp contrast, gifts are rarely exchanged in Germany and are usually not appropriate. Gift giving is not a normal custom in Belgium or the United Kingdom either, although in both countries, flowers are a suitable gift when invited to someone's home.

Customs concerning the exchange of business cards vary, too. Although this point seems of minor importance, observing a country's customs for card giving is a key part of business protocol. In Japan, for example, the Western practice of accepting a business card and pocketing it immediately is considered rude. The proper approach is to carefully look at the card after accepting it, observe the title and organization, acknowledge with a nod that the information has been digested, and perhaps make a relevant comment or ask a polite question.

Negotiating – a complex process even between parties from the same nation – is even more complicated in international transactions because of the added chance of misunderstandings stemming from cultural differences. It is essential to understand the importance of rank in the other country; to know who the decision makers are; to be familiar with the business style of the foreign company; and to understand the nature of agreements in the country, the significance of gestures, and negotiating etiquette.

It is important to acquire, through reading or training, a basic knowledge of the business culture, management attitudes, business methods, and consumer habits of the country being visited. This does not mean that the traveler must go native when conducting business abroad. It does mean that the traveler should be sensitive to the customs and business procedures of the country being visited.

Making the sale

Part

Selling overseas

Many successful exporters first started selling internationally by responding to an inquiry from a foreign firm. Thousands of U.S. firms receive such requests annually, but most firms do not become successful exporters. What separates the successful exporter from the unsuccessful exporter? There is no single answer, but often the firm that becomes successful knows how to respond to inquiries, can separate the wheat from the chaff, recognizes the business practices involved in international selling, and takes time to build a relationship with the client. Although this may seem to be a large number of factors, they are all related and flow out of one another.

Responding to inquiries

Most, but not all, foreign letters of inquiry are in English. A firm may look to certain service providers (such as banks or freight forwarders) for assistance in translating a letter of inquiry in a foreign language. Most large cities have commercial translators who translate for a fee. Many colleges and universities also provide translation services.

A typical inquiry asks for product specifications, information, and price. Some foreign firms want information on purchasing a product for internal use; others (distributors and agents) want to sell the product in their market. A few firms may know a product well enough and want to place an order. Most inquiries want delivery schedules, shipping costs, terms, and, in some cases, exclusivity arrangements.

Regardless of the form such inquiries take, a firm should establish a policy to deal with them. Here are a few suggestions:

- Reply to all correspondents except to those who obviously will not turn into customers. Do not disregard the inquiry merely because it contains grammatical or typographical errors, which may result from the writer knowing English only as a second language. Similarly, if the printing quality of the stationery does not meet usual standards, keep in mind that printing standards in the correspondent's country may be different. Despite first impressions, the inquiry may be from a reputable, well-established firm.

- Reply promptly, completely, and clearly. The correspondent naturally wants to know something about the U.S. firm before doing business with it. The letter should introduce the firm sufficiently and establish it as a reliable supplier. The reply should provide a short but adequate introduction to the firm, including bank references and other sources that confirm reliability. The firm's policy on exports should be stated, including cost, terms, and delivery.

- Enclose information on the firm's goods or services.

- Send the reply airmail. Surface mail can take weeks or even months, whereas airmail usually takes only days. If a foreign firm's letter shows both a street address and a post office box, write to the post office box. In countries where mail delivery is unreliable, many firms prefer to have mail sent to the post office box.

- When speedy communication is called for, send a fax. Unlike telephone communications, fax may be used effectively despite differences in time zones and languages.

- Set up a file for foreign letters. They may turn into definite prospects as export business grows. If the firm has an intermediary handling exports, the intermediary may use the file.

- Sometimes an overseas firm requests a pro forma invoice (see chapter 10), which is a quotation in an invoice format. It is used rarely in domestic business but frequently in international trade.

Separating the wheat from the chaff

How can a firm tell if an overseas inquiry is legitimate and from an established source? A U.S. company can obtain more information about a foreign firm making an inquiry by checking with the following sources of information about foreign firms:

- **Business libraries.** Several publications list and qualify international firms, including Jane's *Major Companies of Europe*, Dun and Bradstreet's *Principal International Business*, and many regional and country directories.

- **International banks.** Bankers have access to vast amounts of information on foreign firms and are usually very willing to assist corporate customers.

- **Foreign embassies.** Foreign embassies are located in Washington, D.C. (see appendix IV), and some have consulates in other major cities. The commercial (business) sections of most foreign embassies have directories of firms located in their countries.

- **U.S. Department of Commerce.** Commerce can provide information on international firms through its

WTDRs (see chapter 7), which are available for a fee through any local Commerce district office (see appendix III).

- *Sources of credit information.* Credit reports on foreign companies are available from many private sector sources, including (in the United States) Dun and Bradstreet and Graydon International. For help in identifying private sector sources of credit reports, contact the nearest Commerce district office. Firms insured by the Foreign Credit Insurance Association (FCIA) can also obtain help from FCIA's headquarters in New York City (telephone 212-306-5000).

Business practices in international selling

Awareness of accepted business practices is paramount to successful international selling. Because cultures vary, there is no single code by which to conduct business. Certain business practices, however, transcend culture barriers:

- Answer requests promptly and clearly.

- Keep promises. The biggest complaint from foreign importers about U.S. suppliers is failure to ship as promised. A first order is particularly important because it shapes a customer's image of a firm as a dependable or an undependable supplier.

- Be polite, courteous, and friendly. It is important, however, to avoid undue familiarity or slang. Some overseas firms feel that the usual brief U.S. business letter is lacking in courtesy.

- Personally sign all letters. Form letters are not satisfactory.

Before traveling to a new market, the traveler should learn as much about the culture as possible to avoid embarrassing situations. For example, in Mexico it is customary to inquire about a colleague's wife and family, whereas in many Middle Eastern countries it is taboo. Patting a U.S. colleague on the back for congratulations is a common practice, but in Japan it would be discourteous. Clothes, expressions, posture, and actions are all important considerations in conducting international business.

Another important consideration is religious and national holidays (see chapter 8). Trying to conduct business on the Fourth of July in the United States would be difficult, if not impossible. Likewise, different dates have special significance in various countries. Some countries have long holidays by U.S. standards, making business difficult. For example, doing business is difficult in Saudi Arabia during the month of fasting before the Ramadan religious festival.

Numerous seminars, film series, books, and publications exist to help the overseas traveler. Try to obtain cultural information from business colleagues who have been abroad or have expertise in a particular market. A little research and observation in cultural behavior can go a long way in international commerce. Likewise, a lack of sensitivity to another's customs can stop a deal in its tracks. Foreign government consulates in U.S. cities offer a wealth of information on business customs and norms for their countries.

Building a working relationship

Once a relationship has been established with an overseas customer, representative, or distributor, it is important that the exporter work on building and maintaining that relationship. Common courtesy should dictate business activity. By following the points outlined in this chapter, a U.S. firm can present itself well. Beyond these points, the exporter should keep in mind that a foreign contact should be treated and served like a domestic contact. For example, the U.S. company should keep customers and contacts notified of all changes, including price, personnel, address, and phone numbers.

Because of distance, a contact can "age" quickly and cease to be useful unless communication is maintained. For many companies, this means monthly or quarterly visits to customers or distributors. This level of service, although not absolutely necessary, ensures that both the company and the product maintain high visibility in the marketplace. If the U.S. exporting firm cannot afford such frequent travel, it may use fax, telex, and telephone to keep the working relationship active and up to date.

Pricing, quotations, and terms

Proper pricing, complete and accurate quotations, and choice of terms of sale and payment are four critical elements in selling a product or service internationally. Of the four, pricing is the most problematic, even for the experienced exporter.

Pricing considerations

- At what price should the firm sell its product in the foreign market?

- Does the foreign price reflect the product's quality?

- Is the price competitive?

- Should the firm pursue market penetration or market-skimming pricing objectives abroad?

- What type of discount (trade, cash, quantity) and allowances (advertising, trade-off) should the firm offer its foreign customers?

- Should prices differ with market segment?

- What should the firm do about product line pricing?

- What pricing options are available if the firm's costs increase or decrease? Is the demand in the foreign market elastic or inelastic?

- Are the prices going to be viewed by the foreign government as reasonable or exploitative?

- Do the foreign country's dumping laws pose a problem?

As in the domestic market, the price at which a product or service is sold directly determines a firm's revenues. It is essential that a firm's market research include an evaluation of all of the variables that may affect the price range for the product or service. If a firm's price is too high, the product or service will not sell. If the price is too low, export activities may not be sufficiently profitable or may create a net loss.

The traditional components for determining proper pricing are costs, market demand, and competition. These categories are the same for domestic and foreign sales and must be evaluated in view of the firm's objective in entering the foreign market. An analysis of each component from an export perspective may result in export prices that are different from domestic prices.

Foreign market objectives

An important aspect of a company's pricing analysis involves determining market objectives. Is the company attempting to penetrate a new market? Looking for long-term market growth? Looking for an outlet for surplus production or outmoded products? For example, many firms view the foreign market as a secondary market and consequently have lower expectations regarding market share and sales volume. Pricing decisions are naturally affected by this view.

Firms also may have to tailor their marketing and pricing objectives for particular foreign markets. For example, marketing objectives for sales to a developing nation where per capita income may be one tenth of per capita income in the United States are necessarily different from the objectives for Europe or Japan.

Costs

The computation of the actual cost of producing a product and bringing it to market or providing a service is the core element in determining whether exporting is financially viable. Many new exporters calculate their export price by the cost-plus method alone. In the cost-plus method of calculation, the exporter starts with the domestic manufacturing cost and adds administration, research and development, overhead, freight forwarding, distributor margins, customs charges, and profit.

The net effect of this pricing approach may be that the export price escalates into an uncompetitive range. For a sample calculation see table 10-1. The table shows clearly that if an export product has the same ex-factory price as the domestic product, its final consumer price is considerably higher.

A more competitive method of pricing for market entry is what is termed marginal cost pricing. This method considers the direct, out-of-pocket expenses of producing and selling products for export as a floor beneath which prices cannot be set without incurring a loss. For example, export products may have to be modified for the export market to accommodate different sizes, electrical systems, or labels. Changes of this nature may increase costs. On the other hand, the export product may be a stripped-down version of the domestic product and therefore cost less. Or, if additional products can be produced without increasing fixed costs, the incremental cost of producing additional products for export should be lower than the earlier average production costs for the domestic market.

In addition to production costs, overhead, and research and development, other costs should be allocated to domestic and export products in proportion to the benefit derived from those expenditures. Additional costs often associated with export sales include

- market research and credit checks;
- business travel;
- international postage, cable, and telephone rates;
- translation costs;
- commissions, training charges, and other costs involving foreign representatives;
- consultants and freight forwarders; and
- product modification and special packaging.

After the actual cost of the export product has been calculated, the exporter should formulate an approximate consumer price for the foreign market.

Market demand

As in the domestic market, demand in the foreign market is a key to setting prices. What will the market bear for a specific product or service?

For most consumer goods, per capita income is a good gauge of a market's ability to pay. Per capita income for most of the industrialized nations is comparable to that of the United States. For the rest of the world, it is much lower. Some products may create such a strong demand – chic goods such as "Levis," for example – that even low per capita income will not affect their selling price. However, in most lower per capita income markets, simplifying the product to reduce selling price may be an answer. The firm must also keep in mind that currency valuations alter the affordability of their goods. Thus, pricing should accommodate wild fluctuations in currency and the relative strength of the dollar, if possible. The firm should also consider who the customers will be. For example, if the firm's main customers in a developing country are expatriates or the upper class, a high price may work even though the average per capita income is low.

Competition

In the domestic market, few companies are free to set prices without carefully evaluating their competitors' pricing policies. This point is also true in exporting, and it is further complicated by the need to evaluate the competition's prices in each export market the exporter intends to enter.

Where a particular foreign market is being serviced by many competitors, the exporter may have little choice but to match the going price or even go below it to establish a market share. If the exporter's product or service is new to a particular foreign market, it may actually be possible to set a higher price than is normally charged domestically.

Pricing summary

- Determine the objective in the foreign market.
- Compute the actual cost of the export product.
- Compute the final consumer price.
- Evaluate market demand and competition.
- Consider modifying the product to reduce the export price.

Quotations and pro forma invoices

Many export transactions, particularly first-time export transactions, begin with the receipt of an inquiry from abroad, followed by a request for a quotation or a pro forma invoice.

A quotation describes the product, states a price for it, sets the time of shipment, and specifies the terms of sale and terms of payment. Since the foreign buyer may not be familiar with the product, the description of it in an overseas quotation usually must be more detailed than in a domestic quotation. The description should include the following 15 points:

1. Buyer's name and address.
2. Buyer's reference number and date of inquiry.
3. Listing of requested products and brief description.
4. Price of each item (it is advisable to indicate whether items are new or used and to quote in U.S. dollars to reduce foreign-exchange risk).
5. Gross and net shipping weight (in metric units where appropriate).
6. Total cubic volume and dimensions (in metric units where appropriate) packed for export.
7. Trade discount, if applicable.
8. Delivery point.
9. Terms of sale.
10. Terms of payment.
11. Insurance and shipping costs.
12. Validity period for quotation.
13. Total charges to be paid by customer.
14. Estimated shipping date to factory or U.S. port (it is preferable to give U.S. port).
15. Estimated date of shipment arrival.

Sellers are often requested to submit a pro forma invoice with or instead of a quotation. Pro forma invoices (see figure 10-2 for a sample) are not for payment purposes but are essentially quotations in an invoice format. In addition to the foregoing list of items, a pro forma invoice should include a statement certifying that the pro forma invoice is true and correct and a statement describing the country of origin of the goods. Also, the invoice should be conspicuously marked "pro forma invoice." These invoices are only models that the buyer uses when applying for an import license or arranging for funds. In fact, it is good business practice to include a pro forma invoice with any international quotation, regardless of whether it has been requested.

When final collection invoices are being prepared at the time of shipment, it is advisable to check with the U.S. Department of Commerce or some other reliable source for special invoicing requirements that may prevail in the country of destination.

It is very important that price quotations state explicitly that they are subject to change without notice. If a specific price is agreed upon or guaranteed by the exporter, the precise period during which the offer remains valid should be specified.

Terms of sale

In any sales agreement, it is important that a common understanding exist regarding the delivery terms. The terms in international business transactions often sound similar to those used in domestic business, but they frequently have very different meanings.

Confusion over terms of sale can result in a lost sale or a loss on a sale. For this reason, the exporter must know the terms before preparing a quotation or a pro forma invoice. A complete list of important terms and their definitions is contained in *Incoterms 1990,* a booklet issued by ICC Publishing Corporation, Inc., 156 Fifth Avenue, Suite 820, New York, NY 10010; telephone 212-206-1150. The cost is $23.95 plus postage, handling, and sales tax if applicable. *Guide to Incoterms 1990,* also available from ICC, uses illustrations and commentary to explain how buyer and seller divide risks and obligations – and therefore costs – in specific kinds of international transactions. The 1990 update of *Incoterms* resulted in several new terms and abbreviations; exporters should, therefore, take care to use the correct terms to avoid confusion.

The following are a few of the more common terms used in international trade:

- CIF (cost, insurance, freight) to a named overseas port of import. Under this term, the seller quotes a price for the goods (including insurance), all transportation, and miscellaneous charges to the point of debarkation from the vessel. (Typically used for ocean shipments only.)

- CFR (cost and freight) to a named overseas port of import. Under this term, the seller quotes a price for the goods that includes the cost of transportation to the named point of debarkation. The cost of insurance is left to the buyer's account. (Typically used for ocean shipments only.)

- CPT (carriage paid to) and CIP (carriage and insurance paid to) a named place of destination. Used in place of CFR and CIF, respectively, for shipment by modes other than water.

- EXW (ex works) at a named point of origin (e.g., ex factory, ex mill, ex warehouse). Under this term, the price quoted applies only at the point of origin and the seller agrees to place the goods at the disposal of the buyer at the specified place on the date or within the period fixed. All other charges are for the account of the buyer.

- FAS (free alongside ship) at a named U.S. port of export. Under this term, the seller quotes a price for the goods that includes charges for delivery of the goods alongside a vessel at the port. The seller handles the cost of unloading and wharfage; loading, ocean transportation, and insurance are left to the buyer.

- FCA (free carrier) to a named place. This term replaces the former "FOB named inland port" to designate the seller's responsibility for the cost of loading goods at the named shipping point. It may be used for multimodal transport, container stations, and any mode of transport, including air.

- FOB (free on board) at a named port of export. The seller quotes the buyer a price that covers all costs up to and including delivery of goods aboard an overseas vessel.

When quoting a price, the exporter should make it meaningful to the prospective buyer. A price for industrial machinery quoted "EXW Saginaw, Michigan, not export packed" would be meaningless to most prospective foreign buyers. Such buyers would have difficulty determining the total cost and, therefore, would hesitate to place an order.

The exporter should quote CIF whenever possible, because it has meaning abroad. It shows the foreign buyer the cost of getting the product to a port in or near the desired country.

If assistance is needed in figuring the CIF price, an international freight forwarder (see chapter 12) can provide help to U.S. firms. The exporter should furnish the freight forwarder with a description of the product to be exported and its weight and cubic measurement when packed; the freight forwarder can then compute the CIF price. There is usually no charge for this service.

If at all possible, the exporter should quote the price in U.S. dollars. Doing so eliminates the risk of possible exchange rate fluctuations and the problems of currency conversion. (As a courtesy, the exporter may also wish to include a second pro forma invoice in the foreign currency of the buyer.)

A simple misunderstanding regarding delivery terms may prevent exporters from meeting contractual obligations or make them responsible for shipping costs they sought to avoid. It is important to understand and use delivery terms correctly.

Table 10-1.
Sample Cost-Plus Calculation of Product Cost

	Domestic Sale	Export Sale
Factory price	$ 7.50	$ 7.50
Domestic freight	.70	.70
	8.20	8.20
Export documentation		.50
		8.70
Ocean freight and insurance		1.20
		9.90
Import duty (12 percent of landed cost)		1.19
		11.09
Wholesaler markup (15 percent)	1.23	
	9.43	
Importer/distributor markup (22 percent)		2.44
		13.53
Retail markup (50 percent)	4.72	6.77
Final consumer price	$14.15	$20.30

Figure 10-2.
Sample Pro Forma Invoice

Tech International
1000 J Street, N.W.
Washington, DC 20005

Telephone 202-555-1212   Fax 202-555-1111

PRO FORMA INVOICE

Date: Jan. 12, 1991

To: Gomez Y. Cartagena   Your Reference: Ltr., Jan. 6, 1991
      Aptdo. Postal 77
      Bogota, Colombia   Our Reference: Col. 91-14

We hereby quote as follows   Terms of Payment: Letter of Credit
                                                    Terms of Sale: CIF Buenaventura

Quantity	Model	Description	Unit	Extension
3	2-50	Separators in accordance with attached specifications	$14,750.00	$44,250.00
3	14-40	First-stage Filter Assemblies per attached specifications	$ 1,200.00	$ 3,600.00
3	custom	Drive Units – 30 hp each (for operation on 3-phase 440 v., 50 cy. current) complete with remote controls	$ 4,235.00	$12,705.00

TOTAL FOB Washington, D.C. domestic packed..$60,555.00
Export processing, packaging, prepaid inland freight
  to Dulles International Airport & forwarder's
  handling charges FOB Dulles Airport, Virginia...$63,670.00
Estimated air freight and insurance ....$ 2,960.00
Est. CIF Buenaventura, Colombia $66,630.00

Estimated gross weight 9,360 lbs.   **Estimated cube 520 cu. ft.**
Export packed 4,212 kg.   **Export packed 15.6 cu. meters**

PLEASE NOTE

1. All prices quoted herein are U.S. dollars.

2. Prices quoted herein for merchandise only are valid for 60 days from this date.

3. Any changes in shipping costs or insurance rates are for account of the buyer.

4. We estimate ex-factory shipment approximately 60 days from receipt here of purchase order and letter of credit.

Export regulations, customs benefits, and tax incentives

This chapter covers a wide range of regulations, procedures, and practices that fall into three categories: (1) regulations that exporters must follow to comply with U.S. law; (2) procedures that exporters should follow to ensure a successful export transaction; and (3) programs and certain tax procedures that open new markets or provide financial benefits to exporters.

Export regulations

Although export licensing is a basic part of exporting, it is one of the most widely misunderstood aspects of government regulations for exporting. The export licensing procedure may appear complex at first, but in most cases it is a rather straightforward process. Exporters should remember, however, that violations of the Export Administration Regulations (EAR) carry both civil and criminal penalties. Export controls are administered by the Bureau of Export Administration (BXA) in the U.S. Department of Commerce. Whenever there is any doubt about how to comply with export regulations, Department of Commerce officials or qualified professional consultants should be contacted for assistance.

The EAR are available by subscription from the Superintendent of Documents, U.S. Government Printing Office, Washington, DC 20401; telephone 202-275-2091. Subscription forms may be obtained from local Commerce Department district offices or from the Office of Export Licensing, Exporter Counseling Division, Room 1099D, U.S. Department of Commerce, Washington, DC 20230; telephone 202-377-4811.

Types of license

Export License

For reasons of national security, foreign policy, or short supply, the United States controls the export and reexport of goods and technical data through the granting of two types of export license: general licenses and individually validated licenses (IVLs). There are also special licenses that are used if certain criteria are met, for example, distribution, project, and service supply. Except for U.S. territories and possessions and, in most cases, Canada, all items exported from the United States require an export license. Several agencies of the U.S. government are involved in the export license procedure.

General License

A general license is a broad grant of authority by the government to all exporters for certain categories of products. Individual exporters do not need to apply for general licenses, since such authorization is already granted through the EAR; they only need to know the authorization is available.

Individually Validated License

An IVL is a specific grant of authority from the government to a particular exporter to export a specific product to a specific destination if a general license is not available. The licenses are granted on a case-by-case basis for either a single transaction or for many transactions within a specified period of time. An exporter must apply to the Department of Commerce for an IVL. One exception is munitions, which require a Department of State application and license. Other exceptions are listed in the EAR.

Determining which license to use

The first step in complying with the export licensing regulations is to determine whether a product requires a general license or an IVL. The determination is based on what is being exported and its destination. The determination is a three-step procedure:

1. *Determine the destination.* Check the schedule of country groups in the EAR (15 CFR Part 770, Supp. 1) to see under which country group the export destination falls.

2. *Determine the export control commodity number (ECCN).* All dual-use items (items used for both military and civilian purposes) are in one of several categories of commodities controlled by the Department of Commerce. To determine what ECCN applies to a particular commodity, see the Commodity Control List in the EAR (15 CFR Part 799.1, Supp. 1).

3. *Determine what destinations require an IVL.* Refer to the specified ECCN in Part 799.1 of the EAR. Look under the paragraph "Validated License Required" to check which country groups require an IVL. If the country group in question is not listed there, no IVL is required. If it is listed there, an IVL is required unless the commodity meets one of the technical exceptions cited under the ECCN.

To avoid confusion, the exporter is strongly advised to seek assistance in determining the proper license. The best source is the Department of Commerce's Exporter

Counseling Division. Telephone or write to Exporter Counseling Division, Room 1099D, U.S. Department of Commerce, Washington, DC 20230; telephone 202-377-4811. Or the exporter may check with the local Commerce district office. An exporter can also request a preliminary, written commodity classification opinion from the Office of Technology and Policy Analysis, U.S. Department of Commerce. P.O. Box 273, Washington, DC 20044.

Shipments under a general license

If, after reviewing the EAR or after consulting with the Department of Commerce, it is determined that an IVL is not required, an exporter may ship its product under a general license.

A general license does not require a specific application. Exporters who are exporting under a general license must determine whether a *destination control statement* is required. (See the "Antidiversion, Antiboycott, and Anti-trust Requirements" section of this chapter.)

Finally, if the shipment is destined for a free-world destination and is valued at more than $2,500 or requires a validated export license, the exporter must complete a shipper's export declaration (SED). SEDs are used by Customs to indicate the type of export license being used and to keep track of what is exported. They are also used by the Bureau of Census to compile statistics on U.S. trade patterns.

Shipments under an individually validated license

If an IVL is required, the U.S. exporter must prepare a Form BXA-622P, "Application for Export License," and submit it to BXA. The applicant must be certain to follow the instructions on the form carefully. In some instances, technical manuals and support documentation must also be included.

If the application is approved, a Validated Export License is mailed to the applicant. The license contains an export authorization number that must be placed on the SED. Unlike some goods exported under a general license, all goods exported under an IVL must be accompanied by an SED.

The final step in complying with the IVL procedure is recordkeeping. The exporter must keep records of all shipments against an IVL. All documents related to an export application should be retained for five years. Section 787.13 of the EAR covers recordkeeping requirements.

Avoiding Delays in Receiving an Individually Validated License

In filling out license applications, exporters commonly make four errors that account for most delays in processing applications:

1. Failing to sign the application.

2. Handwriting, rather than typing, the application.

3. Responding inadequately to section 9b of the application, "Description of Commodity or Technical Data," which calls for a description of the item or items to be exported. The applicant must be specific and is encouraged to attach additional material to explain the product fully.

4. Responding inadequately to section 12 of the application, where the specific end use of the products or technical data is to be described. Again, the applicant must be specific. Answering vaguely or entering "Unknown" is likely to delay the application process.

In an emergency, the Department of Commerce may consider expediting the processing of an IVL application, but this procedure cannot be used as a substitute for the timely filing of an application. An exporting firm that feels it qualifies for emergency handling should contact the Exporter Counseling Division.

Additional Documentation

Certain applications for an IVL must be accompanied by supporting documents supplied by the prospective purchaser or the government of the country of ultimate destination. By reviewing Part 775 of the EAR, the exporter can determine whether any supporting documents are required.

The most common supporting documents are the *international import certificate* and the *statement of ultimate consignee and purchaser*. The international import certificate (Form ITA-645P/ATF-4522/DSP-53) is a statement issued by the government of the country of destination that certifies that the imported products will be disposed of responsibly in the designated country. It is the responsibility of the exporter to notify the consignee to obtain the certificate. The import certificate should be retained in the U.S. exporter's files, and a copy should be submitted with the IVL application.

The statement of ultimate consignee and purchaser (BXA Form 629P) is a written assurance that the foreign purchaser of the goods will not resell or dispose of goods in a manner contrary to the export license under which the goods were originally exported. The exporter must send the statement to the foreign consignee and purchaser for completion. The exporter then submits this form along with the export license application.

In addition to obtaining the appropriate export license, U.S. exporters should be careful to meet all other international trade regulations established by specific legislation or other authority of the U.S. government. The import regulations of foreign countries must also be taken into account. The exporter should keep in mind that even if help is received with the license and documentation from others, such as banks, freight forwarders or consultants, the exporter remains responsible for ensuring that all statements are true and accurate.

Antidiversion, antiboycott, and antitrust requirements

Antidiversion clause

To help ensure that U.S. exports go only to legally authorized destinations, the U.S. government requires a destination control statement on shipping documents. Under this requirement, the commercial invoice and bill of lading (or air waybill) for nearly all commercial shipments leaving the United States must display a statement notifying the carrier and all foreign parties (the ultimate and intermediate consignees and purchaser) that the U.S. material has been licensed for export only to certain destinations and may not be diverted contrary to U.S. law. Exceptions to the use of the destination control statement are (1) shipments to Canada and intended for consumption in Canada and (2) shipments being made under certain general licenses. Advice on the appropriate statement to be used can be provided by the Department of Commerce, the Commerce district office, an attorney, or the freight forwarder.

Antiboycott regulations

The United States has an established policy of opposing restrictive trade practices or boycotts fostered or imposed by foreign countries against other countries friendly to the United States. This policy is implemented through the antiboycott provisions of the Export Administration Act enforced by the Department of Commerce and through the Tax Reform Act of 1977 enforced by the Department of the Treasury.

In general, these laws prohibit U.S. persons from participating in foreign boycotts or taking actions that further or support such boycotts. The antiboycott regulations carry out this general purpose by

- prohibiting U.S. persons from refusing to do business with blacklisted firms and boycotted friendly countries pursuant to foreign boycott demands;

- prohibiting U.S. persons from discriminating against other U.S. persons on the basis of race, religion, sex, or national origin in order to comply with a foreign boycott;

- prohibiting U.S. persons from furnishing information about their business relationships with blacklisted friendly foreign countries or blacklisted companies in response to boycott requirements;

- prohibiting U.S. persons from appearing to perform any of these prohibited acts;

- providing for public disclosure of requests to comply with foreign boycotts; and

- requiring U.S. persons who receive requests to comply with foreign boycotts to disclose publicly whether they have complied with such requests.

The antiboycott provisions of the Export Administration Act apply to all U.S. persons, including intermediaries in the export process, as well as foreign subsidiaries that are "controlled in fact" by U.S. companies and U.S. officials.

The Department of Commerce's Office of Antiboycott Compliance (OAC) administers the program through ongoing investigations of corporate activities. OAC operates an automated boycott-reporting system providing statistical and enforcement data to Congress and to the public, issuing interpretations of the regulations for the affected public, and offering nonbinding informal guidance to the private sector on specific compliance concerns. U.S. firms with questions about complying with antiboycott regulations should call OAC at 202-377-2381 or write to Office of Antiboycott Compliance, Bureau of Export Administration, Room 6098, U.S. Department of Commerce, Washington, DC 20230.

Antitrust laws

The U.S. antitrust laws reflect this nation's commitment to an economy based on competition. They are intended to foster the efficient allocation of resources by providing consumers with goods and services at the lowest price that efficient business operations can profitably offer. Various foreign countries – including the EC, Canada, the United Kingdom, Federal Republic of Germany, Japan, and Australia – also have their own antitrust laws that U.S. firms must comply with when exporting to such nations.

The U.S. antitrust statutes do not provide a checklist of specific requirements. Instead they set forth broad principles that are applied to the specific facts and circumstances of a business transaction. Under the U.S. antitrust laws, some types of trade restraints, known as per se violations, are regarded as conclusively illegal. Per se violations include price-fixing agreements and conspiracies, divisions of markets by competitors, and certain group boycotts and tying arrangements.

Most restraints of trade in the United States are judged under a second legal standard known as the *rule of reason*. The rule of reason requires a showing that (1) certain acts occurred and (2) such acts had an anti-competitive effect. Under the rule of reason, various factors are considered, including business justification, impact on prices and output in the market, barriers to entry, and market shares of the parties.

In the case of exports by U.S. firms, there are special limitations on the application of the per se and rule of reason tests by U.S. courts. Under Title IV of the Export Trading Company Act (also known as the Foreign Trade Antitrust Improvements Act), there must be a "direct, substantial and reasonably foreseeable" effect on the domestic or import commerce of the United States or on the export commerce of a U.S. person before an activity may be challenged under the Sherman Antitrust Act or the Federal Trade Commission Act (two of the primary federal antitrust statutes). This provision clarifies the particular circumstances under which the overseas activities of U.S. exporters may be challenged under these two antitrust statutes. Under Title III of the Export Trading Company Act (see chapter 4) the Department of Commerce, with the concurrence of the U.S. Department of Justice, can issue an export trade certificate of review that provides certain limited immunity from the federal and state antitrust laws.

Although the great majority of international business transactions do not pose antitrust problems, antitrust issues may be raised in various types of transactions, among which are

- overseas distribution arrangements;

- overseas joint ventures for research, manufacturing, construction, and distribution;

- patent, trademark, copyright, and know-how licenses;

- mergers and acquisitions involving foreign firms; and

- raw material procurement agreements and concessions.

The potential U.S. and foreign antitrust problems posed by such transactions are discussed in greater detail in chapter 16. Where potential U.S. or foreign antitrust issues are raised, it is advisable to obtain the advice and assistance of qualified antitrust counsel.

For particular transactions that pose difficult antitrust issues, and for which an export trade certificate of review is not desired, the Antitrust Division of the Department of Justice can be asked to state its enforcement views in a *business review letter.* The business review procedure is initiated by writing a letter to the Antitrust Division describing the particular business transaction that is contemplated and requesting the department's views on the antitrust legality of the transaction.

Certain aspects of the federal antitrust laws and the Antitrust Division's enforcement policies regarding international transactions are explored in the Department of Justice's *Antitrust Enforcement Guidelines for International Operations* (1988).

Foreign Corrupt Practices Act (FCPA)

The FCPA makes it unlawful for any person or firm (as well as persons acting on behalf of the firm) to offer, pay, or promise to pay (or to authorize any such payment or promise) money or anything of value to any foreign official (or foreign political party or candidate for foreign political office) for the purpose of obtaining or retaining business. It is also unlawful to make a payment to any person *while knowing* that all or a portion of the payment will be offered, given, or promised directly or indirectly, to any foreign official (or foreign political party, candidate, or official) for the purposes of assisting the person or firm in obtaining or retaining business. *Knowing* includes the concepts of *conscious disregard* and *willful blindness.* The FCPA also contains provisions applicable to publicly held companies concerning financial recordkeeping and internal accounting controls.

The Department of Justice enforces the criminal provisions of the FCPA and the civil provisions against "domestic concerns." The Securities and Exchange Commission (SEC) is responsible for civil enforcement against "issuers." The Department of Commerce supplies general information to U.S. exporters who have questions about the FCPA and about international developments concerning the FCPA.

There is an exception to the antibribery provisions for "facilitating payments for routine governmental action." Actions "similar" to the examples listed in the statute are also covered by this exception. A person charged with violating the FCPA's antibribery provisions may assert as a defense that the payment was lawful under the written laws and regulations of the foreign country or that the payment was associated with demonstrating a product or performing a contractual obligation.

Firms are subject to a fine of up to $2 million. Officers, directors, employees, agents, and stockholders are subject to a fine of up to $100,000 and imprisonment for up to five years. The U.S. attorney general can bring a civil action against a domestic concern (and the SEC against an issuer) for a fine of up to $10,000 as well as against any officer, director, employee, or agent of a firm or stockholder acting on behalf of the firm, who willfully violates the antibribery provisions. Under federal criminal law other than the FCPA, individuals may be fined up to $250,000 or up to twice the amount of the gross gain or gross loss if the defendant derives pecuniary gain from the offense or causes a pecuniary loss to another person.

The attorney general (and the SEC, where appropriate) may also bring a civil action to enjoin any act or practice whenever it appears that the person or firm (or a person acting on behalf of a firm) is in violation or about to be in violation of the antibribery provisions.

A person or firm found in violation of the FCPA may be barred from doing business with the federal government. Indictment alone can lead to a suspension of the right to do business with the government.

Conduct that constitutes a violation of the FCPA may give rise to a private cause of action under the Racketeer-Influenced and Corrupt Organizations Act.

The Department of Justice is establishing an FCPA opinion procedure to replace the current FCPA review procedure. The details of the opinion procedure will be provided in 28 CFR Part 77 (1991). Under the opinion procedure, any party will be able to request a statement of the Department of Justice's present enforcement intentions under the antibribery provisions of the FCPA regarding any proposed business conduct. Conduct for which Justice has issued an opinion stating that the conduct conforms with current enforcement policy will be entitled in any subsequent enforcement action to a presumption of conformity with the FCPA.

Food and Drug Administration (FDA) and Environmental Protection Agency (EPA) restrictions

In addition to the various export regulations that have been discussed, rules and regulations enforced by FDA and EPA also affect a limited number of exporters.

Food and Drug Administration

FDA enforces U.S. laws intended to assure the consumer that foods are pure and wholesome, that drugs and devices are safe and effective, and that cosmetics are safe. FDA has promulgated a wide range of regulations to enforce these goals. Exporters of products covered by FDA's regulations are affected as follows:

- If the item is intended for export only, meets the specifications of the foreign purchaser, is not in conflict with the laws of the country to which it is to be shipped, and is properly labeled, it is exempt from the adulteration and misbranding provisions of the Federal Food, Drug, and Cosmetic Act (see 801(e)). This exemption does not apply to "new drugs" or "new animal drugs" that have not been approved as safe and effective or to certain devices.

- If the exporter thinks the export product may be covered by FDA, it is important to contact the nearest FDA field office or the Public Health Service, Food and Drug Administration, 5600 Fishers Lane, Rockville, MD 20857.

Environmental Protection Agency

EPA's involvement in exports is limited to hazardous waste, pesticides, and toxic chemicals. Although EPA has no authority to prohibit the export of these substances, it has an established notification system designed to inform receiving foreign governments that materials of possible human health or environmental concern will be entering their country.

Under the Resource Conservation and Recovery Act, generators of waste who wish to export waste considered hazardous are required to notify EPA before shipping a given hazardous waste to a given foreign consignee. EPA then notifies the government of the foreign consignee. Export cannot occur until written approval is received from the foreign government.

As for pesticides and other toxic chemicals, neither the Federal Insecticide, Fungicide, and Rodenticide Act nor the Toxic Substances Control Act requires exporters of banned or severely restricted chemicals to obtain written consent before shipping. However, exporters of unregistered pesticides or other chemicals subject to regulatory control actions must comply with certain notification requirements.

An exporter of hazardous waste, unregistered pesticides, or toxic chemicals should contact the Office of International Activities, U.S. Environmental Protection Agency, 401 M Street, S.W., Washington, DC 20460; telephone 202-382-4880.

Import regulations of foreign governments

Import documentation requirements and other regulations imposed by foreign governments vary from country to country. It is vital that exporters be aware of the regulations that apply to their own operations and transactions. Many governments, for instance, require consular invoices, certificates of inspection, health certification, and various other documents. For sources of information about foreign government import regulations, see chapter 12.

Customs benefits for exporters

Drawback of customs duties

Drawback is a form of tax relief in which a lawfully collected customs duty is refunded or remitted wholly or in part because of the particular use made of the commodity on which the duty was collected. U.S. firms that import materials or components that they process or assemble for reexport may obtain drawback refunds of all duties paid on the imported merchandise, less 1 percent to cover customs costs. This practice encourages U.S. exporters by permitting them to compete in foreign markets without the handicap of including in their sales prices the duties paid on imported components.

The Trade and Tariff Act of 1984 revised and expanded drawbacks. Regulations implementing the act have been promulgated in 19 CFR Part 191. Under existing regulations several types of drawback have been authorized, but only three are of interest to most manufacturers:

1. If articles manufactured in the United States with the use of imported merchandise are exported, then the duties paid on the imported merchandise that was used may be refunded as drawback (less 1 percent).

2. If both imported merchandise and domestic merchandise of the same kind and quality are used to manufacture articles, some of which are exported, then duties that were paid on the imported merchandise are refundable as drawback, regardless of whether that merchandise was used in the exported articles.

3. If articles of foreign origin imported for consumption after December 28, 1980, are exported from the United States or are destroyed under the supervision of U.S. Customs within three years of the date of importation, in the same condition as when imported and without being "used" in the United States, then duties that were paid on the imported merchandise (less 1 percent) are refundable as drawback. Incidental operations on the merchandise (such as testing, cleaning, repacking, or inspection) are not considered to be "uses" of the article.

To obtain drawback, the U.S. firm must file a proposal with a regional commissioner of customs (for the first type of drawback) or with the Entry Rulings Branch, U.S. Customs Headquarters, at the address in the following paragraph (for other types of drawback). These offices may also provide a model drawback proposal for the U.S. company.

Drawback claimants must establish that the articles on which drawback is being claimed were exported within five years after the merchandise in question was imported. Once the request for drawback is approved, the proposal and approval together constitute the manufacturer's drawback rate. For more information contact Entry Rulings

Branch, Room 2107, U.S. Customs Headquarters, 1301 Constitution Avenue, N.W., Washington, DC 20229; telephone 202-566-5856.

U.S. foreign-trade zones

Exporters should also consider the customs privileges of U.S. foreign-trade zones. These zones are domestic U.S. sites that are considered outside U.S. customs territory and are available for activities that might otherwise be carried on overseas for customs reasons. For export operations, the zones provide accelerated export status for purposes of excise tax rebates and customs drawback. For import and reexport activities, no customs duties, federal excise taxes, or state or local ad valorem taxes are charged on foreign goods moved into zones unless and until the goods, or products made from them, are moved into customs territory. This means that the use of zones can be profitable for operations involving foreign dutiable materials and components being assembled or produced here for reexport. Also, no quota restrictions ordinarily apply.

There are now 180 approved foreign-trade zones in port communities throughout the United States. Associated with these projects are some 200 subzones. These facilities are available for operations involving storage, repacking, inspection, exhibition, assembly, manufacturing, and other processing.

More than 2,100 business firms used foreign-trade zones in fiscal year 1990. The value of merchandise moved to and from the zones during that year exceeded $80 billion. Export shipments from zones and subzones amounted to some $12 billion.

Information about the zones is available from the zone manager, from local Commerce district offices, or from the Executive Secretary, Foreign-Trade Zones Board, International Trade Administration, U.S. Department of Commerce, Washington, DC 20230.

Foreign free port and free trade zones

To encourage and facilitate international trade, more than 300 free ports, free trade zones, and similar customs-privileged facilities are now in operation in some 75 foreign countries, usually in or near seaports or airports. Many U.S. manufacturers and their distributors use free ports or free trade zones for receiving shipments of goods that are reshipped in smaller lots to customers throughout the surrounding areas. Information about free trade zones, free ports, and similar facilities abroad may be found in *Tax-Free Trade Zones of the World,* published by Matthew Bender & Co., International Division, 1275 Broadway, Albany, NY 12204; telephone 800-424-4200.

Bonded warehouses

Bonded warehouses can also be found in many locations. Here, goods can be warehoused without duties being assessed. Once goods are released, they are subject to duties.

Foreign sales corporations

One of the most important steps a U.S. exporter can take to reduce federal income tax on export-related income is to set up a foreign sales corporation (FSC). This tax incentive for U.S. exporters replaced the domestic international sales corporation (DISC), except the interest charge DISC. While the interest charge DISC allows exporters to defer paying taxes on export sales, the tax incentive provided by the FSC legislation is in the form of a permanent exemption from federal income tax for a portion of the export income attributable to the offshore activities of FSCs (26 U.S.C., sections 921-927). The tax exemption can be as great as 15 percent on gross income from exporting, and the expenses can be kept low through the use of intermediaries who are familiar with and able to carry out the formal requirements. A firm that is exporting or thinking of exporting can optimize available tax benefits with proper planning, evaluation, and assistance from an accountant or lawyer.

An FSC is a corporation set up in certain foreign countries or in U.S. possessions (other than Puerto Rico) to obtain a corporate tax exemption on a portion of its earnings generated by the sale or lease of export property and the performance of some services. A corporation initially qualifies as an FSC by meeting certain basic formation tests. An FSC (unless it is a small FSC) must also meet several foreign management tests throughout the year. If it complies with those requirements, the FSC is entitled to an exemption on qualified export transactions in which it performs the required foreign economic processes.

FSCs can be formed by manufacturers, nonmanufacturers, or groups of exporters, such as export trading companies. An FSC can function as a principal, buying and selling for its own account, or as a commission agent. It can be related to a manufacturing parent or it can be an independent merchant or broker.

An FSC must be incorporated and have its main office (a shared office is acceptable) in the U.S. Virgin Islands, American Samoa, Guam, the Northern Mariana Islands, or a qualified foreign country. In general, a firm must file for incorporation by following the normal procedures of the host nation or U.S. possession. Taxes paid by an FSC to a foreign country do not qualify for the foreign U.S. tax credit. Some nations, however, offer tax incentives to attract FSCs; to qualify, a company must identify itself as an FSC to the host government. Consult the government tax authorities in the country or U.S. possession of interest for specific information.

A country qualifies as an FSC host if it has an exchange of information agreement with the United States approved by the U.S. Department of the Treasury. As of February 20, 1991, the qualified countries were Australia, Austria, Barbados, Belgium, Bermuda, Canada, Costa Rica, Cyprus, Denmark, Dominican Republic, Egypt, Finland, France, Germany, Grenada, Iceland, Ireland, Jamaica, Korea, Malta, Mexico, Morocco, Netherlands, New Zealand, Norway, Pakistan, Philippines, Sweden, and Trinidad and Tobago. Since the Internal Revenue Service (IRS) does not allow foreign tax credits for foreign taxes imposed on the FSC's qualified income, it is generally advantageous to locate an FSC only in a country where local income taxes and withholding taxes are minimized. Most FSCs are incorporated in the U.S. Virgin Islands or Guam.

The FSC must have at least one director who is not a U.S. resident, must keep one set of its books of account (including copies or summaries of invoices) at its main offshore office, cannot have more than 25 shareholders, cannot have any preferred stock, and must file an election to become an FSC with the IRS. Also, a group may not own both an FSC and an interest charge DISC.

The portion of the FSC gross income from exporting that is exempt from U.S. corporate taxation is 32 percent for a corporate-held FSC if it buys from independent suppliers or contracts with related suppliers at an "arm's-length" price – a price equivalent to that which would have been paid by an unrelated purchaser to an unrelated seller. An FSC supplied by a related entity can also use the special administrative pricing rules to compute its tax exemption. Although an FSC does not have to use the two special administrative pricing rules, these rules may provide additional tax savings for certain FSCs.

Small FSCs and interest charge DISCs are designed to give export incentives to smaller businesses. The tax benefits of a small FSC or an interest charge DISC are limited by ceilings on the amount of gross income that is eligible for the benefits.

The small FSC is generally the same as an FSC, except that a small FSC must file an election with the IRS designating itself as a small FSC – which means it does not have to meet foreign management or foreign economic process requirements. A small FSC tax exemption is limited to the income generated by $5 million or less in gross export revenues.

An exporter can still set up a DISC in the form of an interest charge DISC to defer the imposition of taxes for up to $10 million in export sales. A corporate shareholder of an interest charge DISC may defer the imposition of taxes on approximately 94 percent of its income up to the $10 million ceiling if the income is reinvested by the DISC in qualified export assets. An individual who is the sole shareholder of an interest charge DISC can defer 100 percent of the DISC income up to the $10 million ceiling. An interest charge DISC must meet the following requirements: the taxpayer must make a new election; the tax year of the new DISC must match the tax year of its majority stockholder; and the DISC shareholders must pay interest annually at U.S. Treasury bill rates on their proportionate share of the accumulated taxes deferred.

A *shared FSC* is an FSC that is shared by 25 or fewer unrelated exporter-shareholders to reduce the costs while obtaining the full tax benefit of an FSC. Each exporter-shareholder owns a separate class of stock and each runs its own business as usual. Typically, exporters pay a commission on export sales to the FSC, which distributes the commission back to the exporter.

States, regional authorities, trade associations, or private businesses can sponsor a shared FSC for their state's companies, their association's members, or their business clients or customers, or for U.S. companies in general. A shared FSC is a means of sharing the cost of the FSC. However, the benefits and proprietary information are not shared. The sponsor and the other exporter-shareholders do not participate in the exporter's profits, do not participate in the exporter's tax benefits, and are not a risk for another exporter's debts.

For more information about FSCs, U.S. companies may contact the assistant secretary for trade development (telephone 202-377-1461); the Office of the Chief Counsel for International Commerce, U.S. Department of Commerce (202-377-0937); or a local office of the IRS.

Commerce assistance related to multilateral trade negotiations

The Tokyo Round Trade Agreements, completed in 1979 under General Agreement on Tariff and Trade (GATT) auspices, produced significant tariff reductions and established several nontariff trade barrier (NTB) agreements or codes. The codes currently in effect address the following NTBs:

- Countervailing measures to offset trade-distortive subsidies.
- Antidumping duties used to counter injurious price discrimination.
- Discriminatory government procurement.
- Technical barriers to trade (e.g., product standards).
- Uniform and equitable customs valuation for duty purposes.
- Import licensing procedures.
- Trade in civil aircraft (both tariff and nontariff issues).

An important benefit for U.S. exporters stemming from the Tokyo Round is the GATT Government Procurement Agreement opening many foreign government procurement orders to U.S. suppliers. Commerce's TOP has been designated the primary clearing point for tenders generated under this agreement. Information on the TOP can be obtained by contacting the local Commerce district office or Trade Opportunity Program, U.S. Department of Commerce, Export Promotion Services, Washington, DC 20230; telephone 202-377-4203.

Users can also access TOP leads by tapping in directly to the EBB, a data base service of the Department of Commerce. Subscriptions to this service can be obtained by mail from U.S. Department of Commerce, National Technical Information Service, 5285 Port Royal Road, Springfield, VA 22161.

Other data base information on foreign tenders can be obtained from the *Commerce Business Daily,* available from the U.S. Government Printing Office, Washington, DC 20402; telephone 202-783-3238. Brief summaries of leads also appear in the *Journal of Commerce.*

In 1991, negotiators were engaged in achieving a successful conclusion of the Uruguay Round of multilateral trade negotiations. U.S. objectives included (1) a substantial market access agreement covering tariffs and nontariff measures and (2) improvement in GATT to cover trade in such new areas as services, intellectual property rights, and trade-related investment measures. General information on the Uruguay Round can be obtained from the Office of Multilateral Affairs, H3513, U.S. Department of Commerce/ITA, Washington, DC 20230.

Bilateral trade agreements

The United States has concluded bilateral trade agreements with several Eastern European countries, the Soviet Union, and Mongolia. These congressionally approved agreements are required by the Trade Act of 1974 for these countries to receive most-favored nation (MFN) treatment. In addition to an article providing for reciprocal MFN status, the agreements contain guarantees on intellectual property rights and business facilitation. Such guarantees as the right to establish commercial representation offices in a country by no more than a simple registration process, the right to serve as and hire agents, the right to deal directly with customers and end users of products and services, and the right to hire employees of a company's choice are all included in the agreements. The intellectual property rights provisions include protection for computer software and trade secrets. Trade agreements are in effect with Hungary, Czechoslovakia, and Romania (the MFN provisions of this agreement have been suspended). As of August 14, 1991, the trade agreements with the Soviet Union, Mongolia, and Bulgaria have been signed and submitted to the Congress for approval.

Intellectual property rights considerations

The United States provides a wide range of protection for intellectual property (i.e., patents, trademarks, service marks, copyrights, trade secrets, and semiconductor mask works). Many businesses – particularly high-technology firms, the publishing industry, chemical and pharmaceutical firms, the recording industry, and computer software companies – depend heavily on the protection afforded their creative products and processes.

In the United States, there are five major forms of intellectual property protection. A U.S. patent confers on its owner the exclusive right for 17 years from the date the patent is granted to manufacture, use, and sell the patented product or process within the United States. The United States and the Philippines are the only two countries that award patents on a first-to-invent basis; all other countries award patents to the first to file a patent application. As of November 16, 1989, a trademark or service mark registered with the U.S. Patent and Trademark Office remains in force for 10 years from the date of registration and may be renewed for successive periods of 10 years, provided the mark continues to be used in interstate commerce and has not been previously canceled or surrendered.

A work created (fixed in tangible form for the first time) in the United States on or after January 1, 1978, is automatically protected by a U.S. copyright from the moment of its creation. Such a copyright, as a general rule, has a term that endures for the author's life plus an additional 50 years after the author's death. In the case of works made for hire and for anonymous and pseudonymous works (unless the author's identity is revealed in records of the U.S. Copyright Office of the Library of Congress), the duration of the copyright is 75 years from publication or 100 years from creation, whichever is shorter. Other, more detailed provisions of the Copyright Act of 1976 govern the term of works created before January 1, 1978.

Trade secrets are protected by state unfair competition and contract law. Unlike a U.S. patent, a trade secret does not entitle its owner to a government-sanctioned monopoly of the discovered technology for a particular length of time. Nevertheless, trade secrets can be a valuable and marketable form of technology. Trade secrets are typically protected by confidentiality agreements between a firm and its employees and by trade secret licensing agreement provisions that prohibit disclosures of the trade secret by the licensee or its employees.

Semiconductor mask work registrations protect the mask works embodied in semiconductor chip products. In many other countries, mask works are referred to as integrated circuit layout designs. The Semiconductor Chip Protection Act of 1984 provides the owner of a mask work with the exclusive right to reproduce, import, and distribute such mask works for a period of 10 years from the earlier of two dates: the date on which the mask work is registered with the U.S. Copyright Office or the date on which the mask work is first commercially exploited anywhere in the world.

The rights granted under U.S. patent, trademark, or copyright law can be enforced only in the United States, its territories, and its possessions; they confer no protection in a foreign country. The protection available in each country depends on that country's national laws, administrative practices, and treaty obligations. The relevant international treaties set certain minimum standards for protection, but individual country laws and practices can and do differ significantly.

To secure patent and trademark right outside the United States a company must apply for a patent or register a trademark on a country-by-country basis. However, U.S. individuals and corporations are entitled to a "right of priority" and to "national treatment" in the 100 countries that, along with the United States, are parties to the Paris Convention for the Protection of Industrial Property.

The right of priority gives an inventor 12 months from the date of the first application filed in a Paris Convention country (6 months for a trademark) in which to file in other Paris Convention countries – to relieve companies of the burden of filing applications in many countries simultaneously. A later treaty to which the United States adheres, the Patent Cooperation Treaty, allows companies to file an international application for protection in other member states. Individual national applications, however, must follow within 18 months.

National treatment means that a member country will not discriminate against foreigners in granting patent or trademark protection. Rights conferred may be greater or less than provided under U.S. law, but they must be the same as the country provides its own nationals.

The level and scope of copyright protection available within a country also depends on that country's domestic laws and treaty obligations. In most countries, the place of first publication is an important criterion for determining whether foreign works are eligible for copyright protection. Works first published in the United States on or after March 1, 1989 – the date on which U.S. adherence to the Berne Convention for the Protection of Literary and Artistic Works became effective – are, with few exceptions, automatically protected in the more than 80 countries that comprise the Berne Union. Exporters of goods embodying works protected by copyright in the United States should find out how individual Berne Union countries deal with older U.S. works, including those first published (but not first or simultaneously published in a Berne Union country) before March 1, 1989.

The United States maintains copyright relations with a number of countries under a second international agreement called the Universal Copyright Convention (UCC). UCC countries that do not also adhere to Berne often require compliance with certain formalities to maintain copyright protection. Those formalities can be either or both of the following: (1) registration and (2) the requirement that published copies of a work bear copyright notice, the name of the author, and the date of first publication. The United States has bilateral copyright agreements with a number of countries, and the laws of these countries may or may not be consistent with either of the copyright conventions. Before first publication of a work anywhere, it is advisable to investigate the scope of and requirements for maintaining copyright protection for those countries in which copyright protection is desired.

Intellectual property rights owners should be aware that after valuable intellectual property rights have been secured in foreign markets, enforcement must be accomplished through local law. As a general matter, intellectual property rights are private rights to be enforced by the rights owner. Ease of enforcement varies from country to country and depends on such factors as the attitude of local officials, substantive requirements of the law, and court procedures. U.S. law affords a civil remedy for infringement (with money damages to a successful plaintiff) and criminal penalties (including fines and jail terms) for more serious offenses. The availability of criminal penalties for infringement, either as the exclusive remedy or in addition to private suits, also varies among countries.

A number of countries are parties to only some, or even none, of the treaties that have been discussed here. Therefore, would-be U.S. exporters should carefully evaluate the intellectual property laws of their potential foreign markets, as well as applicable multilateral and bilateral treaties and agreements (including bilateral trade agreements), *before* making a decision to do business there. The intellectual property considerations that arise can be quite complex and, if possible, should be explored in detail with an attorney.

In summary, U.S. exporters with intellectual property concerns should consider taking the following steps:

1. Obtaining protection under all applicable U.S. laws for their inventions, trademarks, service marks, copyrights, and semiconductor mask works.

2. Researching the intellectual property laws of countries where they may conduct business. The US&FCS has information about intellectual property laws and practices of particular countries, although it does not provide legal advice.

3. Securing the services of competent local counsel to file appropriate patent, trademark, or copyright applications within priority periods.

4. Adequately protecting their trade secrets through appropriate confidentiality provisions in employment, licensing, marketing, distribution, and joint venture agreements.

Arbitration of disputes in international transactions

The parties to a commercial transaction may provide in their contract that any disputes over interpretation or performance of the agreement will be resolved through arbitration. In the domestic context, arbitration may be appealing for a variety of reasons. Frequently cited advantages over conventional courtroom litigation include potential savings in time and expense, confidentiality of the proceedings, and expertise of the arbitrators.

For export transactions, in which the parties to the agreement are from different countries, additional important advantages are neutrality (international arbitration allows each party to avoid the domestic courts of the other should a dispute arise) and ease of enforcement (foreign arbitral awards can be easier to enforce than foreign court decisions).

In an agreement to arbitrate (usually just inserted as a term in the contract governing the transaction as a whole), the parties also have broad power to agree on many significant aspects of the arbitration. The arbitration clause may do the following:

- Specify the location (a "neutral site") where the arbitration will be conducted, although care must be taken to select a country that has adopted the UN Convention on the Recognition and Enforcement of Foreign Awards (or another convention providing for the enforcement of arbitral awards).

- Establish the rules that will govern the arbitration, usually by incorporating a set of existing arbitration rules such as the UN Commission on International Trade Law (UNCITRAL) Model Rules.

- Appoint an arbitration institute to administer the arbitration. The International Chamber of Commerce based in Paris, the American Arbitration Association in New York, and the Arbitration Institute of the Stockholm Chamber of Commerce in Sweden are three such prominent institutions.

- Choose the law that will govern procedural issues or the merits of the dispute, for example, the law of the State of New York.

- Place certain limitations on the selection of arbitrators, for example, by agreeing to exclude nationals of the parties to the dispute or by requiring certain qualifications or expertise.

- Designate the language in which the arbitral proceedings will be conducted.

For international arbitration to work effectively, the national courts in the countries of both parties to the dispute must recognize and support arbitration as a legitimate alternative means for resolving disputes. This support is particularly crucial at two stages in the arbitration process. First, should one party attempt to avoid arbitration after a dispute has arisen, the other party must be able to rely on the judicial system in either country to enforce the agreement to arbitrate by compelling arbitration. Second, the party that wins in the arbitration proceeding must be confident that the national courts will enforce the decision of the arbitrators. This will ensure that the arbitration process is not ultimately frustrated at the enforcement stage if the losing party refuses to pay or otherwise satisfy the arbitral award.

The strong policy of U.S. federal law is to approve and support resolution of disputes by arbitration. Through the UN Convention on the Recognition and Enforcement of Foreign Arbitral Awards (popularly known as the New York Convention), which the United States ratified in 1970, more than 80 countries have undertaken international legal obligations to recognize and enforce arbitral awards. While several other arbitration treaties have been concluded, the New York Convention is by far the most important international agreement on commercial arbitration and may be credited for much of the explosive growth of arbitration of international disputes in recent decades.

Providing for arbitration of disputes makes good sense in many international commercial transactions. Because of the complexity of the subject, however, legal advice should be obtained for specific export transactions.

The United Nations sales convention

The UN Convention on Contracts for the International Sale of Goods (CISG) became the law of the United States on January 1, 1988. It establishes uniform legal rules to govern the formation of international sales contracts and the rights and obligations of the buyer and seller. The CISG is expected to facilitate and stimulate international trade.

The CISG applies automatically to all contracts for the sale of goods between traders from two different countries that have both ratified the CISG. This automatic application takes place unless the parties to the contract expressly exclude all or part of the CISG or expressly stipulate to law other than the CISG. Parties can also expressly choose to apply the CISG when it would not automatically apply.

At present, the following nations apply the CISG: Argentina, Australia, Austria, Bulgaria, Byelorussian Socialist Republic, Chile, China, Czechoslovakia, Denmark, Egypt, Finland, France, Germany, Hungary, Iraq, Italy, Lesotho, Mexico, Norway, Spain, Sweden, Switzerland, Syria, Ukrainian Soviet Socialist Republic,

USSR, United States, Yugoslavia, and Zambia. The CISG will enter into force in the Netherlands on January 1, 1992, and in Guinea on February 1, 1992.

The United States made a reservation, the effect of which is that the CISG will apply only when the other party to the transaction also has its place of business in a country that applies the CISG.

Convention provisions

The provisions and scope of the CISG are similar to Article 2 of the Uniform Commercial Code (effective in the United States except Louisiana). The CISG comprises four parts:

- Part I, Sphere of Application and General Provisions (Articles 1-13), provides that the CISG covers the international sale of most commercial goods.

- Part II, Formation of the Contract (Articles 14-24), provides rules on offer and acceptance.

- Part III, Sale of Goods (Articles 25-88), covers obligations and remedies of the seller and buyer and rules governing the passing of risk and damages.

- Part IV, Final Provisions (Articles 89-101), covers the right of a country to disclaim certain parts of the convention.

Applying (or excluding) the CISG

U.S. businesses can avoid the difficulties of reaching agreement with foreign parties on choice-of-law issues because the CISG text is available as a compromise. Using the CISG may decrease the time and legal costs otherwise involved in research of different unfamiliar foreign laws. Further, the CISG may reduce the problems of proof and foreign law in domestic and foreign courts.

Application of the CISG may especially make sense for smaller firms and for American firms contracting with companies in countries where the legal systems are obscure, unfamiliar, or not suited for international sales transactions of goods. However, some larger, more experienced firms may want to continue their current practices, at least with regard to parties with whom they have been doing business regularly.

When a firm chooses to exclude the CISG, it is not sufficient to simply say "the laws of New York apply," because the CISG would be the law of the State of New York under certain circumstances. Rather, one would say "the provisions of the Uniform Commercial Code as adopted by the State of New York, and not the UN Convention on Contracts for the International Sale of Goods, apply."

After it is determined whether or not the CISG governs a particular transaction, the related documentation should be reviewed to ensure consistency with the CISG or other governing law. For agreements about to expire, companies should make sure renewals take into account the applicability (or nonapplicability) of the CISG.

The CISG can be found in the *Federal Register* (Vol. 52, p. 6262, 1987) along with a notice by the U.S. Department of State, and in the pocket part to 15 U.S.C.A. app. at 29. To obtain an up-to-date listing of ratifying or acceding countries and their reservations call the UN at 212-963-3918 or 212-963-7958. For further information contact the Office of the Assistant Legal Adviser for Private International Law, U.S. Department of State (202-653-9851), or the Office of the Chief Counsel for International Commerce, U.S. Department of Commerce (202-377-0937).

After the sale

Part

Documentation, shipping, and logistics

12

When preparing to ship a product overseas, the exporter needs to be aware of packing, labeling, documentation, and insurance requirements. Because the goods are being shipped by unknown carriers to distant customers, the new exporter must be sure to follow all shipping requirements to help ensure that the merchandise is

- packed correctly so that it arrives in good condition;

- labeled correctly to ensure that the goods are handled properly and arrive on time and at the right place;

- documented correctly to meet U.S. and foreign government requirements as well as proper collection standards; and

- insured against damage, loss, and pilferage and, in some cases, delay.

Because of the variety of considerations involved in the physical export process, most exporters, both new and experienced, rely on an international freight forwarder to perform these services.

Freight forwarders

The international freight forwarder acts as an agent for the exporter in moving cargo to the overseas destination. These agents are familiar with the import rules and regulations of foreign countries, methods of shipping, U.S. government export regulations, and the documents connected with foreign trade.

Freight forwarders can assist with an order from the start by advising the exporter of the freight costs, port charges, consular fees, cost of special documentation, and insurance costs as well as their handling fees – all of which help in preparing price quotations. Freight forwarders may also recommend the type of packing for best protecting the merchandise in transit; they can arrange to have the merchandise packed at the port or containerized. The cost for their services is a legitimate export cost that should be figured into the price charged to the customer.

When the order is ready to ship, freight forwarders should be able to review the letter of credit, commercial invoices, packing list, and so on to ensure that everything is in order. They can also reserve the necessary space on board an ocean vessel, if the exporter desires.

If the cargo arrives at the port of export and the exporter has not already done so, freight forwarders may make the necessary arrangements with customs brokers to ensure that the goods comply with customs export documentation

regulations. In addition, they may have the goods delivered to the carrier in time for loading. They may also prepare the bill of lading and any special required documentation. After shipment, they forward all documents directly to the customer or to the paying bank if desired.

Packing

In packing an item for export, the shipper should be aware of the demands that exporting puts on a package. Four problems must be kept in mind when an export shipping crate is being designed: breakage, weight, moisture, and pilferage.

Most general cargo is carried in containers, but some is still shipped as breakbulk cargo. Besides the normal handling encountered in domestic transportation, a breakbulk shipment moving by ocean freight may be loaded aboard vessels in a net or by a sling, conveyor, chute, or other method, putting added strain on the package. In the ship's hold, goods may be stacked on top of one another or come into violent contact with other goods during the voyage. Overseas, handling facilities may be less sophisticated than in the United States and the cargo may be dragged, pushed, rolled, or dropped during unloading, while moving through customs, or in transit to the final destination.

Moisture is a constant problem because cargo is subject to condensation even in the hold of a ship equipped with air conditioning and a dehumidifier. The cargo may also be unloaded in the rain, and some foreign ports do not have covered storage facilities. In addition, unless the cargo is adequately protected, theft and pilferage are constant threats.

Since proper packing is essential in exporting, often the buyer specifies packing requirements. If the buyer does not so specify, be sure the goods are prepared with the following considerations in mind:

- Pack in strong containers, adequately sealed and filled when possible.

- To provide proper bracing in the container, regardless of size, make sure the weight is evenly distributed.

- Goods should be packed in oceangoing containers, if possible, or on pallets to ensure greater ease in handling.

- Packages and packing filler should be made of moisture-resistant material.

- To avoid pilferage, avoid mentioning contents or brand names on packages. In addition, strapping, seals, and shrink wrapping are effective means of deterring theft.

One popular method of shipment is the use of containers obtained from carriers or private leasing concerns. These containers vary in size, material, and construction and can accommodate most cargo, but they are best suited for standard package sizes and shapes. Some containers are no more than semi-truck trailers lifted off their wheels and placed on a vessel at the port of export. They are then transferred to another set of wheels at the port of import for movement to an inland destination. Refrigerated and liquid bulk containers are readily available.

Normally, air shipments require less heavy packing than ocean shipments, but they must still be adequately protected, especially if highly pilferable items are packed in domestic containers. In many instances, standard domestic packing is acceptable, especially if the product is durable and there is no concern for display packaging. In other instances, high-test (at least 250 pounds per square inch) cardboard or tri-wall construction boxes are more than adequate.

For both ocean and air shipments, freight forwarders and carriers can advise on the best packaging. Marine insurance companies are also available for consultation. It is recommended that a professional firm be hired to package for export if the exporter is not equipped for the task. This service is usually provided at a moderate cost.

Finally, because transportation costs are determined by volume and weight, special reinforced and lightweight packing materials have been devised for exporting. Care in packing goods to minimize volume and weight while giving strength may well save money while ensuring that goods are properly packed.

Labeling

Specific marking and labeling is used on export shipping cartons and containers to

- meet shipping regulations,
- ensure proper handling,
- conceal the identity of the contents, and
- help receivers identify shipments.

The overseas buyer usually specifies export marks that should appear on the cargo for easy identification by receivers. Many markings may be needed for shipment. Exporters need to put the following markings on cartons to be shipped:

- Shipper's mark.
- Country of origin (U.S.A.).
- Weight marking (in pounds and in kilograms).
- Number of packages and size of cases (in inches and centimeters).
- Handling marks (international pictorial symbols).

- Cautionary markings, such as "This Side Up" or "Use No Hooks" (in English and in the language of the country of destination).
- Port of entry.
- Labels for hazardous materials (universal symbols adapted by the International Maritime Organization).

Legibility is extremely important to prevent misunderstandings and delays in shipping. Letters are generally stenciled onto packages and containers in waterproof ink. Markings should appear on three faces of the container, preferably on the top and on the two ends or the two sides. Old markings must be completely removed.

In addition to port marks, customer identification code, and indication of origin, the marks should include the package number, gross and net weights, and dimensions. If more than one package is being shipped, the total number of packages in the shipment should be included in the markings. The exporter should also include any special handling instructions on the package. It is a good idea to repeat these instructions in the language of the country of destination. Standard international shipping and handling symbols should also be used.

Exporters may find that customs regulations regarding freight labeling are strictly enforced; for example, most countries require that the country of origin be clearly labeled on each imported package. Most freight forwarders and export packing specialists can supply necessary information regarding specific regulations.

Documentation

Exporters should seriously consider having the freight forwarder handle the formidable amount of documentation that exporting requires; freight forwarders are specialists in this process. The following documents are commonly used in exporting; which of them are actually used in each case depends on the requirements of both the U.S. government and the government of the importing country.

- **Commercial invoice.** As in a domestic transaction, the commercial invoice is a bill for the goods from the buyer to the seller. A commercial invoice should include basic information about the transaction, including a description of the goods, the address of the shipper and seller, and the delivery and payment terms. The buyer needs the invoice to prove ownership and to arrange payment. Some governments use the commercial invoice to assess customs duties.

- **Bill of lading.** Bills of lading are contracts between the owner of the goods and the carrier (as with domestic shipments). There are two types. A *straight bill of lading* is nonnegotiable. A *negotiable* or *shipper's order bill of lading* can be bought, sold, or traded while goods are in transit and is used for letter-of-credit transactions. The customer usually needs the original or a copy as proof of ownership to take possession of the goods.

- **Consular invoice.** Certain nations require a consular invoice, which is used to control and identify goods. The invoice must be purchased from the consulate of the country to which the goods are being shipped and usually must be prepared in the language of that country.

- **Certificate of origin.** Certain nations require a signed statement as to the origin of the export item. Such certificates are usually obtained through a semiofficial organization such as a local chamber of commerce. A certificate may be required even though the commercial invoice contains the information.

- **Inspection certification.** Some purchasers and countries may require a certificate of inspection attesting to the specifications of the goods shipped, usually performed by a third party. Inspection certificates are often obtained from independent testing organizations.

- **Dock receipt and warehouse receipt.** These receipts are used to transfer accountability when the export item is moved by the domestic carrier to the port of embarkation and left with the international carrier for export.

- **Destination control statement.** This statement appears on the commercial invoice, ocean or air waybill of lading, and SED to notify the carrier and all foreign parties that the item may be exported only to certain destinations.

- **Insurance certificate.** If the seller provides insurance, the insurance certificate states the type and amount of coverage. This instrument is negotiable.

- **Shipper's export declaration.** The SED is used to control exports and compile trade statistics and must be prepared and submitted to the customs agent for shipments by mail valued at more than $500 and for shipments by means other than mail valued at more than $2,500. In addition, an SED must be prepared for all shipments covered by an IVL, regardless of value.

- **Export license.** U.S. export shipments are required by the U.S. government to have an export license, either a general license or an IVL. (See chapter 11 for a complete discussion of licensing.)

- **Export packing list.** Considerably more detailed and informative than a standard domestic packing list, an export packing list itemizes the material in each individual package and indicates the type of package: box, crate, drum, carton, and so on. It shows the individual net, legal, tare, and gross weights and measurements for each package (in both U.S. and metric systems). Package markings should be shown along with the shipper's and buyer's references. The packing list should be attached to the outside of a package in a waterproof envelope marked "packing list enclosed." The list is used by the shipper or forwarding agent to determine (1) the total shipment weight and volume and (2) whether the correct cargo is being shipped. In addition, customs officials (both U.S. and foreign) may use the list to check the cargo.

Documentation must be precise. Slight discrepancies or omissions may prevent U.S. merchandise from being exported, result in U.S. firms not getting paid, or even result in the seizure of the exporter's goods by U.S. or foreign government customs. Collection documents are subject to precise time limits and may not be honored by a bank if out of date. Much of the documentation is routine for freight forwarders or customs brokers acting on the firm's behalf, but the exporter is ultimately responsible for the accuracy of the documentation.

The number of documents the exporter must deal with varies depending on the destination of the shipment. Because each country has different import regulations, the exporter must be careful to provide proper documentation. If the exporter does not rely on the services of a freight forwarder, there are several methods of obtaining information on foreign import restrictions:

- Country desk officers (see appendix II) in the Department of Commerce are specialists in individual country conditions.

- Industry specialists in the Department of Commerce can advise on product classifications.

- Foreign government embassies and consulates in the United States can often provide information on import regulations.

- The Bureau of National Affairs *Export Shipping Manual* contains complete country-by-country shipping information as well as tariff systems, import and exchange controls, mail regulations, and other special information. Contact the Bureau of National Affairs, 1231 25th Street, N.W., Washington, DC 20037.

- The *Air Cargo Tariff Guidebook* lists country-by-country regulations affecting air shipments. Other information includes tariff rules and rates, transportation charges, air waybill information, and special carrier regulations. Contact the Air Cargo Tariff, P.O. Box 7627, 1117 ZJ Schiphol Airport, Netherlands.

- The National Council on International Trade Documentation (NCITD) provides several low-cost publications that contain information on specific documentation commonly used in international trade. NCITD provides a free listing of its publications. Contact National Council on International Trade Documentation, 350 Broadway, Suite 1200, New York, NY 10013; telephone 212-925-1400.

Shipping

The handling of transportation is similar for domestic orders and export orders. The export marks should be added to the standard information shown on a domestic bill of lading and should show the name of the exporting carrier and the latest allowed arrival date at the port of export. The exporter should also include instructions for the inland carrier to notify the international freight forwarder by telephone on arrival.

International shipments are increasingly being made on a through bill of lading under a multimodal contract. The multimodal transport operator (frequently one of the modal carriers) takes charge of and responsibility for the entire movement from factory to the final destination.

When determining the method of international shipping, the exporter may find it useful to consult with a freight forwarder. Since carriers are often used for large and bulky shipments, the exporter should reserve space on the carrier well before actual shipment date (this reservation is called the booking contract).

The exporter should consider the cost of shipment, delivery schedule, and accessibility to the shipped product by the foreign buyer when determining the method of international shipping. Although air carriers are more expensive, their cost may be offset by lower domestic shipping costs (because they may use a local airport instead of a coastal seaport) and quicker delivery times. These factors may give the U.S. exporter an edge over other competitors, whose service to their accounts may be less timely.

Before shipping, the U.S. firm should be sure to check with the foreign buyer about the destination of the goods. Buyers often wish the goods to be shipped to a free-trade zone or a free port (see chapter 11), where goods are exempt from import duties.

Insurance

Export shipments are usually insured against loss, damage, and delay in transit by cargo insurance. For international shipments, the carrier's liability is frequently limited by international agreements and the coverage is substantially different from domestic coverage. Arrangements for cargo insurance may be made by either the buyer or the seller, depending on the terms of sale. Exporters are advised to consult with international insurance carriers or freight forwarders for more information.

Damaging weather conditions, rough handling by carriers, and other common hazards to cargo make marine insurance important protection for U.S. exporters. If the terms of sale make the U.S. firm responsible for insurance, it should either obtain its own policy or insure cargo under a freight forwarder's policy for a fee. If the terms of sale make the foreign buyer responsible, the exporter should not assume (or even take the buyer's word) that adequate insurance has been obtained. If the buyer neglects to obtain coverage or obtains too little, damage to the cargo may cause a major financial loss to the exporter.

Figure 12-1.
Sample Shipper's Export Declaration (SED)

U.S. DEPARTMENT OF COMMERCE - BUREAU OF THE CENSUS - INTERNATIONAL TRADE ADMINISTRATION

FORM **7525-V** (1-1-88)　　　　**SHIPPER'S EXPORT DECLARATION**　　　　OMB No. 0607-0018

1a. EXPORTER *(Name and address including ZIP code)*

| ZIP CODE | 2. DATE OF EXPORTATION | 3. BILL OF LADING/AIR WAYBILL NO. |

b. EXPORTER'S EIN (IRS) NUMBER　　c. PARTIES TO TRANSACTION
　☐ Related　　☐ Non-related

4a. ULTIMATE CONSIGNEE

b. INTERMEDIATE CONSIGNEE

5. FORWARDING AGENT

| 6. POINT (STATE) OF ORIGIN OR FTZ NO. | 7. COUNTRY OF ULTIMATE DESTINATION |

8. LOADING PIER *(Vessel only)*　　9 MODE OF TRANSPORT *(Specify)*

10. EXPORTING CARRIER　　11. PORT OF EXPORT

12. PORT OF UNLOADING *(Vessel and air only)*　　13. CONTAINERIZED *(Vessel only)*
　☐ Yes　　☐ No

14. SCHEDULE B DESCRIPTION OF COMMODITIES. *(Use columns 17-19)*

15. MARKS, NOS., AND KINDS OF PACKAGES

D/F (16)	SCHEDULE B NUMBER (17)	CHECK DIGIT	QUANTITY - SCHEDULE B UNIT(S) (18)	SHIPPING WEIGHT (Kilos) (19)	VALUE (U.S. dollars, omit cents) *(Selling price or cost if not sold)* (20)

21. VALIDATED LICENSE NO./GENERAL LICENSE SYMBOL　　22. ECCN *(When required)*

23. Duly Authorized officer or employee | The exporter authorizes the forwarder named above to act as forwarding agent for export control and customs purposes.

24. I certify that all statements made and all information contained herein are true and correct and that I have read and understand the instructions for preparation of this document, set forth in the **"Correct Way to Fill Out the Shipper's Export Declaration."** I understand that civil and criminal penalties, including forfeiture and sale, may be imposed for making false or fraudulent statements herein, failing to provide the requested information or for violation of U.S. laws on exportation (13 U.S.C. Sec. 305; 22 U.S.C. Sec. 401; 18 U.S.C. Sec. 1001; 50 U.S.C. App. 24 10).

Signature | **Confidential** - For use solely for offical purposes authorized by the Secretary of Commerce (13 U.S.C. 301 (g)).

Title | Export shipments are subject to inspection by U.S. Customs Service and/or Office of Export Enforcement.

Date | 25 AUTHENTICATION *(When required)*

The "Correct Way to Fill Out the Shipper's Export Declaration" is available from the Bureau of the Census, Washington, D.C. 20233.
FedEx M-1086　6/91　LOGOS # 103369

Methods of payment

There are several basic methods of receiving payment for products sold abroad. As with domestic sales, a major factor that determines the method of payment is the amount of trust in the buyer's ability and willingness to pay. For sales within the United States, if the buyer has good credit, sales are usually made on open account; if not, cash in advance is required. For export sales, these same methods may be used; however, other methods are also often used in international trade. Ranked in order from most secure for the exporter to least secure, the basic methods of payment are

1. cash in advance,

2. letter of credit,

3. documentary collection or draft,

4. open account, and

5. other payment mechanisms, such as consignment sales.

Since getting paid in full and on time is of utmost concern to exporters, risk is a major consideration. Many factors make exporting riskier than domestic sales. However, there are also several methods of reducing risks. One of the most important factors in reducing risks is to know what risks exist. For that reason, exporters are advised to consult an international banker to determine an acceptable method of payment for each specific transaction.

Cash in advance

Cash in advance before shipment may seem to be the most desirable method of all, since the shipper is relieved of collection problems and has immediate use of the money if a wire transfer is used. Payment by check, even before shipment, may result in a collection delay of four to six weeks and therefore frustrate the original intention of payment before shipment. On the other hand, advance payment creates cash flow problems and increases risks for the buyer. Thus, cash in advance lacks competitiveness; the buyer may refuse to pay until the merchandise is received.

Documentary letters of credit and drafts

The buyer may be concerned that the goods may not be sent if the payment is made in advance. To protect the interests of both buyer and seller, documentary letters of credit or drafts are often used. Under these two methods, documents are required to be presented before payment is made. Both letters of credit and drafts may be paid immediately, at sight, or at a later date. Drafts that are to be paid when presented for payment are called *sight drafts*. Drafts that are to be paid at a later date, which is often after the buyer receives the goods, are called *time drafts* or *date drafts*.

Since payment under these two methods is made on the basis of documents, all terms of sale should be clearly specified. For example, "net 30 days" should be specified as "net 30 days from acceptance" or "net 30 days from date of bill of lading" to avoid confusion and delay of payment. Likewise, the currency of payment should be specified as "US$XXX" if payment is to be made in U.S. dollars. International bankers can offer other suggestions to help.

Banks charge fees – usually a small percentage of the amount of payment – for handling letters of credit and less for handling drafts. If fees charged by both the foreign and U.S. banks for their collection services are to be charged to the account of the buyer, this point should be explicitly stated in all quotations and on all drafts.

The exporter usually expects the buyer to pay the charges for the letter of credit, but some buyers may not accept terms that require this added cost. In such cases the exporter must either absorb the letter of credit costs or lose that potential sale.

Letters of credit

A letter of credit adds a bank's promise of paying the exporter to that of the foreign buyer when the exporter has complied with all the terms and conditions of the letter of credit. The foreign buyer applies for issuance of a letter of credit to the exporter and therefore is called the *applicant;* the exporter is called the *beneficiary.*

Payment under a documentary letter of credit is based on documents, not on the terms of sale or the condition of the goods sold. Before payment, the bank responsible for making payment verifies that all documents are exactly as required by the letter of credit. When they are not as required, a discrepancy exists, which must be *cured* before payment can be made. Thus, the full compliance of documents with those specified in the letter of credit is mandatory.

Often a letter of credit issued by a foreign bank is confirmed by a U.S. bank. This means that the U.S. bank, which is the confirming bank, adds its promise to pay to that of the foreign, or issuing, bank. Letters of credit that are not confirmed are advised through a U.S. bank and are called *advised* letters of credit. U.S. exporters may wish to confirm letters of credit issued by foreign banks not only because they are unfamiliar with the credit risk of the foreign bank but also because there may be concern about the political or economic risk associated with the country in which the bank is located. An international banker or the local U.S. Department of Commerce district office can help exporters evaluate these risks to determine what might be appropriate for each specific export transaction.

A letter of credit may be either *irrevocable* (that is, it cannot be changed unless both the buyer and the seller agree to make the change) or *revocable* (that is, either party may unilaterally make changes). A revocable letter of credit is inadvisable. A letter of credit may be *at sight*, which means immediate payment upon presentation of documents, or it may be a *time* or *date* letter of credit with payment to be made in the future. See the "Drafts" section of this chapter.

Any change made to a letter of credit after it has been issued is called an amendment. The fees charged by the banks involved in amending the letter of credit may be paid by either the exporter or the foreign buyer, but who is to pay which charges should be specified in the letter of credit. Since changes can be time-consuming and expensive, every effort should be made to get the letter of credit right the first time.

An exporter is usually not paid until the advising or confirming bank receives the funds from the issuing bank. To expedite the receipt of funds, wire transfers may be used. Bank practices vary, however, and the exporter may be able to receive funds by discounting the letter of credit at the bank, which involves paying a fee to the bank for this service. Exporters should consult with their international bankers about bank policy.

A Typical Letter of Credit Transaction

Here is what typically happens when payment is made by an irrevocable letter of credit confirmed by a U.S. bank:

1. After the exporter and customer agree on the terms of a sale, the customer arranges for its bank to open a letter of credit. (Delays may be encountered if, for example, the buyer has insufficient funds.)

2. The buyer's bank prepares an irrevocable letter of credit, including all instructions to the seller concerning the shipment.

3. The buyer's bank sends the irrevocable letter of credit to a U.S. bank, requesting confirmation. The exporter may request that a particular U.S. bank be the confirming bank, or the foreign bank selects one of its U.S. correspondent banks.

4. The U.S. bank prepares a letter of confirmation to forward to the exporter along with the irrevocable letter of credit.

5. The exporter reviews carefully all conditions in the letter of credit. The exporter's freight forwarder should be contacted to make sure that the shipping date can be met. If the exporter cannot comply with one or more of the conditions, the customer should be alerted at once.

6. The exporter arranges with the freight forwarder to deliver the goods to the appropriate port or airport.

7. When the goods are loaded, the forwarder completes the necessary documents.

8. The exporter (or the forwarder) presents to the U.S. bank documents indicating full compliance.

9. The bank reviews the documents. If they are in order, the documents are airmailed to the buyer's bank for review and transmitted to the buyer.

10. The buyer (or agent) gets the documents that may be needed to claim the goods.

11. A draft, which may accompany the letter of credit, is paid by the exporter's bank at the time specified or may be discounted at an earlier date.

Example of a Confirmed Irrevocable Letter of Credit

The example of a confirmed irrevocable letter of credit in figure 13-1 illustrates the various parts of a typical letter of credit. In this sample, the letter of credit was forwarded to the exporter, The Walton Building Supplies Company (A) by the drawee bank, C&S/Sovran Corporation (B) as a result of the letter of credit being issued by the First Hong Kong Bank, Hong Kong (C), for the account of the importer, BBH Hong Kong (D). The date of issue was March 8, 1991 (E), and the exporter must submit proper documents (e.g., a commercial invoice in one original and three copies) (F) by June 23, 1991 (G) in order for a sight draft (H) to be honored.

Tips on Using a Letter of Credit

When preparing quotations for prospective customers, exporters should keep in mind that banks pay only the amount specified in the letter of credit – even if higher charges for shipping, insurance, or other factors are documented.

Upon receiving a letter of credit, the exporter should carefully compare the letter's terms with the terms of the exporter's pro forma quotation. This point is extremely important, since the terms must be precisely met or the letter of credit may be invalid and the exporter may not be paid. If meeting the terms of the letter of credit is impossible or any of the information is incorrect or misspelled, the exporter should get in touch with the customer immediately and ask for an amendment to the letter of credit to correct the problem.

The exporter must provide documentation showing that the goods were shipped by the date specified in the letter of credit or the exporter may not be paid. Exporters should check with their freight forwarders to make sure that no unusual conditions may arise that would delay shipment. Similarly, documents must be presented by the date specified for the letter of credit to be paid. Exporters should verify with their international bankers that sufficient time will be available for timely presentation.

International letters of credit are usually governed by uniform customs and practices or by ICC Publication No. 400. International bankers may be consulted for more information.

Exporters should always request that the letter of credit specify that partial shipments and transshipment will be allowed. Doing so prevents unforeseen problems at the last minute.

Drafts

A draft, sometimes also called a bill of exchange, is analogous to a foreign buyer's check. Like checks used in domestic commerce, drafts sometimes carry the risk that they will be dishonored.

Sight Drafts

A sight draft is used when the seller wishes to retain title to the shipment until it reaches its destination and is paid for. Before the cargo can be released, the original ocean bill of lading must be properly endorsed by the buyer and surrendered to the carrier, since it is a document that evidences title.

Air waybills of lading, on the other hand, do not need to be presented in order for the buyer to claim the goods. Hence, there is a greater risk when a sight draft is being used with an air shipment.

In actual practice, the bill of lading or air waybill is endorsed by the shipper and sent via the shipper's bank to the buyer's bank or to another intermediary along with a sight draft, invoices, and other supporting documents specified by either the buyer or the buyer's country (e.g., packing lists, consular invoices, insurance certificates). The bank notifies the buyer when it has received these documents; as soon as the amount of the draft is paid, the bank releases the bill of lading, enabling the buyer to obtain the shipment.

When a sight draft is being used to control the transfer of title of a shipment, some risk remains because the buyer's ability or willingness to pay may change between the time the goods are shipped and the time the drafts are presented for payment. Also, the policies of the importing country may change. If the buyer cannot or will not pay for and claim the goods, then returning or disposing of them becomes the problem of the exporter.

Exporters should also consider which foreign bank should negotiate the sight draft for payment. If the negotiating bank is also the buyer's bank, the bank may favor its customer's position, thereby putting the exporter at a disadvantage. Exporters should consult their international bankers to determine an appropriate strategy for negotiating drafts.

Time Drafts and Date Drafts

If the exporter wants to extend credit to the buyer, a time draft can be used to state that payment is due within a certain time after the buyer accepts the draft and receives the goods, for example, 30 days after acceptance. By signing and writing "accepted" on the draft, the buyer is formally obligated to pay within the stated time. When this is done the draft is called a *trade acceptance* and can be either kept by the exporter until maturity or sold to a bank at a discount for immediate payment.

A date draft differs slightly from a time draft in that it specifies a date on which payment is due, for example, December 1, 19XX, rather than a time period after the draft is accepted. When a sight draft or time draft is used, a buyer can delay payment by delaying acceptance of the draft. A date draft can prevent this delay in payment but still must be accepted.

When a bank accepts a draft, it becomes an obligation of the bank and a negotiable investment known as a banker's acceptance is created. A *banker's acceptance* can also be sold to a bank at a discount for immediate payment.

Credit cards

Many U.S. exporters of consumer and other products (generally of low dollar value) that are sold directly to the end user accept Visa and MasterCard in payment for export sales. In international credit card transactions, merchants are normally required to deposit drafts in the currency of their country; for example, a U.S. exporter would deposit a draft in U.S. dollars. U.S. merchants may find that domestic rules and international rules governing credit card transactions differ somewhat and should contact their credit card processor for more specific information.

International credit card transactions are typically placed by telephone or fax, methods that facilitate fraudulent transactions. Merchants should determine the validity of transactions and obtain proper authorizations.

Open account

In a foreign transaction, an open account is a convenient method of payment and may be satisfactory if the buyer is well established, has demonstrated a long and favorable payment record, or has been thoroughly checked for creditworthiness. Under open account, the exporter simply bills the customer, who is expected to pay under agreed terms at a future date. Some of the largest firms abroad make purchases only on open account.

Open account sales do pose risks, however. The absence of documents and banking channels may make legal enforcement of claims difficult to pursue. The exporter may have to pursue collection abroad, which can be difficult and costly. Also, receivables may be harder to finance, since drafts or other evidence of indebtedness are unavailable.

Before issuing a pro forma invoice to a buyer, exporters contemplating a sale on open account terms should thoroughly examine the political, economic, and commercial risks and consult with their bankers if financing will be needed for the transaction.

Other payment mechanisms

Consignment sales

In international consignment sales, the same basic procedure is followed as in the United States. The material is shipped to a foreign distributor to be sold on behalf of the exporter. The exporter retains title to the goods until they are sold by the distributor. Once the goods are sold, payment is sent to the exporter. With this method, the exporter has the greatest risk and least control over the goods and may have to wait quite a while to get paid.

When this type of sale is contemplated, it may be wise to consider some form of risk insurance. In addition, it may be necessary to conduct a credit check on the foreign distributor (see the section of this chapter titled "Decreasing Credit Risks Through Credit Checks"). Furthermore, the contract should establish who is responsible for property risk insurance covering merchandise until it is sold and payment received.

Foreign currency

A buyer and a seller in different countries rarely use the same currency. Payment is usually made in either the buyer's or the seller's currency or in a mutually agreed-on currency that is foreign to both parties.

One of the uncertainties of foreign trade is the uncertainty of the future exchange rates between currencies. The relative value between the dollar and the buyer's currency may change between the time the deal is made and the time payment is received. If the exporter is not properly protected, a devaluation in the foreign currency could cause the exporter to lose dollars in the transaction. For example, if the buyer has agreed to pay 500,000 French francs for a shipment and the franc is valued at 20 cents, the seller would expect to receive $100,000. If the franc later decreased in value to be worth 19 cents, payment under the new rate would be only $95,000, a loss of $5,000 for the seller. On the other hand, if the foreign currency increases in value the exporter would get a windfall in extra profits. However, most exporters are not interested in speculating on foreign exchange fluctuations and prefer to avoid risks.

One of the simplest ways for a U.S. exporter to avoid this type of risk is to quote prices and require payment in U.S. dollars. Then the burden and risk are placed on the buyer to make the currency exchange. Exporters should also be aware of problems of currency convertibility; not all currencies are freely or quickly convertible into U.S. dollars. Fortunately, the U.S. dollar is widely accepted as an international trading currency, and American firms can often secure payment in dollars.

If the buyer asks to make payment in a foreign currency, the exporter should consult an international banker before negotiating the sales contract. Banks can offer advice on the foreign exchange risks that exist; further, some international banks can help one hedge against such a risk if necessary, by agreeing to purchase the foreign currency at a fixed price in dollars regardless of the value of the currency when the customer pays. The bank charges a fee or discount on the transaction. If this mechanism is used, the fee should be included in the price quotation.

Countertrade and barter

International countertrade is a trade practice whereby a supplier commits contractually, as a condition of sale, to undertake specified initiatives that compensate and benefit the other party. The resulting linked trade fulfills financial (e.g., lack of foreign exchange), marketing, or public policy objectives of the trading parties. Not all suppliers consider countertrade an objectionable imposition; many U.S. exporters consider countertrade a necessary cost of doing business in markets where U.S. exports would otherwise not occur.

Simple barter is the direct exchange of goods or services between two parties; no money changes hands. Pure barter arrangements in international commerce are rare, because the parties' needs for the goods of the other seldom coincide and because valuation of the goods may pose problems. The most common form of compensatory trade practiced today involves contractually linked, parallel trade transactions each of which involves a separate financial settlement. For example, a countertrade contract may provide that the U.S. exporter will be paid in a convertible currency as long as the U.S. exporter (or another entity designated by the exporter) agrees to export a related quantity of goods from the importing country.

U.S. exporters can take advantage of countertrade opportunities by trading through an intermediary with countertrade expertise, such as an international broker, an international bank, or an export management company. Some export management companies offer specialized countertrade services. Exporters should bear in mind that countertrade often involves higher transaction costs and greater risks than simple export transactions.

The Department of Commerce can advise and assist U.S. exporters faced with countertrade requirements. The Finance and Countertrade Division of the Office of Finance, Industry, and Trade Information monitors countertrade trends, disseminates information (including lists of potentially beneficial countertrade opportunities), and provides general assistance to enterprises seeking barter and countertrade opportunities. For information, contact Finance and Countertrade Division, Office of Finance, Industry, and Trade Information, International Trade Administration, U.S. Department of Commerce, Washington, D.C.; telephone 202-377-4471. UNCITRAL is expected to publish a legal guide to countertrade contracts in 1992.

Decreasing credit risks through credit checks

Generally, it is a good idea to check a buyer's credit even if credit risk insurance or relatively safe payment methods are employed. Banks are often able to provide credit reports on foreign companies, either through their own foreign branches or through a correspondent bank.

The Department of Commerce's WTDRs (see chapter 7) also provide useful information for credit checks. For a fee, a WDTR may be requested on any foreign company. Although the WTDR is itself not a credit report, it does contain some financial information and also identifies other U.S. companies that do business with the reported firm. The exporter may then contact those companies directly to find out about their payment experience.

Private credit reporting services also are available. Several U.S. services compile financial information on foreign firms (particularly larger firms) and make it available to subscribers. Reliable evaluations can also be obtained from foreign credit reporting services, many of which are listed in *The Exporter's Guide to Foreign Sources for Credit Information*, published by Trade Data Reports, Inc., 6 West 37th Street, New York, NY 10018.

Collection problems

In international trade, problems involving bad debts are more easily avoided than rectified after they occur. Credit checks and the other methods that have been discussed can limit the risks involved. Nonetheless, just as in a company's domestic business, exporters occasionally encounter problems with buyers who default on payments. When these problems occur in international trade, obtaining payment can be both difficult and expensive. Even when the exporter has insurance to cover commercial credit risks, a default by a buyer still requires time, effort, and cost. The exporter must exhaust all reasonable means of obtaining payment before an insurance claim is honored, and there is often a significant delay before the insurance payment is made.

The simplest (and least costly) solution to a payment problem is to contact and negotiate with the customer. With patience, understanding, and flexibility, an exporter can often resolve conflicts to the satisfaction of both sides.

This point is especially true when a simple misunderstanding or technical problem is to blame and there is no question of bad faith. Even though the exporter may be required to compromise on certain points – perhaps even on the price of the committed goods – the company may save a valuable customer and profit in the long run.

If, however, negotiations fail and the sum involved is large enough to warrant the effort, a company should obtain the assistance and advice of its bank, legal counsel, and other qualified experts. If both parties can agree to take their dispute to an arbitration agency, this step is preferable to legal action, since arbitration is often faster and less costly. The International Chamber of Commerce handles the majority of international arbitrations and is usually acceptable to foreign companies because it is not affiliated with any single country. For information contact the vice president for arbitration, U.S. Council of the International Chamber of Commerce, telephone 212-354-4480. The American Arbitration Association is also a reputable arbitration agency that handles international disputes; for information telephone 212-484-4000.

U.S. Government Trade Complaint Service

The Trade Complaint Service is available to aid U.S. exporters who find themselves in a trade dispute as a result of a specific overseas commercial transaction. These disputes, which are processed through the Department of Commerce's district offices, must meet certain criteria. After a firm has made every effort to settle the complaint without U.S. government assistance, cases are accepted when it can be clearly shown that communications have broken down and the value of the claim is more than $1,000. Simple collection claims are not accepted.

Commerce makes every effort to restore communications between the parties to the dispute in order to arrive at an amicable settlement. When legal proceedings are initiated, U.S. government assistance is normally withdrawn.

Figure 13-1.
Sample Confirmed Irrevocable Letter of Credit

INTERNATIONAL BANKING GROUP   **ORIGINAL**

C&S/Sovran Corporation
P.O. BOX 4899, ATLANTA, GEORGIA 30302-4899
CABLE ADDRESS: CITSOUTH
TELEX NO. 3737650
SWIFT NO. CSBKUS 33

OUR ADVICE NUMBER: EA00000091
ADVICE DATE: 08MAR91   ****AMOUNT****
ISSUE BANK REF: 3312/HBI/22341   USD****25,000.00
EXPIRY DATE: 23JUN91

BENEFICIARY: APPLICANT:
THE WALTON BUILDING SUPPLIES CO.   BBH HONG KONG
2356 SOUTH BELK STREET   34 INDUSTRIAL DRIVE
ATLANTA, GEORGIA 30345   CENTRAL, HONG KONG

WE HAVE BEEN REQUESTED TO ADVISE TO YOU THE FOLLOWING LETTER OF CREDIT AS
ISSUED BY:
FIRST HONG KONG BANK
1 CENTRAL TOWER
HONG KONG

PLEASE BE GUIDED BY ITS TERMS AND CONDITIONS AND BY THE FOLLOWING:
CREDIT IS AVAILABLE BY NEGOTIATION OF YOUR DRAFT(S) IN DUPLICATE AT
SIGHT FOR 100 PERCENT OF INVOICE VALUE DRAWN ON US ACCOMPANIED BY THE
FOLLOWING DOCUMENTS:

1. SIGNED COMMERCIAL INVOICE IN 1 ORIGINAL AND 3 COPIES.

2. FULL SET 3/3 OCEAN BILLS OF LADING CONSIGNED TO THE ORDER OF FIRST HONG KONG
   BANK, HONG KONG NOTIFY APPLICANT AND MARKED FREIGHT COLLECT.

3. PACKING LIST IN 2 COPIES.

EVIDENCING SHIPMENT OF: 5000 PINE LOGS – WHOLE – 8 TO 12 FEET
                        FOB SAVANNAH, GEORGIA

SHIPMENT FROM: SAVANNAH, GEORGIA   TO: HONG KONG
LATEST SHIPPING DATE: 02JUN91

PARTIAL SHIPMENTS NOT ALLOWED   TRANSHIPMENT NOT ALLOWED

ALL BANKING CHARGES OUTSIDE HONG KONG ARE FOR BENEFICIARYS ACCOUNT.
DOCUMENTS MUST BE PRESENTED WITHIN 21 DAYS FROM B/L DATE.

AT THE REQUEST OF OUR CORRESPONDENT, WE CONFIRM THIS CREDIT AND ALSO ENGAGE
WITH YOU THAT ALL DRAFTS DRAWN UNDER AND IN COMPLIANCE WITH THE TERMS OF THIS
CREDIT WILL BE DULY HONORED BY US.

PLEASE EXAMINE THIS INSTRUMENT CAREFULLY. IF YOU ARE UNABLE TO COMPLY WITH
THE TERMS OR CONDITIONS, PLEASE COMMUNICATE WITH YOUR BUYER TO ARRANGE FOR
AN AMENDMENT.

Financing export transactions

Exporters naturally want to get paid as quickly as possible, and importers usually prefer delaying payment at least until they have received and resold the goods. Because of the intense competition for export markets, being able to offer good payment terms is often necessary to make a sale. Exporters should be aware of the many financing options open to them so that they may choose the one that is most favorable for both the buyer and the seller.

An exporter may need (1) preshipment financing to produce or purchase the product or to provide a service or (2) postshipment financing of the resulting account or accounts receivable, or both. The following factors are important to consider in making decisions about financing:

- **The need for financing to make the sale.** In some cases, favorable payment terms make a product more competitive. If the competition offers better terms and has a similar product, a sale can be lost. In other cases, the exporter may need financing to produce the goods that have been ordered or to finance other aspects of a sale, such as promotion and selling expenses, engineering modifications, and shipping costs. Various financing sources are available to exporters, depending on the specifics of the transaction and the exporter's overall financing needs.

- **The cost of different methods of financing.** Interest rates and fees vary. The total costs and their effect on price and profit should be well understood before a pro forma invoice is submitted to the buyer.

- **The length of time financing is required.** Costs increase with the length of terms. Different methods of financing are available for short, medium, and long terms. However, exporters also need to be fully aware of financing limitations so that they can obtain the financing required to complete the transaction.

- **The risks associated with financing the transaction.** The greater the risks associated with the transaction – whether they actually exist or are only perceived by the lender – the greater the costs to the exporter as well as the more difficult financing will be to obtain. Financing will also be more costly.

The creditworthiness of the buyer directly affects the probability of payment to the exporter, but it is not the only factor of concern to a potential lender. The political and economic stability of the buyer's country also can be of concern. To provide financing for either accounts receivable or the production or purchase of the product for sale, the lender may require the most secure methods of payment, a letter of credit (possibly confirmed), or export credit insurance.

If a lender is uncertain about the exporter's ability to perform, or if additional credit capacity is needed, a government guarantee program may enable the lender to provide additional financing.

- **The availability of the exporter's own financial resources.** The company may be able to extend credit without seeking outside financing, or the company may have sufficient financial strength to establish a commercial line of credit. If neither of these alternatives is possible or desirable, other options may exist, but the exporter should fully explore the available options before issuing the pro forma invoice.

For assistance in determining which financing options may be available, the following sources may be consulted:

- The exporter's international or domestic banker.

- The exporter's state export promotion or export finance office.

- The Department of Commerce district office.

- The SBA.

- The Eximbank, Washington, D.C.

Extending credit to foreign buyers

Exporters need to weigh carefully the credit or financing they extend to foreign customers. Exporters should follow the same careful credit principles they follow for domestic customers. An important reason for controlling the credit period is the cost incurred, either through use of working capital or through interest and fees paid. If the buyer is not responsible for paying these costs, then the exporter should factor them into the selling price.

A useful guide for determining the appropriate credit period is the normal commercial terms in the exporter's industry for internationally traded products. Buyers generally expect to receive the benefits of such terms. With few exceptions, normal commercial terms range from 30 to 180 days for off-the-shelf items like consumer goods, chemicals, and other industrial raw materials, agricultural commodities, and spare parts and components. Custom-made or higher-value capital equipment, on the other hand, may warrant longer repayment periods. An allowance may have to be made for longer shipment times than are found in domestic trade, because foreign buyers are often unwilling to have the credit period start before receiving the goods.

Foreign buyers often press exporters for longer payment periods, and it is true that liberal financing is a means of enhancing export competitiveness. The exporter should recognize, however, that longer credit periods increase any risk of default for which the exporter may be liable.

Thus, the exporter must exercise judgment in balancing competitiveness against considerations of cost and safety. Also, credit terms once extended to a buyer tend to set the precedent for future sales, so the exporter should carefully consider any credit terms extended to first-time buyers.

Customers are frequently charged interest on credit periods of a year or longer but infrequently on short-term credit (up to 180 days). Most exporters absorb interest charges for short-term credit unless the customer pays after the due date.

Obtaining cash immediately is usually a high priority with exporters. One way they do so is by converting their export receivables to cash at a discount with a bank. Another way is to expand working capital resources. A third approach, suitable when the purchase involves capital goods and the repayment period extends a year or longer, is to arrange for project financing. In this case, a lender makes a loan directly to the buyer for the project and the exporter is paid immediately from the loan proceeds while the bank waits for payment and earns interest. A fourth method, when financing is difficult to obtain for a buyer or market, is to engage in countertrade (see chapter 13) to afford the customer an opportunity to generate earnings with which to pay for the purchase.

The options that have been mentioned normally involve the payment of interest, fees, or other costs. Some options are more feasible when the amounts are in larger denominations. Exporters should also determine whether they incur financial liability should the buyer default.

Commercial banks

The same type of commercial loans that finance domestic activities – including loans for working capital and revolving lines of credit – are often sought to finance export sales until payment is received. However, banks do not usually extend credit solely on the basis of an order.

A logical first step in obtaining financing is for an exporter to approach its local commercial bank. If the exporter already has a loan for domestic needs, then the lender already has experience with the exporter's ability to perform. Many exporters have very similar, if not identical, preshipment needs for both their international and their domestic transactions. Many lenders, therefore, would be willing to provide financing for export transactions if there were a reasonable certainty of repayment. By using letters of credit or export credit insurance, an exporter can reduce the lender's risk.

When a lender wishes greater assurance than is afforded by the transaction, a government guarantee program (see the "Government Assistance Programs" section of this chapter) may enable a lender to extend credit to the exporter.

For a company that is new to exporting or is a small or medium-sized business, it is important to select a bank

that is sincerely interested in serving businesses of similar type or size. If the exporter's bank lacks an international department, it will refer the exporter to a correspondent bank that has one. The exporter may want to visit the international department – of the exporter's own bank or a correspondent bank – to discuss its export plans, available banking facilities, and applicable fees.

When selecting a bank, the exporter should ask the following questions:

- What are the charges for confirming a letter of credit, processing drafts, and collecting payment?

- Does the bank have foreign branches or correspondent banks? Where are they located?

- Can the bank provide buyer credit reports? At what cost?

- Does it have experience with U.S. and state government financing programs that support small business export transactions? If not, is it willing to consider participating in these programs?

- What other services, such as trade leads, can it provide?

Banker's acceptances and discounting

A time draft under an irrevocable letter of credit confirmed by a prime U.S. bank presents relatively little risk of default. Also, some banks or other lenders may be willing to buy time drafts that a creditworthy foreign buyer has accepted or agreed to pay at a specified future date. In some cases, banks agree to accept the obligations of paying a draft, usually of a customer, for a fee; this is called a *banker's acceptance.*

However, to convert these instruments to cash immediately, an exporter must obtain a loan using the draft as collateral or sell the draft to an investor or a bank for a fee. When the draft is sold to an investor or bank, it is sold at a discount. The exporter receives an amount less than the face value of the draft so that when the draft is paid at its face value at the specified future date, the investor or bank receives more than it paid to the exporter. The difference between the amount paid to the exporter and the face amount paid at maturity is called a *discount* and represents the fees or interest (or both) the investor or bank receives for holding the draft until maturity. Some drafts are discounted by the investor or bank without recourse to the exporter in case the party that is obligated to pay the draft defaults; others may be discounted with recourse to the exporter, in which case the exporter must reimburse the investor or bank if the party obligated to pay the draft defaults. The exporter should be certain of the terms and conditions of any financing arrangement of this nature.

Project finance

Some export sales, especially sales of capital equipment, may sometimes require financing terms tailored to the buyer's cash flow and may involve payments over several years. Often the buyer obtains a loan from its own bank or arranges for other financing to enable it to pay cash to the exporter. If other project financing is required, either the exporter or the foreign buyer can initiate the proposal.

U.S. exporters frequently benefit from project finance in which federal agencies such as the Eximbank and OPIC participate. Although these programs are designed to support the purchase of U.S. goods and services, many U.S. companies export without being parties to the project finance or even being aware of its existence.

Other private sources

Factoring, forfaiting, and confirming

Factoring is the discounting of a foreign account receivable that does not involve a draft. The exporter transfers title to its foreign accounts receivable to a factoring house (an organization that specializes in the financing of accounts receivable) for cash at a discount from the face value. Although factoring is often done without recourse to the exporter, the specific arrangements should be verified by the exporter. Factoring of foreign accounts receivable is less common than factoring of domestic receivables.

Forfaiting is the selling, at a discount, of longer term accounts receivable or promissory notes of the foreign buyer. These instruments may also carry the guarantee of the foreign government. Both U.S. and European forfaiting houses, which purchase the instruments at a discount from the exporter, are active in the U.S. market. Because forfaiting may be done either with or without recourse to the exporter, the specific arrangements should be verified by the exporter.

Confirming is a financial service in which an independent company confirms an export order in the seller's country and makes payment for the goods in the currency of that country. Among the items eligible for confirmation (and thereby eligible for credit terms) are the goods themselves; inland, air, and ocean transportation costs; forwarding fees; custom brokerage fees; and duties. For the exporter, confirming means that the entire export transaction from plant to end user can be fully coordinated and paid for over time. Although confirming is common in Europe, it is still in its infancy in the United States.

Export intermediaries

In addition to acting as export representatives, many export intermediaries, such as ETCs and EMCs, can help finance export sales. Some of these companies may provide short-term financing or may simply purchase the goods to be exported directly from the manufacturer, thus eliminating any risks associated with the export transaction as well as the need for financing. Some of the larger companies may make countertrade arrangements that substitute for financing in some cases.

Buyers and suppliers as sources of financing

Foreign buyers may make down payments that reduce the need for financing from other sources. In addition, buyers may make progress payments as the goods are completed, which also reduce other financing requirements. Letters of credit that allow for progress payments upon inspection by the buyer's agent or receipt of a statement of the exporter that a certain percentage of the product has been completed are not uncommon.

In addition, suppliers may be willing to offer terms to the exporter if they are comfortable that they will receive payment. Suppliers may be willing to accept assignment of a part of the proceeds of a letter of credit or a partial transfer of a transferable letter of credit. However, some banks allow only a single transfer or assignment of a letter of credit. Therefore, the exporter should investigate the policy of the bank that will be advising or confirming the letter of credit.

Government assistance programs

Several federal government agencies, as well as a number of state and local ones, offer programs to assist exporters with their financing needs. Some are guarantee programs that require the participation of an approved lender; others provide loans or grants to the exporter or a foreign government.

Government programs generally aim to improve exporters' access to credit rather than to subsidize the cost at below-market levels. With few exceptions, banks are allowed to charge market interest rates and fees; part of those fees is paid to the government agencies to cover the agencies' administrative costs and default risks.

Government guarantee and insurance programs are used by commercial banks to reduce the risk associated with loans to exporters. Lenders concerned with an exporter's ability to perform under the terms of sale, and with an exporter's ability to be paid, often use government programs to reduce the risks that would otherwise prevent them from providing financing.

In overview, the Eximbank is the federal government's general trade finance agency, offering numerous programs to address a broad range of needs. Credit insurance provided through its affiliate, the FCIA, protects against default on exports sold under open account terms and drafts and letters of credit that are not the obligation of a U.S. entity. (Excluded are drafts that have been accepted by a U.S. bank or corporation and letters of credit confirmed by a U.S. bank.) Other guarantee and loan programs extend project finance and medium-term credit for durable goods.

Other agencies fill various market niches. USDA offers a variety of programs to foster agricultural exports. The TDP (see chapter 7) provides grant financing for project planning activities conducted by U.S. firms and thereby seeks to give a U.S. "imprint" on project feasibility studies and design. SBA offers programs to address the needs of smaller exporters. OPIC provides specialized assistance to U.S. firms through its performance bond and contractor insurance programs. AID provides grants to developing nations that can be used to purchase U.S. goods and services (see chapter 7).

Although the Department of Commerce does not offer any financing programs of its own, export counseling is available through its district offices. In addition, current articles on export finance programs are periodically published in *Business America*.

The following descriptions provide a basic overview.

Export-Import Bank of the United States

Eximbank is an independent U.S. government agency with the primary purpose of facilitating the export of U.S. goods and services. Eximbank meets this objective by providing loans, guarantees, and insurance coverage to U.S. exporters and foreign buyers, normally on market-related credit terms.

Eximbank's insurance and guarantee programs (see table 14-1) are structured to encourage private financial institutions to fund U.S. exports by reducing the commercial risks (such as buyer insolvency and failure to pay) and political risks (such as war and currency inconvertibility) exporters face. The financing made available under Eximbank's guarantees and insurance is generally on market terms, and most of the commercial and political risks are borne by Eximbank.

Eximbank's loan program, on the other hand, is structured to neutralize interest rate subsidies offered by foreign governments. By responding with its own subsidized loan assistance, Eximbank enables U.S. financing to be competitive on specific sales with that offered by foreign exporters.

Preexport Financing

The Working Capital Guarantee program enables lenders to provide financing an exporter may need to purchase or produce a product for export as well as finance short-term accounts receivable. If the exporter defaults on a loan guaranteed under this program, Eximbank reimburses the lender for the guaranteed portion – generally, 90 percent of the loan – thereby reducing the lender's overall risk. The Working Capital Guarantee program can be used either to support ongoing export sales or to meet a temporary cash flow demand arising from a single export transaction.

The loan principal can be up to 90 percent of the value of the collateral put up by the exporter, a relatively generous percentage. Eligible collateral includes foreign receivables, exportable inventory purchased with the proceeds of the loan, and goods in production. The term of the guaranteed line of credit is generally one year, but a longer period may be acceptable.

Postexport Financing

Eximbank offers commercial and political risk insurance through its affiliate, the FCIA. The insurance protects mostly short-term credit extended for the sale of consumer goods, raw materials, commodities, spare parts, and other items normally sold on terms of up to 180 days. Coverage is also available for some bulk commodities sold on 360-day terms and capital and quasi-capital goods sold on terms of up to five years.

FCIA's insurance policies for exporters include the New-to-Export Policy, Single-Buyer Policy, and Multi-Buyer Policy. In addition, the Umbrella Policy enables an administrator to handle most administrative duties for the exporter. With prior written approval, exporters can assign the rights to any proceeds to a lender as collateral for financing.

FCIA's policies cover up to 100 percent of loans due to specified political risks, such as war and expropriation, and up to 95 percent due to loans from other commercial risks, such as buyer default and insolvency. Exporters generally must meet U.S. content requirements and, under some policies, must insure all eligible foreign sales.

FCIA premiums reflect various risk factors, including length of credit period, payment method, and the country of the buyer. In keeping with insurance principles, FCIA seeks a reasonable spread of risk among the different export markets and avoids unduly concentrated credit exposure.

Several private companies also offer export credit insurance covering political and commercial risks. Private insurance is available for established exporters with a proven track record, often at competitive premium rates, although underwriting capacity in particular markets may be limited. Coverage for contract repudiation and wrongful calling of a bid or performance bond may also be available in the private market. Contact an insurance broker for more information.

To encourage exporters and lenders to make export loans to creditworthy foreign buyers of U.S.-produced goods and services, Eximbank offers its guarantee program. Eximbank guarantees the repayment of medium-term (up to seven years and less than $10 million) loans to foreign buyers of U.S. goods and services. Lenders charge market rate interest on the loan. A minimum 15 percent cash payment is required from the buyer; the remaining 85 percent is financed. Eximbank's guarantee covers 100 percent of the political risk and 85 percent of the commercial risk of the principal on medium-term loans. Coverage for the loan's interest is also provided. Eximbank guarantees loans made in U.S. dollars or any other freely convertible currency.

Eximbank offers fixed-rate financing for long-term sales (repayment periods up to 10 years) for projects such as telecommunications, power plants, and transportation. The interest rates, which are set under international agreement and regularly adjusted in step with market conditions, reflect the per capita income of the importing country and the repayment period of the loan. Eximbank loans to developed countries are charged market interest rates; loans to less developed countries may be slightly less. In practice, Eximbank seldom lends to buyers in developed countries. To qualify for an Eximbank loan, an exporter must show evidence of foreign government-supported competition. This qualification may be waived for small businesses requesting loans of $2.5 million or less. Like the guarantee program, Eximbank's loans require a 15 percent cash payment in advance.

For more information on Eximbank's programs contact the Marketing and Program Division, Export-Import Bank, 811 Vermont Avenue N.W., Washington, DC 20571; telephone 202-566-8873. The toll-free hotline telephone number for advice and assistance to small businesses interested in exporting is 800-424-5201.

Department of Agriculture

The FAS of USDA administers several programs to help make U.S. exporters competitive in international markets and make U.S. products affordable to countries that have greater need than they have ability to pay.

One effort to boost U.S. agricultural sales overseas is the Export Credit Guarantee Program, which offers risk protection for U.S. exporters against nonpayment of foreign banks. The program guarantees payment for commercial as well as noncommercial risks. Private U.S. banking institutions provide the operating funds. The guarantee program makes it easier for exporters to obtain bank financing and to meet credit competition from other exporting countries.

FAS also helps carry out food aid programs that provide emergency food donations and long-term concessional and commercial financing for U.S. agricultural products. These sales are intended to stimulate long-range improvements in foreign economies and development of export markets for U.S. farm products.

Firms may obtain additional information on these financial programs by contacting General Sales Manager, Export Credits, Foreign Agricultural Service, 14th Street and Independence Avenue, S.W., Washington, DC 20250; telephone 202-447-3224.

Overseas Private Investment Corporation

OPIC facilitates U.S. foreign direct investment in developing nations and Eastern Europe. OPIC is an independent, financially self-supporting corporation, fully owned by the U.S. government.

OPIC encourages U.S. investment projects overseas by offering political risk insurance, guaranties, and direct loans. OPIC political risk insurance protects U.S. investment ventures abroad against the risks of civil strife and other violence, expropriation, and inconvertibility of currency. In addition, OPIC can cover business income loss due to political violence or expropriation. Congress has authorized OPIC to support selected equity investments under a pilot program.

OPIC also provides guaranties, limited to $50 million, that protect against both commercial and political risk. OPIC's direct lending is aimed exclusively toward U.S. small and medium-sized companies investing in projects overseas. OPIC direct loans do not exceed $6 million.

U.S. exporters and contractors operating abroad can benefit from OPIC programs covering wrongful calling of performance, bid, and down payment bonds and contract repudiation. Under other programs, OPIC ensures against expropriation of construction equipment temporarily located abroad, spare parts warehoused abroad, and some cross-border operating and capital loans.

OPIC also provides services to facilitate wider participation by smaller U.S. businesses in overseas investment, including investment missions, a computerized data bank, and investor information services.

For more information on any of these programs contact OPIC's Public Affairs Office, Overseas Private Investment Corporation, 1613 M Street N.W., Washington, DC 20537; telephone 800-424-6742 (202-457-7010 in the Washington metropolitan area).

Small Business Administration

SBA also provides financial assistance programs for U.S. exporters. Applicants must qualify as small businesses under the SBA's size standards and meet other eligibility criteria.

Under SBA's Export Revolving Line of Credit (ERLC) Loan program, any number of withdrawals and repayments can be made as long as the dollar limit of the line is not exceeded and disbursements are made within the stated maturity period (not more than 18 months). Proceeds can be used only to finance labor and materials needed for manufacturing, to purchase inventory to meet an export order, and to penetrate or develop foreign markets. Examples of eligible expenses for developing foreign markets include professional export marketing advice or services, foreign business travel, and trade show participation. Under the ERLC program, funds may not be used to purchase fixed assets.

However, under the International Trade Loan program, SBA can guarantee up to $1 million for facilities and equipment (including land and buildings; construction of new facilities; renovation, improvement, or expansion of existing facilities; and purchase or reconditioning of machinery, equipment, and fixtures), plus $250,000 in working capital. Applicants must establish either that (1) loan proceeds will enable them to expand significantly existing export markets or develop new ones or (2) they have been adversely affected by import competition.

Although SBA loans are generally limited to $750,000, larger loans can be financed by using a cooperative agreement between SBA and Eximbank. This option may be attractive to a company with an existing SBA loan or one whose bank would prefer to work through a local SBA office, since Eximbank is based in Washington, D.C.

Both the ERLC and the International Trade Loan programs are guarantee programs that require the participation of an eligible commercial bank. Most bankers are familiar with SBA's guarantee programs.

In addition, other SBA programs may meet specific needs of exporters. For example, SBA's contractor bond program may help small exporters obtain bid or performance bonds if the transaction is structured in accordance with SBA requirements.

For more specific information on SBA's financial assistance programs, policies, and requirements, contact the nearest SBA field office or SBA's Office of Business Loans, Small Business Administration, 409 3rd Street, S.W., Washington, DC 20416; telephone 202-205-6570.

State and local export finance programs

Several cities and states have funded and operational export financing programs, including preshipment and postshipment working capital loans and guarantees, accounts receivable financing, and export insurance. To be eligible for these programs, an export sale must generally be made under a letter of credit or with credit insurance coverage. A certain percentage of state or local content may also be required. However, some programs may require only that certain facilities, such as a state or local port, be used; therefore, exporters may have several options.

Exporters should contact a Department of Commerce district office (see appendix III) or their state economic development agency for more information.

Table 14-1.
Loan and Guarantee Programs of the Export-Import Bank of the United States

Exports	Appropriate Programs
Short-term (up to 180 days)	
Consumables, small manufactured items, spare parts, raw materials	FCIA, Working Capital Guarantee
Medium-term (181 days to 5 years)	
Mining, refining, construction, and agricultural equipment; general aviation aircraft; planning and feasibility studies	FCIA, Commercial Bank Guarantees, Small Business Credit, Medium-Term Credit, Working Capital Guarantee
Long-term (5 years and longer)	
Power plants, LPG and gas-producing plants, other major projects, commercial jet aircraft or locomotives, other heavy capital goods	Direct Loans, Financial Guarantees

After-sales service

Three factors are critical to the success of any export sales effort: quality, price, and service. Quality and price are dealt with in other chapters. Service should be an integral part of any company's export strategy from the start. Properly handled, service can be a foundation for growth. Ignored or left to chance, it can cause an export effort to fail.

Service is the prompt delivery of the product. It is courteous sales personnel. It is a localized user manual or service manual. It is ready access to a service facility. It is knowledgeable, cost-effective maintenance, repair, or replacement. Service is location. Service is dealer support.

Service varies by the product type, the quality of the product, the price of the product, and the distribution channel employed. For export products that require no service – such as food products, some consumer goods, and commercial disposables – the issue is resolved once distribution channels, quality criteria, and return policies have been identified.

On the other hand, the characteristics of consumer durables and some consumables demand that service be available. For such products, service is a feature expected by the consumer. In fact, foreign buyers of industrial goods typically place service at the forefront of the criteria they evaluate when making a purchase decision.

All foreign markets are sophisticated, and each has its own expectations of suppliers and vendors. U.S. manufacturers or distributors must therefore ensure that their service performance is comparable to that of the predominant competitors in the market. This level of performance is an important determinant in ensuring a reasonable competitive position, given the other factors of product quality, price, promotion, and delivery.

An exporting firm's strategy and market entry decision may dictate that it does not provide after-sale service. It may determine that its export objective is the single or multiple opportunistic entry into export markets. Although this approach may work in the short term, subsequent product offerings will be less successful as buyers recall the failure to provide expected levels of service. As a result, market development and sales expenditures may result in one-time sales. Instead of saving money by cutting back on service, the company will see lower profits (because expenses are not spread over longer production runs), ongoing sales programs, and multiple sales to developed buyers.

Service delivery options

Service is an important factor in the initial export sale and ongoing success of products in foreign markets. U.S. firms have many options for the delivery of service to foreign buyers.

A high-cost option – and the most inconvenient for the foreign retail, wholesale, commercial, or industrial buyer – is for the product to be returned to the manufacturing or distribution facility in the United States for service or repair. The buyer incurs a high cost and loses the use of the product for an extended period, while the seller must incur the export cost of the same product a second time to return it. Fortunately, there are practical, cost-effective alternatives to this approach.

If the selected export distribution channel is a joint venture or other partnership arrangement, the overseas partner may have a service or repair capability in the markets to be penetrated. An exporting firm's negotiations and agreements with its partner should include explicit provisions for repairs, maintenance, and warranty service. The cost of providing this service should be negotiated into the agreement.

For goods sold at retail outlets, a preferred service option is to identify and use local service facilities. Doing so requires front-end expenses to identify and train local service outlets, but such costs are more than repaid in the long run.

An excellent case study on this issue involves a foreign firm's service approach to the U.S. market. A leading Canadian manufacturer of consumer personal care items uses U.S. distributors and sales representatives to generate purchases by large and small retailers across the United States. The products are purchased at retail by individual consumers. The Canadian firm contracted with local consumer electronic repair facilities in leading U.S. cities to provide service or replacement for its product line. Consequently, the manufacturer can include a certificate with each product listing "authorized" local warranty and service centers.

There are administrative, training, and supervisory overhead costs associated with such a warranty and service program. The benefit, however, is that the company is now perceived to be a local company that competes on equal footing with domestic U.S. manufacturers. U.S. exporters should keep this example in mind when entering foreign markets.

Exporting a product into commercial or industrial markets may dictate a different approach. For the many U.S. companies that sell through distributors, selection of a representative to serve a region, a nation, or a market should be based not only on the distributing company's ability to sell effectively but also on its ability and willingness to service the product.

Assessing that ability to service requires that the exporter ask questions about existing service facilities; about the types, models, and age of existing service equipment; about training practices for service personnel; and about the firm's experience in servicing similar products.

If the product being exported is to be sold directly to end users, service and timely performance are critical to success. The nature of the product may require delivery of on-site service to the buyer within very specific time parameters. These are negotiable issues for which the U.S. exporter must be prepared. Such on-site service may be available from service organizations in the buyer's country; or the exporting company may have to send personnel to the site to provide service. The sales contract should anticipate a reasonable level of on-site service and should include the associated costs. Existing performance and service history can serve as a guide for estimating service and warranty requirements on export sales, and sales can be costed accordingly. This practice is accepted among small and large exporters alike.

At some level of export activity, it may become cost-effective for a U.S. company to establish its own branch or subsidiary operation in the foreign market. The branch or subsidiary may be a one-person operation or a more extensive facility staffed with sales, administration, service, and other personnel, most of whom are nationals in the market. This high-cost option enables the exporter to ensure sales and service quality, provided that personnel are trained in sales, products, and service on an ongoing basis. The benefits of this option include the control it gives to the exporter and the ability to serve multiple markets in a single region.

Manufacturers of similar or related products may find it cost-effective to consolidate service, training, and support in each export market. Service can be delivered by U.S.-based personnel, a foreign facility under contract, or a jointly owned foreign-based service facility. Despite its cost benefits, this option raises a number of issues. Such joint activity may be interpreted as being in restraint of trade or otherwise market controlling or monopolistic. Exporters that are considering it should therefore obtain competent legal counsel when developing this joint operating arrangement. Exporters may wish to consider obtaining an export trade certificate of review, which provides limited immunity from U.S. antitrust laws.

Legal considerations

Service is a very important part of many types of representation agreements. For better or worse, the quality of service in a country or region affects the U.S. manufacturer's reputation there.

Quality of service also affects the intellectual property rights of the manufacturer. A trademark is a mark of source, with associated quality and performance. If quality control is not maintained, the manufacturer can lose its rights to the product, because one can argue that, within that foreign market, the manufacturer has abandoned the trademark to the distributor.

It is, therefore, imperative that agreements with a representative be specific about the form of the repair or service facility, the number of people on the staff, inspection provisions, training programs, and payment of costs associated with maintaining a suitable facility. The depth or breadth of a warranty in a given country or region should be tied to the service facility to which the manufacturer has access in that market; it is important to promise only what can be delivered.

Another part of the representative agreement may detail the training the exporter will provide to its foreign representative. This detail can include frequency of training, who must be trained, where the training is provided, and which party absorbs travel and per diem costs.

New sales opportunities and improved customer relations

Foreign buyers of U.S.-manufactured products typically have limited contact with the manufacturer or its personnel. The foreign service facility is, in fact, one of the major contact points between the exporter and the buyer. To a great extent, the U.S. manufacturer's reputation is made by the overseas service facility.

The service experience can be a positive and reinforcing sales and service encounter. It can also be an excellent sales opportunity if the service personnel are trained to take advantage of the situation. Service personnel can help the customer make life cycle decisions regarding the efficient operation of the product, how to update it for more and longer cost-effective operation, and when to replace it as the task expands or changes. Each service contact is an opportunity to educate the customer and expand the exporter's sales opportunities.

Service is also an important aspect of selling solutions and benefits rather than product features. More than one leading U.S. industrial products exporter sells its products as a "tool to do the job" rather than as a "truck" or a "cutting machine" or "software." Service capability enables customers to complete their jobs more efficiently with the exporter's "tool." Training service managers and personnel in this type of thinking vitalizes service facilities and generates new sales opportunities.

Each foreign market offers a unique opportunity for the U.S. exporter. Care and attention to the development of in-country sales and distribution capabilities is paramount. Delivery of after-sales service is critical to the near- and long-term success of the U.S. company's efforts in any market.

Senior personnel should commit to a program of regular travel to each foreign market to meet with the company's representatives, clients, and others who are important to the success of the firm in that market. Among those persons would be the commercial officer at the US&FCS post and representatives of the American chamber of commerce and the local chamber of commerce or business association.

The benefits of such a program are twofold. First, executive management learns more about the foreign marketplace and the firm's capabilities. Second, the in-country representative appreciates the attention and understands the importance of the foreign market in the exporter's long-term plans. As a result, such visits help build a strong, productive relationship.

Technology licensing and joint ventures

Technology licensing

Technology licensing is a contractual arrangement in which the licenser's patents, trademarks, service marks, copyrights, or know-how may be sold or otherwise made available to a licensee for compensation negotiated in advance between the parties. Such compensation, known as *royalties*, may consist of a *lump sum royalty*, a *running royalty* (royalty based on volume of production), or a combination of both. U.S. companies frequently license their patents, trademarks, copyrights, and know-how to a foreign company that then manufactures and sells products based on the technology in a country or group of countries authorized by the licensing agreement.

A technology licensing agreement usually enables a U.S. firm to enter a foreign market quickly, yet it poses fewer financial and legal risks than owning and operating a foreign manufacturing facility or participating in an overseas joint venture. Licensing also permits U.S. firms to overcome many of the tariff and nontariff barriers that frequently hamper the export of U.S.-manufactured products. For these reasons, licensing can be a particularly attractive method of exporting for small companies or companies with little international trade experience, although licensing is profitably employed by large and small firms alike. Technology licensing can also be used to acquire foreign technology (e.g., through cross-licensing agreements or *grantback clauses* granting rights to improvement technology developed by a licensee).

Technology licensing is not limited to the manufacturing sector. Franchising is also an important form of technology licensing used by many service industries. In franchising, the franchisor (licenser) permits the franchisee (licensee) to employ its trademark or service mark in a contractually specified manner for the marketing of goods or services. The franchisor usually continues to support the operation of the franchisee's business by providing advertising, accounting, training, and related services and in many instances also supplies products needed by the franchisee.

As a form of exporting, technology licensing has certain potential drawbacks. The negative aspects of licensing are that (1) control over the technology is weakened because it has been transferred to an unaffiliated firm and (2) licensing usually produces fewer profits than exporting goods or services produced in the United States. In certain Third World countries, there also may be problems in adequately protecting the licensed technology from unauthorized use by third parties.

In considering the licensing of technology, it is important to remember that foreign licensees may attempt to use the licensed technology to manufacture products that are marketed in the United States or third countries in direct competition with the licenser or its other licensees. In many instances, U.S. licensers may wish to impose territorial restrictions on their foreign licensees, depending on U.S. or foreign antitrust laws and the licensing laws of the host country. Also, U.S. and foreign patent, trademark, and copyright laws can often be used to bar unauthorized sales by foreign licensees, provided that the U.S. licenser has valid patent, trademark, or copyright protection in the United States or the other countries involved. In addition, unauthorized exports to the United States by foreign licensees can often be prevented by filing unfair import practices complaints under section 337 of the Tariff Act of 1930 with the U.S. International Trade Commission and by recording U.S. trademarks and copyrights with the U.S. Customs Service.

As in all overseas transactions, it is important to investigate not only the prospective licensee but the licensee's country as well. The government of the host country often must approve the licensing agreement before it goes into effect. Such governments, for example, may prohibit royalty payments that exceed a certain rate or contractual provisions barring the licensee from exporting products manufactured with or embodying the licensed technology to third countries.

The prospective licenser must always take into account the host country's foreign patent, trademark, and copyright laws; exchange controls; product liability laws; possible countertrading or barter requirements; antitrust and tax laws; and attitudes toward repatriation of royalties and dividends. The existence of a tax treaty or bilateral investment treaty between the United States and the prospective host country is an important indicator of the overall commercial relationship. Prospective U.S. licensers, especially of advanced technology, also should determine whether they need to obtain an export license from the U.S. Department of Commerce.

International technology licensing agreements, in a few instances, can unlawfully restrain trade in violation of U.S. or foreign antitrust laws. U.S. antitrust law, as a general rule, prohibits international technology licensing agreements that unreasonably restrict imports of competing goods or technology into the United States or unreasonably restrain U.S. domestic competition or exports by U.S. persons.

Whether or not a restraint is reasonable is a fact-specific determination that is made after consideration of the availability of competing goods or technology; market shares; barriers to entry; the business justifications for and the duration of contractual restraints; valid patents, trademarks, and copyrights; and certain other factors. The U.S. Department of Justice's *Antitrust Enforcement Guidelines for International Operations* (1988) contains useful advice regarding the legality of various types of international transactions, including technology licensing. In those instances in which significant federal antitrust issues are presented, U.S. licensers may wish to consider applying for an export trade certificate of review from the Department of Commerce (see chapter 4) or requesting a Department of Justice business review letter.

Foreign countries, particularly the EC, also have strict antitrust laws that affect technology licensing. The EC has issued detailed regulations governing patent and know-how licensing. These *block exemption* regulations are entitled "Commission Regulation (EEC) No. 2349/84 of 23 July 1984 on the Application of Article 85(3) of the Treaty [of Rome] to Certain Categories of Patent Licensing Agreements" and "Commission Regulation (EEC) No. 556/89 of 30 November 1988 on the Application of Article 85(3) of the Treaty to Certain Categories of Know-how Licensing Agreements." These regulations should be carefully considered by anyone currently licensing or contemplating the licensing of technology to the EC.

Because of the potential complexity of international technology licensing agreements, firms should seek qualified legal advice in the United States before entering into such an agreement. In many instances, U.S. licensors should also retain qualified legal counsel in the host country in order to obtain advice on applicable local laws and to receive assistance in securing the foreign government's approval of the agreement. Sound legal advice and thorough investigation of the prospective licensee and the host country increase the likelihood that the licensing agreement will be a profitable transaction and help decrease or avoid potential problems.

Joint ventures

There are a number of business and legal reasons why unassisted exporting may not be the best export strategy for a U.S. company. In such cases, the firm may wish to consider a joint venture with a firm in the host country. International joint ventures are used in a wide variety of manufacturing, mining, and service industries and are frequently undertaken in conjunction with technology licensing by the U.S. firm to the joint venture.

The host country may require that a certain percentage (often 51 percent) of manufacturing or mining operations be owned by nationals of that country, thereby requiring U.S. firms to operate through joint ventures. In addition to such legal requirements, U.S. firms may find it desirable to enter into a joint venture with a foreign firm to help spread the high costs and risks frequently associated with foreign operations.

Moreover, the local partner may bring to the joint venture its knowledge of the customs and tastes of the people, an established distribution network, and valuable business and political contacts. Having local partners also decreases the foreign status of the firm and may provide some protection against discrimination or expropriation, should conditions change.

There are, of course, possible disadvantages to international joint ventures. A major potential drawback to joint ventures, especially in countries that limit foreign companies to 49 percent or less participation, is the loss of effective managerial control. A loss of effective managerial control can result in reduced profits, increased operating costs, inferior product quality, and exposure to product liability and environmental litigation and fines. U.S. firms that wish to retain effective managerial control will find this issue an important topic in negotiations with the prospective joint venture partner and frequently the host government as well.

Like technology licensing agreements, joint ventures can raise U.S. or foreign antitrust issues in certain circumstances, particularly when the prospective joint venture partners are major existing or potential competitors in the affected national markets. Firms may wish to consider applying for an export trade certificate of review from the Department of Commerce (see chapter 4) or a business review letter from the Department of Justice when significant federal antitrust issues are raised by the proposed international joint venture.

Because of the complex legal issues frequently raised by international joint venture agreements, it is very important, before entering into any such agreement, to seek legal advice from qualified U.S. counsel experienced in this aspect of international trade. Many of the export counseling sources in chapter 2 can help direct a U.S. company to local counsel suitable for its needs.

U.S. firms contemplating international joint ventures also should consider retaining experienced counsel in the host country. U.S. firms can find it very disadvantageous to rely upon their potential joint venture partners to negotiate host government approvals and advise them on legal issues, since their prospective partners' interests may not always coincide with their own. Qualified foreign counsel can be very helpful in obtaining government approvals and providing ongoing advice regarding the host country's patent, trademark, copyright, tax, labor, corporate, commercial, antitrust, and exchange control laws.

Appendices

Export glossary

Acceptance – This term has several related meanings: (1) A time draft (or bill of exchange) that the drawee has accepted and is unconditionally obligated to pay at maturity. The draft must be presented first for acceptance – the drawee becomes the "acceptor" – then for payment. The word "accepted" and the date and place of payment must be written on the face of the draft. (2) The drawee's act in receiving a draft and thus entering into the obligation to pay its value at maturity. (3) Broadly speaking, any agreement to purchase goods under specified terms. An agreement to purchase goods at a stated price and under stated terms.

Ad valorem – According to value. See **Duty.**

Advance against documents – A loan made on the security of the documents covering the shipment.

Advising bank – A bank, operating in the exporter's country, that handles letters of credit for a foreign bank by notifying the export firm that the credit has been opened in its favor. The advising bank fully informs the exporter of the conditions of the letter of credit without necessarily bearing responsibility for payment.

Advisory capacity – A term indicating that a shipper's agent or representative is not empowered to make definitive decisions or adjustments without approval of the group or individual represented. Compare **Without reserve.**

Agent – See **Foreign sales agent.**

Air waybill – A bill of lading that covers both domestic and international flights transporting goods to a specified destination. This is a nonnegotiable instrument of air transport that serves as a receipt for the shipper, indicating that the carrier has accepted the goods listed and obligates itself to carry the consignment to the airport of destination according to specified conditions. Compare **Inland bill of lading, Ocean bill of lading,** and **Through bill of lading.**

Alongside – The side of a ship. Goods to be delivered "alongside" are to be placed on the dock or barge within reach of the transport ship's tackle so that they can be loaded aboard the ship.

Antidiversion clause – See **Destination control statement.**

Arbitrage – The process of buying foreign exchange, stocks, bonds, and other commodities in one market and immediately selling them in another market at higher prices.

Asian dollars – U.S. dollars deposited in Asia and the Pacific Basin. Compare **Eurodollars.**

ATA Carnet – See **Carnet.**

Balance of trade – The difference between a country's total imports and exports. If exports exceed imports, a favorable balance of trade exists; if not, a trade deficit is said to exist.

Barter – Trade in which merchandise is exchanged directly for other merchandise without use of money. Barter is an important means of trade with countries using currency that is not readily convertible.

Beneficiary – The person in whose favor a letter of credit is issued or a draft is drawn.

Bill of exchange – See **Draft.**

Bill of lading – A document that establishes the terms of a contract between a shipper and a transportation company under which freight is to be moved between specified points for a specified charge. Usually prepared by the shipper on forms issued by the carrier, it serves as a document of title, a contract of carriage, and a receipt for goods. Also see **Air waybill, Inland bill of lading, Ocean bill of lading,** and **Through bill of lading.**

Bonded warehouse – A warehouse authorized by customs authorities for storage of goods on which payment of duties is deferred until the goods are removed.

Booking – An arrangement with a steamship company for the acceptance and carriage of freight.

Buying agent – See **Purchasing agent.**

Carnet – A customs document permitting the holder to carry or send merchandise temporarily into certain foreign countries (for display, demonstration, or similar purposes) without paying duties or posting bonds.

Cash against documents (CAD) – Payment for goods in which a commission house or other intermediary transfers title documents to the buyer upon payment in cash.

Cash in advance (CIA) – Payment for goods in which the price is paid in full before shipment is made. This method is usually used only for small purchases or when the goods are built to order.

Cash with order (CWO) – Payment for goods in which the buyer pays when ordering and in which the transaction is binding on both parties.

Certificate of inspection – A document certifying that merchandise (such as perishable goods) was in good condition immediately prior to its shipment (see chapter 12).

Certificate of manufacture – A statement (often notarized) in which a producer of goods certifies that manufacture has been completed and that the goods are now at the disposal of the buyer.

Certificate of origin – A document, required by certain foreign countries for tariff purposes, certifying the country of origin of specified goods (see chapter 12).

CFR – Cost and freight. A pricing term indicating that the cost of the goods and freight charges are included in the quoted price; the buyer arranges for and pays insurance (see chapter 10).

Charter party – A written contract, usually on a special form, between the owner of a vessel and a "charterer" who rents use of the vessel or a part of its freight space. The contract generally includes the freight rates and the ports involved in the transportation.

CIF – Cost, insurance, freight. A pricing term indicating that the cost of the goods, insurance, and freight are included in the quoted price (see chapter 10).

Clean bill of lading – A receipt for goods issued by a carrier that indicates that the goods were received in "apparent good order and condition," without damages or other irregularities. Compare **Foul bill of lading.**

Clean draft – A draft to which no documents have been attached.

Collection papers – All documents (commercial invoices, bills of lading, etc.) submitted to a buyer for the purpose of receiving payment for a shipment.

Commercial attache – The commerce expert on the diplomatic staff of his or her country's embassy or large consulate.

Commercial invoice – An itemized list of goods shipped, usually included among an exporter's collection papers (see chapter 12).

Commission agent – See **Purchasing agent.**

Common carrier – An individual, partnership, or corporation that transports persons or goods for compensation.

Confirmed letter of credit – A letter of credit, issued by a foreign bank, the validity of which has been confirmed by a U.S. bank. An exporter whose payment terms are a confirmed letter of credit is assured of payment by the U.S. bank even if the foreign buyer or the foreign bank defaults. See **Letter of credit.** (Also see chapter 13.)

Consignment – Delivery of merchandise from an exporter (the consignor) to an agent (the consignee) under agreement that the agent sell the merchandise for the account of the exporter. The consignor retains title to the goods until the consignee has sold them. The consignee sells the goods for commission and remits the net proceeds to the consignor.

Consular declaration – A formal statement, made to the consul of a foreign country, describing goods to be shipped.

Consular invoice – A document, required by some foreign countries, describing a shipment of goods and showing information such as the consignor, consignee, and value of the shipment. Certified by a consular official of the foreign country, it is used by the country's customs officials to verify the value, quantity, and nature of the shipment (see chapter 12).

Convertible currency – A currency that can be bought and sold for other currencies at will.

Correspondent bank – A bank that, in its own country, handles the business of a foreign bank.

Countertrade – The sale of goods or services that are paid for in whole or in part by the transfer of goods or services from a foreign country. (See **Barter.**)

Countervailing duty – A duty imposed to counter unfairly subsidized products.

CPT (carriage paid to) and **CIP (carriage and insurance paid to)** – Pricing terms indicating that carriage, or carriage and insurance, are paid to the named place of destination. They apply in place of **CFR** and CIF, respectively, for shipment by modes other than water.

Credit risk insurance – Insurance designed to cover risks of nonpayment for delivered goods. Compare **Marine insurance.**

Customhouse broker – An individual or firm licensed to enter and clear goods through customs.

Customs – The authorities designated to collect duties levied by a country on imports and exports. The term also applies to the procedures involved in such collection.

Date draft – A draft that matures in a specified number of days after the date it is issued, without regard to the date of acceptance. See **Draft, Sight draft,** and **Time draft.** (Also see chapter 13.)

Deferred payment credit – Type of letter of credit providing for payment some time after presentation of shipping documents by exporter.

Demand draft – See **Sight draft.**

Destination control statement – Any of various statements that the U.S. government requires to be displayed on export shipments and that specify the destinations for which export of the shipment has been authorized (see chapter 12).

Devaluation – The official lowering of the value of one country's currency in terms of one or more foreign currencies. For example, if the U.S. dollar is devalued in relation to the French franc, one dollar will "buy" fewer francs than before.

DISC – Domestic international sales corporation (see chapter 11).

Discrepancy – Letter of credit – When documents presented do not conform to the letter of credit it is referred to as a discrepancy.

Dispatch – An amount paid by a vessel's operator to a charterer if loading or unloading is completed in less time than stipulated in the charter party.

Distributor – A foreign agent who sells for a supplier directly and maintains an inventory of the supplier's products.

Dock receipt – A receipt issued by an ocean carrier to acknowledge receipt of a shipment at the carrier's dock or warehouse facilities. Also see **Warehouse receipt.**

Documentary draft – A draft to which documents are attached.

Documents against acceptance (D/A) – Instructions given by a shipper to a bank indicating that documents transferring title to goods should be delivered to the buyer (or drawee) only upon the buyer's acceptance of the attached draft.

Draft (or Bill of exchange) – An unconditional order in writing from one person (the drawer) to another (the drawee), directing the drawee to pay a specified amount to a named drawer at a fixed or determinable future date (see chapter 13). See **Date draft, Sight draft, Time draft.**

Drawback – Articles manufactured or produced in the United States with the use of imported components or raw materials and later exported are entitled to a refund of up to 99 percent of the duty charged on the imported components. The refund of duty is known as a drawback.

Drawee – The individual or firm on whom a draft is drawn and who owes the stated amount. Compare **Drawer.** Also see **Draft.**

Drawer – The individual or firm that issues or signs a draft and thus stands to receive payment of the stated amount from the drawee. Compare **Drawee.** Also see **Draft.**

Dumping – Selling merchandise in another country at a price below the price at which the same merchandise is sold in the home market or selling such merchandise below the costs incurred in production and shipment.

Duty – A tax imposed on imports by the customs authority of a country. Duties are generally based on the value of the goods (ad valorem duties), some other factor such as weight or quantity (specific duties), or a combination of value and other factors (compound duties).

EMC – See **Export management company.**

ETC – See **Export trading company.**

Eurodollars – U.S. dollars placed on deposit in banks outside the United States; usually refers to deposits in Europe.

Ex – **From.** When used in pricing terms such as "ex factory" or "ex dock," it signifies that the price quoted applies only at the point of origin (in the two examples, at the seller's factory or a dock at the import point). In practice, this kind of quotation indicates that the seller agrees to place the goods at the disposal of the buyer at the specified place within a fixed period of time.

Exchange permit – A government permit sometimes required by the importer's government to enable the import firm to convert its own country's currency into foreign currency with which to pay a seller in another country.

Exchange rate – The price of one currency in terms of another, that is, the number of units of one currency that may be exchanged for one unit of another currency.

Eximbank – Export-Import Bank of the United States.

Export broker – An individual or firm that brings together buyers and sellers for a fee but does not take part in actual sales transactions.

Export commission house – An organization which, for a commission, acts as a purchasing agent for a foreign buyer.

Export declaration – See **Shipper's export declaration.**

Export license – A government document that permits the licensee to export designated goods to certain destinations. See **General export license** and **Individually validated export license.** (Also see chapter 11.)

Export management company – A private firm that serves as the export department for several producers of goods or services, either by taking title or by soliciting and transacting export business on behalf of its clients in return for a commission, salary, or retainer plus commission (see chapter 4).

Export trading company – A firm similar or identical to an export management company. (See chapter 4.)

Factoring houses – See chapter 14.

FAS – **Free alongside ship.** A pricing term indicating that the quoted price includes the cost of delivering the goods alongside a designated vessel (see chapter 10).

FCA – **"Free carrier"** to named place. Replaces the former term "FOB named inland port" to designate the seller's responsibility for the cost of loading goods at the named shipping point. May be used for multimodal transport, container stations, and any mode of transport, including air.

FCIA – **Foreign Credit Insurance Association** (see chapter 14).

FI – **Free in.** A pricing term indicating that the charterer of a vessel is responsible for the cost of loading and unloading goods from the vessel.

Floating policy – See **Open policy.**

FO – **Free out.** A pricing term indicating that the charterer of a vessel is responsible for the cost of loading goods from the vessel.

FOB – **"Free on board"** at named port of export. A pricing term indicating that the quoted price covers all expenses up to and including delivery of goods upon an overseas vessel provided by or for the buyer.

Force majeure – The title of a standard clause in marine contracts exempting the parties for nonfulfillment of their obligations as a result of conditions beyond their control, such as earthquakes, floods, or war.

Foreign exchange – The currency or credit instruments of a foreign country. Also, transactions involving purchase or sale of currencies.

Foreign freight forwarder – See **Freight forwarder.**

Foreign sales agent – An individual or firm that serves as the foreign representative of a domestic supplier and seeks sales abroad for the supplier.

Foreign trade zone – See **Free-trade zone.**

Foul bill of lading – A receipt for goods issued by a carrier with an indication that the goods were damaged when received. Compare **Clean bill of lading.**

Free port – An area such as a port city into which merchandise may legally be moved without payment of duties.

Free-trade zone – A port designated by the government of a country for duty-free entry of any nonprohibited goods. Merchandise may be stored, displayed, used for manufacturing, etc., within the zone and reexported without duties being paid. Duties are imposed on the merchandise (or items manufactured from the merchandise) only when the goods pass from the zone into an area of the country subject to the customs authority.

Freight forwarder – An independent business that handles export shipments for compensation. (A freight forwarder is among the best sources of information and assistance on U.S. export regulations and documentation, shipping methods, and foreign import regulations.)

GATT – **General Agreement on Tariffs and Trade.** A multilateral treaty intended to help reduce trade barriers between signatory countries and to promote trade through tariff concessions.

General export license – Any of various export licenses covering export commodities for which **Individually validated export licenses** are not required. No formal application or written authorization is needed to ship exports under a general export license (see chapter 11).

Gross weight – The full weight of a shipment, including goods and packaging. Compare **Tare weight.**

Import license – A document required and issued by some national governments authorizing the importation of goods into their individual countries.

Individually validated export license – A required document issued by the U.S. Government authorizing the export of specific commodities. This license is for a specific transaction or time period in which the exporting is to take place. Compare **General export license.** (Also see chapter 11.)

Inland bill of lading – A bill of lading used in transporting goods overland to the exporter's international carrier. Although a through bill of lading can sometimes be used, it is usually necessary to prepare both an inland bill of lading and an ocean bill of lading for export shipments. Compare **Air waybill, Ocean bill of lading,** and **Through bill of lading.**

International freight forwarder – See **Freight forwarder.**

Irrevocable letter of credit – A letter of credit in which the specified payment is guaranteed by the bank if all terms and conditions are met by the drawee. Compare **Revocable letter of credit.** (Also see chapter 13.)

Letter of credit (L/C) – A document, issued by a bank per instructions by a buyer of goods, authorizing the seller to draw a specified sum of money under specified terms, usually the receipt by the bank of certain documents within a given time (see chapter 13).

Licensing – A business arrangement in which the manufacturer of a product (or a firm with proprietary rights over certain technology, trademarks, etc.) grants permission to some other group or individual to manufacture that product (or make use of that proprietary material) in return for specified royalties or other payment.

Manifest – See **Ship's manifest.**

Marine insurance – Insurance that compensates the owners of goods transported overseas in the event of loss that cannot be legally recovered from the carrier. Also covers air shipments. Compare **Credit risk insurance.**

Marking (or marks) – Letters, numbers, and other symbols placed on cargo packages to facilitate identification.

Ocean bill of lading – A bill of lading (B/L) indicating that the exporter consigns a shipment to an international carrier for transportation to a specified foreign market. Unlike an inland B/L, the ocean B/L also serves as a collection document. If it is a "straight" B/L, the foreign buyer can obtain the shipment from the carrier by simply showing proof of identity. If a "negotiable" B/L is used, the buyer must first pay for the goods, post a bond, or meet other conditions agreeable to the seller. Compare **Air waybill, Inland bill of lading,** and **Through bill of lading.**

On board bill of lading – A bill of lading in which a carrier certifies that goods have been placed on board a certain vessel.

Open account – A trade arrangement in which goods are shipped to a foreign buyer without guarantee of payment. The obvious risk this method poses to the supplier makes it essential that the buyer's integrity be unquestionable.

Open insurance policy – A marine insurance policy that applies to all shipments made by an exporter over a period of time rather than to one shipment only.

Order bill of lading – A negotiable bill of lading made out to the order of the shipper.

Packing list – A list showing the number and kinds of items being shipped, as well as other information needed for transportation purposes (see chapter 12).

Parcel post receipt – The postal authorities' signed acknowledgment of delivery to receiver of a shipment made by parcel post.

PEFCO – **Private Export Funding Corporation.** A corporation that lends to foreign buyers to finance exports from the United States (see chapter 14).

Perils of the sea – A marine insurance term used to designate heavy weather, stranding, lightning, collision, and sea water damage.

Phytosanitary inspection certificate – A certificate, issued by the U.S. Department of Agriculture to satisfy import regulations for foreign countries, indicating that a U.S. shipment has been inspected and is free from harmful pests and plant diseases.

Political risk – In export financing, the risk of loss due to such causes as currency inconvertibility, government action preventing entry of goods, expropriation or confiscation, and war.

Pro forma invoice – An invoice provided by a supplier prior to the shipment of merchandise, informing the buyer of the kinds and quantities of goods to be sent, their value, and important specifications (weight, size, etc.).

Purchasing agent – An agent who purchases goods in his or her own country on behalf of foreign importers such as government agencies and large private concerns.

Quota – The quantity of goods of a specific kind that a country permits to be imported without restriction or imposition of additional duties.

Quotation – An offer to sell goods at a stated price and under specified conditions.

Remitting bank – The bank that sends the draft to the overseas bank for collection.

Representative – See **Foreign sales agent.**

Revocable letter of credit – A letter of credit that can be canceled or altered by the drawee (buyer) after it has been issued by the drawee's bank. Compare **Irrevocable letter of credit.** (Also see chapter 13.)

Schedule B – Refers to Schedule B, Statistical Classification of Domestic and Foreign Commodities Exported from the United States. All commodities exported from the United States must be assigned a seven-digit Schedule B number.

Shipper's export declaration – A form required for all shipments by the U.S. Treasury Department and prepared by a shipper, indicating the value, weight, destination, and other basic information about an export shipment (see chapter 12).

Ship's manifest – An instrument in writing, signed by the captain of a ship, that lists the individual shipments constituting the ship's cargo.

Sight draft (S/D) – A draft that is payable upon presentation to the drawee. Compare **Date draft** and **Time draft** (see chapter 13).

Spot exchange – The purchase or sale of foreign exchange for immediate delivery.

Standard industrial classification (SIC) – A standard numerical code system used by the U.S. government to classify products and services.

Standard international trade classification (SITC) – A standard numerical code system developed by the United Nations to classify commodities used in international trade.

Steamship conference – A group of steamship operators that operate under mutually agreed-upon freight rates.

Straight bill of lading – A nonnegotiable bill of lading in which the goods are consigned directly to a named consignee.

Tare weight – The weight of a container and packing materials without the weight of the goods it contains. Compare **Gross weight.**

Tenor (of a draft) – Designation of a payment as being due at sight, a given number of days after sight, or a given number of days after date.

Through bill of lading – A single bill of lading converting both the domestic and international carriage of an export shipment. An air waybill, for instance, is essentially a through bill of lading used for air shipments. Ocean shipments, on the other hand, usually require two separate documents – an inland bill of lading for domestic carriage and an ocean bill of lading for international carriage. Through bills of lading are insufficient for ocean shipments. Compare **Air waybill, Inland bill of lading,** and **Ocean bill of lading.**

Time draft – A draft that matures either a certain number of days after acceptance or a certain number of days after the date of the draft. Compare **Date draft** and **Sight draft** (see chapter 13).

Tramp steamer – A ship not operating on regular routes or schedules.

Transaction statement – A document that delineates the terms and conditions agreed upon between the importer and exporter.

Trust receipt – Release of merchandise by a bank to a buyer in which the bank retains title to the merchandise. The buyer, who obtains the goods for manufacturing or sales purposes, is obligated to maintain the goods (or the proceeds from their sale) distinct from the remainder of his or her assets and to hold them ready for repossession by the bank.

Warehouse receipt – A receipt issued by a warehouse listing goods received for storage.

Wharfage – A charge assessed by a pier or dock owner for handling incoming or outgoing cargo.

Without reserve – A term indicating that a shipper's agent or representative is empowered to make definitive decisions and adjustments abroad without approval of the group or individual represented. Compare **Advisory capacity.**

Directory of federal export assistance

II

A. Department of Commerce
B. Small Business Administration
C. Export-Import Bank
D. Department of Agriculture
E. Overseas Private Investment Corporation
F. Department of State
G. Department of the Treasury
H. Agency for International Development
I. Office of the U.S. Trade Representative

A. Department of Commerce

The U.S. Department of Commerce can provide a wealth of information to exporters. The first step an exporter should take is to contact the nearest Department of Commerce district office (listed by state in appendix III), which can help guide the exporter to the right person or office.

Addresses on mail to the following offices should include the office name and room number, followed by U.S. Department of Commerce, 14th and Constitution Avenue, N.W., Washington, DC 20230 (exceptions noted).

Phone
Area Code: 202

U.S. and Foreign Commercial Service

Office of Domestic Operations, Room 3810 482-4767

Export Promotion Services

- Office of Export Promotion Resources, Room 1322 (Information on foreign markets, customers, trade leads, *Commercial News USA,* and other Commerce export-related publications) 482-2432

- Office of Export Marketing Programs, Room 2116 (trade show and trade mission information) 482-4231

Office of International Operations

Regional Directors for

- Africa, Near East, and South Asia, Room 1223 482-4836

- East Asia and Pacific, Room 1223 482-8422

- Europe, Room 3130 482-1599

- Western Hemisphere, Room 3130 482-2736

- Fax (Europe and Western Hemisphere)...... 482-3159

- Fax (ANESA and EAP) 482-5179

Trade Development

Product/Service Specialists

- Aerospace, Room 2130 482-2835

- Automotive Affairs and Consumer Goods, Room 4324 482-0823

- Basic Industries, Room 4045 482-0614

- Capital Goods & International Construction: Rm 2001B 482-5023

- Export Trading Company Affairs, Room 1800 482-5131

- International Major Projects, Room 2015B 482-5225

- Science and Electronics, Room 1009 482-3548

- Services, Room 1128A 482-5261

- Textiles and Apparel, Room 3100 482-3737

- Trade Information and Analysis, Room 3814B 482-1316

Industry desk officers can provide information on the competitive strengths of U.S. industries in domestic and international markets. The following is a list of industry desk officers.

Industry	Contact	Phone
A	Area code 202-482-	
Abrasive Products	Presbury, Graylin	5157
Accounting	Chittum, J Marc	0345
Adhesives/Sealants	Prat, Raimundo	0128
Advertising	Chittum, J Marc	0345
Aerospace Financing Issues	Jackson, Jeff	0222
Aerospace Industry Analysis	Walsh, Hugh	0678
Aerospace Market Development	Bowie, David C	8228
Aerospace/Space Programs	Pajor, Peter	4222
Aerospace Trade Policy	Bath, Sally	4222
Aerospace (Trade Promo)	Bowie, David	8228
Agribusiness (Major Proj)	Ruan, Robert	0355
Agricultural Chemicals	Maxey, Francis P	0128
Agricultural Machinery	Wiening, Mary	4708
Air Couriers	Elliott, Frederick	1134
Air Conditioning Eqmt	Greer, Damon	5456
Air, Gas Compressors	McDonald, Edward	0680
Air, Gas Compressors (Trade Promo)	Zanetakos, George	0552
Air Pollution Control Eqmt	Jonkers, Loretta	0564
Aircraft & Aircraft Engines	Driscoll, George	8228
Aircraft & Aircraft Engines (Trade Promo)	Bowie, David	8228
Aircraft Auxiliary Eqmt	Driscoll, George	8228
Aircraft Parts (Market Support)	Driscoll, George	8228
Aircraft Parts/Aux Eqmt (Trade Promo)	Bowie, David	8228
Airlines	Johnson, C William	5071
Airport Equipment	Driscoll, George	8228
Airport Eqmt (Trade Promo)	Bowie, David	8228
Airports, Ports, Harbors (Major Proj)	Piggot, Deboorne	3352
Air Traffic Control Eqmt	Driscoll, George	8228
Alcoholic Beverages	Kenney, Cornelius	2428
Alternate Energy Systems (Trade Promo)	Garden, Les	0556
Aluminum Sheet, Plate/Foil	Cammarota, David	0575
Aluminum Forgings, Electro	Cammarota, David	0575
Aluminum Extrud Alum Rolling	Cammarota, David	0575
Analytical Instruments	Nealon, Marguerite	8411
Analytical/Scientific Instruments (Trade Promo)	Manzolillo, Franc	2991
Animal Feeds	Janis, William V	2250
Apparel	Dulka, William	4058
Apparel (Trade Promo)	Molnar, Ferenc	2043
Asbestos/Cement Prod	Pitcher, Charles	0132
Assembly Equipment	Abrahams, Edward	0312
Audio Text	Inoussa, Mary C	5820
Audio Visual Equipment (Trade Promo)	Beckham, Reginald	5478
Audio Visual Services	Siegmund, John	4781
Automotive Affairs (Trade Promo)	Allison, Loretta	5479
Auto Parts/Suppliers	Reck, Robert	1418

Industry	Contact	Phone
	Area code 202-482-	
Auto Parts/Suppliers (Trade Promo)	White, John	0671
Auto Industry Affairs	Keitz, Stuart	0554
Air Transport Services	Johnson, C William	5071
Avionics and Ground Support Eqmt (Trade Promo)	Bowie, David	8228
Avionics Marketing	Driscoll, George	8228
B		
Bakery Products	Janis, William V	2250
Ball Bearings	Reise, Richard	3489
Basic Paper & Board Mfg	Smith, Leonard S	0375
Bauxite, Alumina, Prim Alum	Cammarota, David	0575
Beer	Kenney, Neil	2428
Belting & Hose	Prat, Raimundo	0128
Beryllium	Duggan, Brian	0575
Beverages	Kenney, Cornelius	2428
Bicycles	Vanderwolf, John	0348
Biotechnology	Arakaki, Emily	3888
Biotechnology (Trade Promo)	Gwaltney, G P	3090
Boat Building (Major Proj)	Piggot, Deboorne	3352
Boats/Pleasure	Vanderwolf, John	0348
Books	Lofquist, William S	0379
Books (Trade Promo)	Kimmel, Edward	3640
Brooms & Brushes	Harris, John	1178
Breakfast Cereal	Janis, William V	2250
Building Materials & Construction	Pitcher, Charles B	0132
Business Eqmt (Trade Promo)	Fogg, Judy	4936
Business Forms	Bratland, Rose Marie	0380
C		
CAD/CAM	McGibbon, Patrick	0314
CAD/Graphics Software	Swann, Vera	4930
Cable TV	Siegmund, John	4781
Canned Food Products	Hodgen, Donald A	3346
Capital Goods (Trade Promo)	Brandes, Jay	0560
Capital Goods	Harrison, Joseph	5455
Carbon Black	Prat, Raimundo	0128
Cellular Radio Telephone Eqmt	Gossack, Linda	4466
Cement	Pitcher, Charles	0132
Cement Plants (Major Proj)	White, Barbara	4160
Ceramics (Advanced)	Siessinger, Fred	0128
Ceramics Machinery	Shaw, Eugene	3494
Cereals	Janis, William V	2250
Cheese	Janis, William V	2250
Chemicals (Liaison & Policy)	Kelly, Michael J	0128
Chemical Industries Machinery (Trade Promo)	Shaw, Eugene	3494
Chemical Plants (Major Proj)	Haraguchi, Wally	4877
Chemicals & Allied Products	Kamenicky, Vincent	0128
Civil Aircraft Agreement	Bath, Sally	4222
Civil Aviation Policy	Johnson, C William	5071
Coal Exports	Yancik, Joseph J	1466
Cobalt	Cammarota, David	0575
Cocoa Products	Manger, Jon	5124
Coffee Products	Manger, Jon	5124
Commercial Aircraft (Trade Policy)	Bath, Sally	4222
Commercial Lighting Fixtures	Whitley, Richard A	0682
Commercial/Indus Refrig Eqmt	Holley, Tyrena	3509

Industry	Contact	Phone
		Area code 202-482-
Commercial Printing	Lofquist, William S	0379
Composites, Advanced	Manion, James	5157
Computer and DP Services	Atkins, Robert G/	4781
	Inoussa, Mary C	5820
Computers, AI	Kader, Vicky	0572
Computer Displays	Hoffman, Heidi	2053
Computers, Laptops	Hoffman, Heidi	2053
Computers, Mainframes	Miles, Timothy	2996
Computer Networking	Spathopoulos, Vivian	0572
Computers (Personal)	Woods, R Clay	3013
Computers and Peripherals, Software (Trade Promo)	Fogg, Judy A	4936
Computers, Workstations	Miles, Timothy	2996
Computers and Business Eqmt	McPhee, John E.	0572
Computer Consulting	Atkins, Robert G	4781
Confectionery Products	Kenney, Cornelius	2428
Construction	MacAuley, Patrick	0132
Construction Machinery	Heimowitz, Leonard	0558
Construction Services	Ruan, Robert	0359
Consumer Electronics	Fleming, Howard	5163
Consumer Goods	Bodansky, Harry	5783
Containers & Packaging	Copperthite, Kim	5159
Cosmetics (Trade Promo)	Kimmel, Edward	3640

D

Industry	Contact	Phone
Dairy Products	Janis, William V	2250
Data Base Services	Inoussa, Mary C	5820
Data Processing Services	Inoussa, Mary C	5820
Desalination/Water Reuse	Wheeler, Frederica	3509
Direct Marketing	Elliott, Frederick	1134
Distilled Spirits	Kenney, Neil	2428
Disk Drives	Kader, Victoria	0571
Drugs	Hurt, William	0128
Durable Consumer Goods	Ellis, Kevin	1176

E

Industry	Contact	Phone
Education Facilities (Major Proj)	White, Barbara	4160
Education Svcs/Manpower Training (Trade Promo)	Chittum, J Marc	0345
Electric Industrial Apparatus Nec	Whitley, Richard A	0682
Elec/Power Gen/Transmission & Dist Eqmt (Trade Promo)	Brandes, Jay	0560
Electrical Power Plants (Major Proj)	Dollison, Robert	2733
Electrical Test & Measuring	Hall, Sarah	2846
Electricity	Sugg, William	1466
ElectroOptical Instruments (Trade Promo)	Manzolillo, Franc	2991
Electronics (Legislation)	Donnelly, Margaret	5466
Electronic Components	Mussehl, Jodee	3360
Electronic Components/ Production & Test Eqmt (Trade Promo)	Burke, Joseph J	5014
Electronic Data Interchange (EDI)	Inoussa, Mary C	5820
Electronic Database Services	Inoussa, Mary C	5820
Elevators, Moving Stairways	Wiening, Mary	4708
Employment Services (Trade Promo)	Chittum, J Marc	0345
Energy & Environment	Greer, Damon	5456

Industry	Contact	Phone
		Area code 202-482-
Energy (Commodities)	Yancik, Joseph J	1466
Energy, Renewable	Rasmussen, John	1466
Energy, Renewable (Tech & Eqmt)	Garden, Les	0556
Engineering/Construction Services (Trade Promo)	Ruan, Robert	0359
Entertainment Industries	Siegmund, John	4781
Entertainment Svcs (Trade Promo)	Siegmund, John	4781
Explosives	Maxey, Francis P	0128
Export Trading Companies	Muller, George	5131

F

Industry	Contact	Phone
Fabricated Metal Construction Materials	Williams, Franklin	0132
Farm Machinery	Wiening, Mary	4708
Fasteners (Industrial)	Reise, Richard	3489
Fats and Oils	Janis, William V	2250
Fencing (Metal)	Shaw, Robert	0132
Ferroalloys Products	Presbury, Graylin	5158
Ferrous Scrap	Sharkey, Robert	0606
Fertilizers	Maxey, Francis P	0128
Filters/Purifying Eqmt	Jonkers, Loretta	0564
Finance & Management Industries	Candilis, Wray O	0339
Financial Svcs (Trade Promo)	Muir, S Cassin	0349
Fisheries (Major Proj)	Ruan, Robert	0359
Flexible Mftg Systems	McGibbon, Patrick	0314
Flour	Janis, William V	2250
Flowers	Janis, William V	2250
Fluid Power	McDonald, Edward	0680
Food Processing/Packaging Machinery (Trade Promo)	Shaw, Eugene	3494
Food Products Machinery	Shaw, Eugene	3494
Food Retailing	Kenney, Cornelius	2428
Footwear	Byron, James E.	4034
Forest Products	Smith, Leonard S	0375
Forest Products, Domestic Construction	Kristensen, Chris	0384
Forest Products (Trade Policy)	Hicks, Michael	0375
Forestry/Woodworking Eqmt (Trade Promo)	McDonald, Ed	0680
Forgings Semifinished Steel	Bell, Charles	0609
Fossil Fuel Power Generation (Major Proj)	Dollison, Robert	2733
Foundry Eqmt	Kemper, Alexis	5956
Foundry Industry	Bell, Charles	0609
Fruits	Hodgen, Donald	3346
Frozen Foods Products	Hodgen, Donald	3346
Fur Goods	Byron, James E.	4034
Furniture	Enright, Joseph	3459

G

Industry	Contact	Phone
Gallium	Cammarota, David	0575
Games & Children's Vehicles	Corea, Judy	5479
Gaskets/Gasketing Materials	Reise, Richard	3489
General Aviation Aircraft	Walsh, Hugh	4222
Gen Indus Mach Nec,	Shaw, Eugene	3494
Generator Sets/Turbines (Major Proj)	Dollison, Robert	2733
Germanium	Cammarota, David	0575
Glass, Flat	Williams, Franklin	0132

Industry	Contact	Phone
		Area code 202-482-
Glassware (Household)	Harris, John	1178
Gloves (Work)	Byron, James	4034
Giftware (Trade Promo)	Beckham, Reginald	5478
Grain Mill Products	Janis, William V	2250
Greeting Cards	Bratland, Rose Marie	0380
Grocery Retailing	Kenney, Cornelius	2428
Ground Water Exploration & Development	Wheeler, Frederica	3509

H

Industry	Contact	Phone
Hand Saws, Saw Blades	Abrahams, Edward	0312
Hand/Edge Tools Ex Mach TI/Saws	Abrahams, Edward	0312
Handbags	Byron, James E.	4034
Hard Surfaced Floor Coverings	Shaw, Robert	0132
Hardware (Export Promo)	Johnson, Charles E	3422
Hazardous Wastes Treatment	Jonkers, Loretta	0564
Health (Eastern Europe)	Plock, Ernest	5820
Health Services	Walsh, James	5131
Heat Treating Equipment	Kemper, Alexis	5956
Heating Eqmt Ex Furnaces	Greer, Damon	5456
Helicopters	Walsh, Hugh	4222
Helicopters (Market Support)	Driscoll, George	8228
High Tech Trade, U.S. Competitiveness	Hatter, Victoria L	3913
Hoists, Overhead Cranes	Wiening, Mary	4708
Home Video	Siegmund, John	4781
Hose & Belting	Prat, Raimundo	0128
Hotel, Restaurants, Catering Eqmt (Trade Promo)	Kimmel, Edward K	3640
Hotels And Motels	Sousane, J Richard	4582
Household Appliances	Harris, John M	1178
Household Appliances (Trade Promo)	Johnson, Charles E	3422
Household Furniture	Enright, Joseph	3459
Housewares (Export Promo)	Johnson, Charles E	3422
Housing Construction	Cosslett, Patrick	0132
Housing (Manufactured)	Tasnadi, Diana	0132
Housing & Urban Development (Major Proj)	White, Barbara	4160
Hydro Power, Plants (Major Proj)	Healey, Mary Alice	4333

I

Industry	Contact	Phone
Ice Cream	Janis, William V	2250
Industrial Chemicals	Hurt, William	0128
Industrial Controls	Whitley, Richard A	0682
Industrial Drives/Gears	Reise, Richard	3489
Industrial Eqmt (Trade Promo)	Shaw, Eugene	3494
Industrial Gases	Kostalas, Antonios	0128
Industrial Organic Chemicals	Hurt, William	0128
Industrial Process Controls	Nealon, Margurite	8411
Industrial Robots	McGibbon, Patrick	0314
Industrial Sewing Machines	Miles, Max	0679
Industrial Structure	Davis, Lester A	4924
Industrial Trucks	Wiening, Mary	4608
Information Services	Inoussa, Mary C	5820
Inorganic Chemicals	Kamenicky, Vincent	0128
Inorganic Pigments	Kamenicky, Vincent	0128
Insulation	Shaw, Robert	0132
Insurance	McAdam, Bruce	0346

Industry	Contact	Phone
		Area code 202-482-
Intellectual Property Rights (Services)	Siegmund, John E	4781
International Commodities	Siesseger, Fred	5124
International Major Projects	Thibeault, Robert	5225
Investment Management	Muir, S Cassin	0349
Irrigation Equipment	Wheeler, Frederica	3509
Irrigation (Major Proj)	Ruan, Robert	0359

J

Industry	Contact	Phone
Jams & Jellies	Hodgen, Donald A	3346
Jewelry	Harris, John	1178
Jewelry (Trade Promo)	Beckham, Reginald	5478
Jute Products	Manger, Jon	5124
Juvenile Products	Bodansky, Harry	5783

K

Industry	Contact	Phone
Kitchen Cabinets	Wise, Barbara	0375

L

Industry	Contact	Phone
Laboratory Instruments	Nealon, Marguerite	8411
Laboratory Instruments (Trade Promo)	Manzolillo, Franc	2991
Lasers/ElectroOptics (Trade Promo)	Manzolillo, Franc	2991
Lawn & Garden Eqmt	Vanderwolf, John	0348
Lead Products	Larrabee, David	0575
Leasing: Eqmt, Svcs	Shuman, John	3050
Leather Apparel	Byron, James E	4034
Leather Tanning	Byron, James E	4034
Leather Products	Byron, James E	4034
Legal Services	Chittum, J Marc	0345
LNG Plants (Major Proj)	Bell, Richard	2460
Local Area Networks	Spathopoulos, Vivian	0572
Logs, Wood	Hicks, Michael	0375
Luggage	Byron, James	4034
Lumber	Wise, Barbara	0375

M

Industry	Contact	Phone
Machine Tool Accessories	McGibbon, Patrick	0314
Magazines	Bratland, Rose Marie	0380
Magnesium	Cammarota, David	0575
Major Projects	Thibeault, Robert	5225
Management and Research Svcs (Trade Promo)	Chittum, J Marc	0345
Management Consulting	Chittum, J Marc	0345
Manifold Business Forms	Bratland, Rose Marie	0380
Manmade Fiber	Dulka, William	4058
Margarine	Janis, William V	2250
Marine Recreational Eqmt (Trade Promo)	Beckham, Reginald	5478
Marine Insurance	Johnson, C William	5012
Marine Port/Shipbuilding Eqmt (Trade Promo)	Heimowitz, Len	0558
Maritime Shipping	Johnson, C William	5012
Materials, Advanced	Cammarota, David	0575
Materials Handling Machinery (Trade Promo)	Wiening, Mary	4708
Meat Products	Hodgen, Donald A	3346
Mech Power Transmission Eqmt	Reise, Richard	3489
Medical Facilities (Major Proj)	White, Barbara	4160
Medical Instruments	Fuchs, Michael	0550

Industry	Contact	Phone
		Area code 202-482-
Medical Instruments & Eqmt (Trade Promo)	Keen, George B	2010
Mercury, Fluorspar	Manion, James J	5157
Metal Building Products	Williams, Franklin	0132
Metal Cutting Machine Tools	McGibbon, Patrick	0314
Metal Forming Machine Tools	McGibbon, Patrick	0314
Metal Powders	Duggan, Brian	0575
Metals, Secondary	Bell, Charles	0606
Metalworking	Mearman, John	0315
Metalworking Eqmt Nec	McGibbon, Patrick	0314
Milk	Janis, William V	2250
Millwork	Wise, Barbara	0375
Mineral Based Construction Materials (Clay, Concrete, Gypsum, Asphalt, Stone)	Pitcher, Charles	0132
Mining Machinery	McDonald, Edward	0680
Mining Machinery (Trade Promo)	Zanetakos, George	0552
Mobile Homes	Cosslett, Patrick	0132
Molybdenum	Cammarota, David	0575
Monorails (Trade Promo)	Wiening, Mary	4708
Motion Pictures	Siegmund, John	4781
Motor Vehicles	Warner, Albert T	0669
Motorcycles	Vanderwolf, John	0348
Motors, Electric	Whitley, Richard A	0682
Music (Prerecorded)	Siegmund, John	4781
Musical Instruments (Trade Promo)	Johnson, Charles	3422
Mutual Funds	Muir, S Cassin	0349

N

Industry	Contact	Phone
Natural Gas	Gillett, Tom	1466
Natural, Synthetic Rubber	Prat, Raimundo	0128
Newspapers	Bratland, Rose Marie	0380
Nickel Products	Presbury, Graylin	0575
Non-alcoholic Beverages	Kenney, Cornelius	2428
Noncurrent Carrying Wiring Devices	Whitley, Richard A	0682
Nondurable Goods	Simon, Les	0341
Nonferrous Foundries	Duggan, Brian	0610
Nonferrous Metals	Manion, James J	0575
Nonmetallic Minerals Nec	Manion, James J	0575
Nonresidential Constr	MacAuley, Patrick	0132
Nuclear Power Plants/ Machinery	Whitley, Richard A	0682
Nuclear Power Plants (Major Proj)	Dollison, Robert	2733
Numerical Controls for Mach Tools	McGibbon, Patrick	0314
Nuts, Edible	Janis, William V	2250
Nuts, Bolts, Washers	Reise, Richard	3489

O

Industry	Contact	Phone
Ocean Shipping	Johnson, C William	5012
Oil & Gas Development & Refining (Major Proj)	Bell, Richard	2460
Oil & Gas (Fuels Only)	Gillett, Tom	1466
Oil Field Machinery	McDonald, Edward	0680
Oil & Gas Field Machinery (Trade Promo)	Miles, Max	0679
Oil & Gas Field Svcs (Trade Promo)	Miles, Max	0679
Oil Shale (Major Proj)	Bell, Richard	2460

Industry	Contact	Phone
		Area code 202-482-
Operations & Maintenance	Chittum, J Marc	0345
Organic Chemicals	Hurt, William	0128
Outdoor Lighting Fixtures	Whitley, Richard A	0682
Outdoor Power Eqmt (Trade Promo)	Johnson, Charles E	3422

P

Industry	Contact	Phone
Packaging & Containers	Copperthite, Kim	0575
Packaging Machinery	Shaw, Eugene	2204
Paints/Coatings	Prat, Raimundo	0128
Paper	Smith, Leonard S	0375
Paper & Board Packaging	Smith, Leonard S	0375
Paper Industries Machinery	Abrahams, Edward	0312
Pasta	Janis, William V	2250
Paving Materials (Asphalt & Concrete)	Pitcher, Charles	0132
Pectin	Janis, William V	2250
Periodicals	Bratland, Rose Marie	0380
Pet Food	Janis, William V	2250
Pet Products (Trade Promo)	Kimmel, Edward K	3640
Petrochemicals	Hurt, William	0128
Petrochem, Cyclic Crudes	Hurt, William	0128
Petrochemicals Plants (Major Proj)	Haraguchi, Wally	4877
Petroleum, Crude & Refined Products	Gillett, Tom	1466
Pharmaceuticals	Hurt, William	0128
Pipelines (Major Proj)	Bell, Richard	2460
Photographic Eqmt & Supplies	Watson, Joyce	0574
Plastic Construction Products (Most)	Williams, Franklin	0132
Plastic Materials/Resins	Prat, Raimundo	0128
Plastic Products	Prat, Raimundo	0128
Plastic Products Machinery	Shaw, Eugene	3494
Plumbing Fixtures & Fittings	Shaw, Robert	0132
Plywood/Panel Products	Wise, Barbara	0375
Point-of-Use Water Treatment	Holley, Tyrena	3509
Pollution Control Equipment	Jonkers, Loretta	0564
Porcelain Electrical Supplies	Whitley, Richard A	0682
Potato Chips	Janis, William V	2250
Poultry Products	Hodgen, Donald A	3346
Power Hand Tools	Abrahams, Edward	0312
Precious Metal Jewelry	Harris, John M	1178
Prefabricated Buildings (Wood)	Cosslett, Patrick	0132
Prefabricated Buildings (Metal)	Williams, Franklin	0132
Prepared Meats	Hodgen, Donald A	3346
Pretzels	Janis, William V	2250
Primary Commodities	Siesseger, Fred	5124
Printing & Publishing	Lofquist, William S	0379
Printing Trade Services	Bratland, Rose Marie	0380
Printing Trades Mach/Eqmt	Kemper, Alexis	5956
Process Control Instruments	Nealon, Marguerite	8411
Process Control Instruments (Trade Promo)	Manzolillo, Franc	2991
Pulp and Paper Machinery (Trade Promo)	Abrahams, Edward	0312
Pulp And Paper Mills (Major Proj)	White, Barbara	4160
Pulpmills	Stanley, Gary	0375
Pumps, Pumping Eqmt	McDonald, Edward	0680

Industry	Contact	Phone
		Area code 202-482-
Pumps, Valves, Compressors (Trade Promo)	Zanetakos, George	0552
R		
Radio & TV Broadcasting	Siegmund, John	4781
Radio & TV Communications Eqmt	Gossack, Linda	2872
Recorded Music	Siegmund, John	4781
Recreational Eqmt (Trade Promo)	Beckham, Reginald	5478
Refractory Products	Duggan, Brian	0575
Refrigeration Eqmt	Greer, Damon	5456
Renewable Energy Eqmt	Garden, Les	0556
Residential Lighting Fixtures	Whitley, Richard A	0682
Retail Trade	Margulies, Marvin J	5086
Rice Milling	Janis, William V	2250
Roads, Railroads, Mass Trans (Major Proj)	Smith, Jay L	4642
Robots/Factory Automation	McGibbon, Patrick	0314
Roofing, Asphalt	Pitcher, Charles	0132
Roller Bearings	Reise, Richard	3489
Rolling Mill Machinery	Abrahams, Edward	0312
Rubber	Prat, Raimundo	0128
Rubber Products	Prat, Raimundo	0128
S		
Saddlery & Harness Products	Byron, James E	4034
Safety & Security Eqmt (Trade Promo)	Umstead, Dwight	8410
Space Services	Plock, Ernest	5620
Satellites & Space Vehicles (Marketing)	Bowie, David C	8228
Satellites, Communications	Cooper, Patricia	4466
Science & Electronics (Trade Promo)	Moose, Jake	4125
Scientific Instruments (Trade Promo)	Manzolillo, Franc	2991
Scientific Measurement/ Control Eqmt	Podolske, Lewis	3360
Screw Machine Products	Reise, Richard	3489
Screws, Washers	Reise, Richard	3489
Security Management Svcs.	Chittum, J Marc	0345
Security/Safety Eqmt (Trade Promo)	Umstead, Dwight	8410
Semiconductor Prod Eqmt & Materials	Finn, Erin	2795
Semiconductors (except Japan)	Mussehl, Judee	3360
Semiconductors, Japan	Scott, Robert	2795
Service Industries (Uruguay Round)	Elliot, Fred	1134
Services Data Base Development	Atkins, Robert G	4781
Services, Telecom	Shefrin, Ivan	4466
Shingles (Wood)	Wise, Barbara	0375
Shoes	Byron, James E	4034
Silverware	Harris, John	1178
Sisal Products	Manger, Jon	5124
Small Arms, Ammunition	Vanderwolf, John	0348
Small Business	Burroughs, Helen	4806
Snackfood	Janis, William V	2250
Soaps, Detergents, Cleaners	Siessinger, Fred	0128
Soft Drinks	Kenney, Cornelius	2428

Industry	Contact	Phone
		Area code 202-482-
Software	Hyikata, Heidi	0572
Software (Trade Promo)	Fogg, Judy	4936
Solar Cells/Photovoltaic Devices	Garden, Les	0556
Solar Equip Ocean/Biomass/ Geothermal	Garden, Les	0556
Solid Wastes Treatment/ Disposal	Jonkers, Loretta	0564
Soy Products	Janis, William V	2250
Space Commercialization (Equipment)	Bowie, David C	8228
Space Policy Development	Pajor, Peter	4222
Special Industry Machinery	Shaw, Eugene	3494
Speed Changers	Reise, Richard	3489
Sporting & Athletic Goods	Vanderwolf, John	0348
Sporting Goods (Trade Promo)	Beckham, Reginald	5478
Steel Industry Products	Bell, Charles	0608
Steel Industry	Brueckmann, Al	0606
Steel Markets	Bell, Charles	0608
Storage Batteries	Larrabee, David	5124
Sugar Products	Siesseger, Fred	5124
Supercomputers	Streeter, Jonathan	0572
Superconductors	Chiarodo, Roger	0402
Switchgear & Switchboard Apparatus	Whitley, Richard A	0682
Systems Integration	Atkins, Robert G	4781
T		
Tea	Janis, William V	2250
Technology Affairs	Shykind, Edwin B	4694
Telecommunications	Stechschulte, Roger	4466
Telecommunications (Major Proj)	Paddock, Richard	4466
Telecommunications (Trade Promo)	Rettig, Theresa E	2952
Telecommunications (Network Eqmt)	Henry, John	4466
Telecommunications (Military Communications Eqmt)	Mocenigo, Anthony	4466
Telecommunications Services	Atkins, Robert G	4781
Telecommunications, Terminal Eqmt	Edwards, Dan	4466
Teletext Services	Inoussa, Mary C	5820
Textile Machinery	McDonald, Edward	0680
Textiles	Dulka, William A	4058
Textiles (Trade Promo)	Molnar, Ferenc	2043
Timber Products (Tropical)	Tasnadi, Diana	5124
Tin Products	Manger, Jon	5124
Tires	Prat, Raimundo	0128
Toiletries (Trade Promo)	Kimmel, Edward K	3640
Tools/Dies/Jigs/Fixtures	McGibbon, Patrick	0314
Tourism (Major Proj)	White, Barbara	4160
Tourism Services	Sousane, J Richard	4582
Toys & Games (Trade Promo)	Beckham, Reginald	5478
Trade Related Employment	Davis, Lester A	4924
Transborder Data Flows	Inoussa, Mary C	5820
Transformers	Whitley, Richard A	0682
Transportation Industries	Alexander, Albert	4581
Transportation Svcs (Trade Promo)	Johnson, Bill	5012
Travel Services	Sousanne, J Richard	4582

Industry	Contact	Phone
	Area code 202-482-	
Tropical Commodities	Tasnadi, Diana	5124
Trucking Services	Sousane, J Richard	4581
Trucks, Trailers, Buses (Trade Promo)	White, John	0669
Tungsten Products	Manger, Jon	5124
Turbines, Steam	Brandes, Jay	0560

U

Industry	Contact	Phone
Uranium	Sugg, William	1466
Used, Reconditioned Eqmt (Trade Promo)	Bodson, John	0681

V

Industry	Contact	Phone
Value Added Telecommunications Serv	Atkins, Robert G	4781
Valves, Pipe Fittings (Except Brass)	Reise, Richard	3489
Vegetables	Hodgen, Donald A	3346
Video Services	Siegmund, John	4781
Videotex Services	Inoussa, Mary C	5820
	Siegmund, John	4781

W

Industry	Contact	Phone
Wallets, Billfolds, Flatgoods	Byron, James	4034
Warm Air Heating Eqmt	Greer, Damon	5456

Industry	Contact	Phone
	Area code 202-482-	
Wastepaper	Stanley, Gary	0375
Watches	Harris, John	1178
Water and Sewerage Treatment Plants (Major Proj)	Healey, Mary Alice	4333
Water Resource Eqmt	Wheeler, Frederica	3509
Water Supply & Distribution	Wheeler, Frederica	3509
Water Treatment/Point of Use	Wheeler, Frederica	3509
Welding/Cutting Apparatus	Kemper, Alexis	5956
Whiskey	Kenney, Cornelius	2428
Wholesale Trade	Margulis, Marvin	5086
Wine	Kenney, Cornelius	2428
Windmill Components	Garden, Les	0556
Wire & Wire Products	Bell, Charles	0606
Wire Cloth, Industrial	Reise, Richard	3489
Wire Cloth	Williams, Franklin	0132
Wood Containers	Hicks, Michael	0375
Wood Preserving	Hicks, Michael	0375
Wood Products	Smith, Leonard S	0375
Wood Working Machinery	McDonald, Edward	0680

Y

Industry	Contact	Phone
Yarns (Trade Promo)	Molnar, Ferenc	2043
Yeast	Janis, William V	2250
Yogurt	Janis, William V	2250

International economic policy

Eastern Europe Business Information Center 482.2645
Latin America/Caribbean Business Information Center 482-0703
Gulf Reconstruction Center.. 482-5767

Country desk officers can provide specific country information relating to international trade. Following is a list of country desk officers.

Country	Desk Officer	Phone (202)	Room
Afghanistan	Timothy Gilman	482-2954	2029B
Albania	Lynn Fabrizio	482-4915	3413
Algeria	Jeffrey Johnson	482-4652	2039
Angola	Sally Miller	482-5148	3317
Anguilla	Robert Dormitzer	482-2527	3021
Argentina	Randy Mye	482-1548	3021
Aruba	Robert Dormitzer	482-2527	3020
ASEAN	George Paine	482-3875	2308
Antigua/Barbuda	Robert Dormitzer	482-2527	3021
Australia	Simone Altfeld	482-3647	2308
Austria	Philip Combs	482-2920	3039
Bahamas	Robert Dormitzer	482-2527	3021
Bahrain	Claude Clement	482-5545	2039
Baltics Republic	Susan Lewenz	482-3952	3318
Bangladesh	Cheryl McQueen	482-2954	2029B
Barbados	Robert Dormitzer	482-2527	3021
Belgium	Simon Bensimon	482-5373	3042
Belize	Robert Dormitzer	482-2527	3021
Benin	Reginald Biddle	482-4388	3317
Bermuda	Robert Dormitzer	482-2527	3021
Bhutan	Timothy Gilman	482-2954	2029B
Bolivia	Laura Zeiger	482-2521	3029
Botswana	Sally Miller	482-5148	3317
Brazil	Roger Turner/Larry Farris	482-3871	3017
Brunei	Raphael Cung	482-3875	2308
Bulgaria	Jeremy Keller	482-4915	3413
Burkina Faso	Philip Michelini	482-4388	3317
Burma(Myanmar)	George Paine	482-3875	2308
Burundi	Debra Henke	482-5149	3317
Cambodia	Hong-Phong B. Pho	482-3875	2308
Cameroon	Debra Henke	482-5149	3317
Canada	Kathleen Keim/ Joseph Payne	482-3101	3033
Cape Verde	Philip Michelini	482-4388	3317
Caymans	Robert Dormitzer	482-2527	3020
Central Africa Rep.	Debra Henke	482-5149	3317
Chad	Debra Henke	482-5149	3317
Chile	Randy Mye	482-1548	3017
Colombia	Laurie MacNamar	482-1659	3025
Comoros	Chandra Watkins	482-4564	3317
Congo	Debra Henke	482-5149	3317
Costa Rica	Laura Subrin	482-2527	3021
Cuba	Mark Siegelman	482-2527	3021
Cyprus	Ann Corro	482-3945	3044
Czechoslovakia	Mark Mowrey	482-4915	3413
Denmark	Maryanne Lyons	482-3254	3413
D'Jibouti	Chandra Watkins	482-4564	3317
Dominica	Robert Dormitzer	482-2527	3021
Dominican Rep.	Theodore Johnson	482-2527	3021
East Caribbean	Robert Dormitzer	482-2527	3021
Ecuador	Laurie McNamara	482-1659	3025
Egypt	Thomas Sams	482-4441	2039
El Salvador	Theodore Johnson	482-2527	3020
Equatorial Guinea	Debra Henke	482-5149	3317

Country	Desk Officer	Phone (202)	Room
Ethiopia	Chandra Watkins	482-4564	3317
European Community	Charles Ludolph	482-5276	3036
Finland	Maryanne Lyons	482-3254	3413
France	Kelly Jacobs/		
	Elena Mikalis	482-8008	3042
Gabon	Debra Henke	482-5149	3317
Gambia	Reginald Biddle	482-4388	3317
Germany	Brenda Fisher	482-2435	3409
	Joan Kloepfer	482-2841	3409
Ghana	Reginald Biddle	482-4388	3317
Greece	Ann Corro	482-3945	3044
Grenada	Robert Dormitzer	482-2527	3021
Guadeloupe	Robert Dormitzer	482-2527	3021
Guatemala	Theodore Johnson	482-2527	3021
Guinea	Philip Michelini	482-4388	3317
Guinea-Bissau	Philip Michelini	482-4388	3317
Guyana	Robert Dormitzer	482-2527	3021
Haiti	Laura Subrin	482-2527	3021
Honduras	Theodore Johnson	482-2527	3020
Hong Kong	Jenelle Matheson	482-2462	2317
Hungary	Russell Johnson	482-4915	3413
Iceland	Maryanne Lyons	482-3254	3037
India	John Simmons/John Crown		
	Tim Gilman	482-2954	2029B
Indonesia	Karen Goddin	482-3875	2308
Iran	Claude Clement	482-5545	2039
Iraq	Thomas Sams	482-4441	2039
Ireland	Boyce Fitzpatrick	482-5401	3039
Israel	Kate FitzGerald-Wilks	482-4652	2039
Italy	Vacant	482-2177	3045
Ivory Coast	Philip Michelini	482-4388	3317
Jamaica	Laura Subrin	482-2527	3021
Japan	Ed Leslie/Cantwell Walsh		
	Eric Kennedy	482-2425	2318
Jordan	Jeffrey Hawkins	482-1860	2039
Kenya	Chandra Watkins	482-4564	3317
Korea	Dan Duvall/Renato Amapor	482-4957	2308
Kuwait	Jeffrey Hawkins	482-1860	2039
Laos	Hong-Phong B. Pho	482-3875	2308
Lebanon	Jeffrey Hawkins	482-1860	2039
Lesotho	Stephen Lamar	482-5148	3317
Liberia	Reginald Biddle	482-4388	3317
Libya	Claude Clement	482-5545	2039
Luxembourg	Simon Bensimon	482-5373	3046
Macao	Jenelle Matheson	482-3583	2317
Madagascar	Chandra Watkins	482-4564	3317
Malawi	Sally Miller	482-5148	3317
Malaysia	Raphael Cung	482-3875	2308
Maldives	John Simons	482-2954	2029B
Mali	Philip Michelini	482-4388	3317
Malta	Robert McLaughlin	482-3748	3049
Martinique	Robert Dormitzer	482-2527	3021
Mauritania	Philip Michelini	482-4564	3317
Mauritius	Chandra Watkins	482-4564	3317
Mexico	Elise Pinkow/Andrew Lowry		
	Ingrid Mohn	482-4464	3028
Mongolia	Jenelle Matheson	482-3583	2317
Montserrat	Robert Dormitzer	482-2527	3314
Morocco	Claude Clement	482-5545	2039
Mozambique	Sally Miller	482-5148	3317
Namibia	Emily Solomon	482-5148	3317
Nepal	Timothy Gilman	482-2954	2029B
Netherlands	Boyce Fitzpatrick	482-5401	3039
Netherlands Antilles	Robert Dormitzer	482-2527	3021

Country	Desk Officer	Phone (202)	Room
New Zealand	Simone Altfeld	482-3647	2308
Nicaragua	Laura Subrin	482-2527	3021
Niger	Philip Michelini	482-4388	3317
Nigeria	Reginald Biddle	482-4388	3317
Norway	James Devlin	482-4414	3037
Oman	Claude Clement	482-5545	2039
Pacific Islands	Karen Goddin	482-3875	2308
Pakistan	Cheryl McQueen	482-2954	2029B
Panama	Laura Subrin	482-2527	3020
Paraguay	Randy Mye	482-1548	3021
People's Rep. of China	Robert Chu/Laura McCall	482-3583	2317
Peru	Laura Zeiger	482-2521	3029
Philippines	George Paine	482-3875	2308
Poland	Audrey Zuck	482-4915	3413
Portugal	Ann Corro	482-3945	3044
Puerto Rico	Theodore Johnson	482-2527	3021
Qatar	Claude Clement	482-5545	2039
Romania	Lynn Fabrizio	482-2645	6043
Rwanda	Debra Henke	482-5149	3317
Sao Tome & Principe	Debra Henke	482-5149	3317
Saudi Arabia	Jeffrey Johnson	482-4652	2039
Senegal	Philip Michelini	482-4388	3317
Seychelles	Chandra Watkins	482-4564	3317
Sierra Leone	Reginald Biddle	482-4388	3317
Singapore	Raphael Cung	482-3875	2308
Somalia	Chandra Watkins	482-4564	3317
South Africa	Emily Solomon	482-5148	3317
Spain	Mary Beth Double	482-4508	3045
Sri Lanka	John Simmons	482-2954	2029B
St. Barthelemy	Robert Dormitzer	482-2527	3021
St. Kitts-Nevis	Robert Dormitzer	482-2527	3021
St. Lucia	Robert Dormitzer	482-2527	3021
St. Martin	Robert Dormitzer	482-2527	3021
St. Vincent-Grenadines	Robert Dormitzer	482-2527	3021
Sudan	Chandra Watkins	482-4564	3317
Suriname	Robert Dormitzer	482-2527	3021
Swaziland	Sally Miller	482-5148	3317
Sweden	James Devlin	482-4414	3037
Switzerland	Philip Combs	482-2920	3039
Syria	Jeffrey Hawkins	482-1860	2039
Taiwan	Ian Davis/Paul Carroll/ Dan Duvall	482-4957	2308
Tanzania	Sally Miller	482-5148	3317
Thailand	Jean Kelly	482-3875	2308
Togo	Reginald Biddle	482-4388	3317
Trinidad & Tobago	Robert Dormitzer	482-2527	3021
Tunisia	Jeffrey Hawkins	482-1860	2039
Turkey	Vacant	482-2177	3045
Turks & Caicos Islands	Robert Dormitzer	482-2527	3021
Uganda	Chandra Watkins	482-4564	3317
United Arab Emirates	Claude Clement	482-5545	2039
United Kingdom	Robert McLaughlin	482-3748	3045
Uruguay	Randy Mye	482-1548	3021
USSR	Susan Lewenz/Linda Nemac	482-4655	3318
Venezuela	Herbert Lindow	482-4303	3029
Vietnam	Hong-Phong B. Pho	482-3875	2308
Virgin Islands (UK)	Robert Dormitzer	482-2527	3020
Virgin Islands (US)	Theodore Johnson	482-2527	3021
Yemen, Rep. of	Jeffrey Hawkins	482-1860	2039
Yugoslavia	Jeremy Keller	482-4915	3413
Zaire	Debra Henke	482-5149	3317
Zambia	Sally Miller	482-5148	3317
Zimbabwe	Sally Miller	482-5148	3317

Bureau of Export Administration

Office of Export Licensing

- Exporter Counseling Division, Room 1099
  (Export licensing, controls, etc.) 482-4811

- Office of Antiboycott Compliance,
  Room 3886 482-2381

Minority Business Development Agency

- Office of Program Development,
  Room 5093 482-3237

B. Small Business Administration

All export programs administered through the Small Business Administration (SBA) are available through SBA field offices (see appendix III). More information about the programs can be obtained through

Small Business Administration
Office of International Trade
409 Third Street S.W., 6th Floor
Washington, DC 20416 202-205-6720

C. Export-Import Bank

Export-Import Bank
811 Vermont Ave., N.W.
Washington, DC 20571

Area Code: 202

Small Business Assistance Hotline 566-8860

Export Trading Company Assistance....................566-8944

Engineering Division 566-8802

D. Department of Agriculture

U.S. Department of Agriculture
14th Street and Independence Avenue, S.W.
Washington, DC 20250   Area Code: 202

Foreign Agricultural Service

Commodity and Marketing Programs:

Dairy, Livestock, and Poultry....................447-8031
Grain and Feed...447-6219
Horticultural and Tropical Products...........447-6590
Oilseed and Oilseed Products 447-7037
Tobacco, Cotton, and Seed 382-9516
Forest Products 382-8138

High-Value Product Services Division 447-3031

AgExport Connections..................................447-7103

E. Overseas Private Investment Corporation

Overseas Private Investment Corp.
7th Floor
1129 20th Street, N.W.
Washington, DC 20527 202-457-7010

F. Department of State

U.S. Department of State Commercial Coordinators:

Bureau of Economic and Business Affairs
Commercial Coordinator 202-647-1942

Bureau of African Affairs
Commercial Coordinator 202-647-3503

Bureau of Inter-American Affairs
Commercial Coordinator 202-647-2066

Bureau of East Asian and Pacific Affairs
Commercial Coordinator 202-647-4835

Bureau of Near Eastern and South Asian
Affairs Commercial Coordinator 202-647-9583

Bureau of European and Canadian Affairs
Commercial Coordinator 202-647-2395

Bureau of International Communications
and Information Policy 202-647-5832

G. Department of the Treasury

U.S. Department of the Treasury
15th Street and Pennsylvania Avenue, N.W.
Washington, DC 20220

U.S. Customs Strategic Investigation Division
(Exodus Command Center) 202-566-9464

H. Agency for International Development

Agency for International Development
Department of State Building
320 21st Street, N.W.
Washington, DC 20523

Office of Business Relations.....................202-235-1840

I. Office of the U.S. Trade Representative

Office of the United States Trade Representative
Winder Building
600 17th Street, N.W.
Washington, DC 20506

Area Code: 202

General Counsel 395-3150
Private Sector Liaison 395-6120
Agricultural Affairs & Commodity Policy 395-6127
The Americas Trade Policy 395-6135
East-West & Non-Market Economies 395-4543
Europe & Japan 395-4620
General Agreement on Tariffs &
     Trade (GATT)...395-6843
Industrial & Energy Trade Policy 395-7320
Investment Policy...395-3510
Pacific, Asia, Africa, &
     North-South Trade Policy 395-3430

State and local sources of assistance

Alabama

U.S. Department of Commerce
US&FCS District Office
3rd Floor, Berry Building
2015 2nd Avenue North
Birmingham, Alabama 35203
(205) 731-1331; fax (205) 731-0076

U.S. Small Business Administration
2121 8th Avenue North, Suite 200
Birmingham, Alabama 35203-2398
(205) 731-1344; fax (205) 731-1404

Alabama Development Office
International Development Office
135 South Union Street
(Mailing address: c/o State Capitol)
Montgomery, Alabama 36130
(205) 263-0048; fax (205) 265-5078

Alabama International Trade Center
University of Alabama, Tuscaloosa
P.O. Box 870396
Tuscaloosa, Alabama 35487-0396
(205) 348-7621; fax (205) 348-6974

North Alabama International Trade Association
Madison County Courthouse, 7th Floor
Huntsville, Alabama 35801
(205) 532-3505; fax (205) 532-3704

Department of Planning and Economic Development
Madison County Courthouse, 7th Floor
Huntsville, Alabama 35801
(205) 532-3505; fax (205) 532-3704

Center for International Trade & Commerce
250 North Water Street, Suite 131
Mobile, Alabama 36602
(205) 433-1151; fax (205) 438-2711

Alabama World Trade Association
International Trade Center
250 North Water Street, Suite 131
Mobile, Alabama 36602
(205) 433-3174; fax (205) 438-2711

Alabama Export Council
2015 2nd Avenue North, Room 302
Birmingham, Alabama 35203
(205) 731-1331

Birmingham Area Chamber of Commerce
International Department
P.O. Box 10127
Birmingham, Alabama 35202
(205) 323-5461; fax (205) 324-2320

Alaska

U.S. Department of Commerce
US&FCS District Office
World Trade Center
4201 Tudor Center Drive, Suite 319
Anchorage, Alaska 99508-5916
(907) 271-6237; fax (907) 271-6242

U.S. Small Business Administration
222 West 8th Avenue, # 67
Anchorage, Alaska 99513-7559
(907) 271-4022; fax (907) 271-4545

Alaska Department of Commerce
  and Economic Development
International Trade Division
3601 C Street, Suite 798
Anchorage, Alaska 99503
(907) 561-5585; fax (907) 561-4557

World Trade Center Alaska/Anchorage
World Trade Center
4201 Tudor Center Drive, Suite 320
Anchorage, Alaska 99508-5916
(907) 561-1516; fax (907) 561-1541

Alaska Center for International Business
World Trade Center
4201 Tudor Center Drive, Suite 120
Anchorage, Alaska 99508-5916
(907) 561-2322; fax (907) 561-1541

Alaska State Chamber of Commerce – Juneau
310 Second Street
Juneau, Alaska 99801
(907) 586-2322; fax (907) 586-3744

Alaska State Chamber of Commerce – Anchorage
801 B Street, Suite 405
Anchorage, Alaska 99501
(907) 278-2722; fax (907) 278-6643

Anchorage Chamber of Commerce
437 E Street, Suite 300
Anchorage, Alaska 99501-2365
(907) 272-2401; fax (907) 272-4117

Fairbanks Chamber of Commerce
First National Center
100 Cushman Street
Fairbanks, Alaska 99707
(907) 452-1105

Arizona

U.S. Department of Commerce
US&FCS District Office
Federal Building & U.S. Courthouse
230 North First Avenue, Room 3412
Phoenix, Arizona 85025
(602) 379-3285; fax (602) 379-4324

U.S. Small Business Administration
Central and One Thomas, Suite 800
2828 North Central Avenue
Phoenix, Arizona 85004-1025
(602) 379-3732

U.S. Small Business Administration
300 West Congress, Box FB33
Tucson, Arizona 85701
(602) 670-6715

Arizona Department of Commerce
International Trade and Investment Division
3800 North Central Avenue, Suite 1500
Phoenix, Arizona 85012
(602) 280-1371

Foreign Trade Zone No. 48
7800 South Nogales Highway
Tucson, Arizona 85706
(602) 741-1940

Arizona World Trade Association
34 West Monroe, Suite 900
Phoenix, Arizona 85003
(602) 254-5521

Arkansas

U.S. Department of Commerce
US&FCS District Office
Room 811, Savers Building
320 West Capitol
Little Rock, Arkansas 72201
(501) 324-5794; fax (501) 324-7380

U.S. Small Business Administration
Little Rock Field Office
Room 600, Savers Building
320 West Capitol
Little Rock, Arkansas 72201
(501) 324-5871

Marketing Division
Arkansas Industrial Development Commission
1 Capitol Mall
Little Rock, Arkansas 72201
(501) 682-7690; fax (501) 682-7691

The World Trade Club
c/o Marketing Division
Arkansas Industrial Development Commission
1 Capitol Mall
Little Rock, Arkansas 72201
(501) 682-7690

Export Finance Office
Arkansas Development Finance Authority
100 South Main
Little Rock, Arkansas 72201
(501) 682-5909

Arkansas International Center
University of Arkansas at Little Rock
2801 South University
Little Rock, Arkansas 72204
(501) 569-3282

Mid-South International Trade Association
P.O. Box 888
100 South Main, Room 438
Little Rock, Arkansas 72201
(501) 374-1957; fax (501) 375-8317

Arkansas Small Business Development Center
100 South Main, Suite 401
Little Rock, Arkansas 72201
(501) 324-9043

California

U.S. Department of Commerce
US&FCS District Office
11000 Wilshire Boulevard, Suite 9200
Los Angeles, California 90024
(213) 575-7104; fax (213) 575-7220

U.S. Department of Commerce
US&FCS District Office
250 Montgomery Street, 14th Floor
San Francisco, California 94104
(415) 705-2300; fax (415) 705-2299

U.S. Department of Commerce
US&FCS District Office
6363 Greenwich Drive, Suite 145
San Diego, California 92122
(619) 557-5395; fax (619) 557-6176

U.S. Department of Commerce
US&FCS Branch Office
Suite #1, 116-A West 4th Street
Santa Ana, California 92701
(714) 836-2461; fax (714) 836-2330

U.S. Department of Commerce
Bureau of Export Administration
5201 Great America Parkway, Suite 226
Santa Clara, California 95050
(408) 748-7450; fax (408) 748-7470

U.S. Small Business Administration
2719 N Air Fresno Drive
Fresno, California 93727-1547
(209) 487-5189

U.S. Small Business Administration
330 North Brand Boulevard, Suite 190
Glendale, California 91203-2304
(213) 688-2956; fax (213) 894-5665

U.S. Small Business Administration
660 J Street, Room 215
Sacramento, California 95814-2413
(916) 551-1445

U.S. Small Business Administration
880 Front Street, Room 4-S-29
San Diego, California 92188
(619) 557-7252

U.S. Small Business Administration (Regional Office)
71 Stevenson Street, 20th Floor
San Francisco, California 94105
(415) 744-6418

U.S. Small Business Administration (District Office)
211 Main Street, 4th Floor
San Francisco, California 94105-1988
(415) 744-6801

U.S. Small Business Administration
901 West Civic Center Drive, Suite 160
Santa Ana, California 92703
(714) 836-2494; fax (714) 836-2528

California State World Trade Commission
1121 L Street, Suite 310
Sacramento, California 95814
(916) 324-5511; fax (916) 324-5791

California State World Trade Commission
Office of Export Development
One World Trade Center, Suite 990
Long Beach, California 90831-0990
(213) 590-5965; fax (213) 590-5958

California Export Finance Office
425 Market Street, Suite 2838
San Francisco, California 94105
(415) 557-9812; fax (415) 557-7770

California Export Finance Office
107 South Broadway, Suite 8039
Los Angeles, California 90012
(213) 620-2433; fax (213) 620-6102

California Chamber of Commerce,
International Trade Department
1201 K Street, 12th Floor
P.O. Box 1736
Sacramento, California 95812-1736
(916) 444-6670

California Council for International Trade
700 Montgomery Street, Suite 305
San Francisco, California 94111
(415) 788-4127

California Department of Food and Agriculture
Agriculture Export Program
1220 N Street, Room 104
Sacramento, California 95814
(916) 322-4339; fax (916) 324-1681

Economic Development Corporation
  of Los Angeles County
6922 Hollywood Boulevard, Suite 415
Los Angeles, California 90028
(213) 462-5111; fax (213) 462-2228

Long Beach Area Chamber of Commerce
International Business Association
One World Trade Center, Suite 350
Long Beach, California 90853
(213) 436-1251; fax (213) 436-7088

Century City Chamber of Commerce
International Business Council
1801 Century Park East, Suite 300
Century City, California 90067
(213) 553-4062

Los Angeles Area Chamber of Commerce
International Commerce Division
404 South Bixel Street
Los Angeles, California 90017
(213) 629-0602; fax (213) 629-0708

San Diego Chamber of Commerce
402 West Broadway, Suite 1000
San Diego, California 92101
(619) 232-0124

San Francisco Chamber of Commerce
San Francisco World Trade Association
465 California Street, 9th Floor
San Francisco, California 94104
(415) 392-4511

The Greater Los Angeles World Trade
  Center Association
One World Trade Center, Suite 295
Long Beach, California 90831-0295
(213) 495-7070; fax (213) 495-7071

Citrus College Center for International
  Trade Development
363 South Park Avenue, Suite 105
Pomona, California 91766
(714) 629-2223; fax (714) 622-4217

Riverside Community College Center
  for International Trade Development
1760 Chicago Avenue, Building K
Riverside, California 92507
(714) 276-3400

Custom Brokers & Freight Forwarders Association
303 World Trade Center
San Francisco, California 94111
(415) 536-2233

Export Managers Association of California
124 East Olympic Boulevard, Suite 517
Los Angeles, California 90015
(213) 749-8698

Foreign Trade Association of Southern California
350 South Figueroa Street, #226
Los Angeles, California 90071
(213) 627-0634

International Marketing Association of Orange County
Cal State Fullerton
Marketing Department
Fullerton, California 92634
(714) 773-2223

Santa Clara Valley World Trade Association
P.O. Box 611208
San Jose, California 95161
(408) 998-7000

Valley International Trade Association
(San Fernando Valley)
1323 Carmelina Avenue, Suite 214
Los Angeles, California 90025
(213) 207-1802

World Trade Association of Orange County
1 Park Plaza, Suite 150
Irvine, California 92714
(714) 549-8151

World Trade Association of San Diego
6363 Greenwich Drive, Suite 140
San Diego, California 92122
(619) 453-4605

San Mateo County Economic Development Association
951 Mariners Island Boulevard, Suite 200
San Mateo, California 94404
(415) 345-8300; fax (415) 345-6896

San Jose Center for International Trade
and Development
50 West San Fernando Street, Suite 900
San Jose, California 95113
(408) 277-4060; fax (408) 277-3615

Santa Clara Chamber of Commerce
P.O. Box 387
Santa Clara, California 95052
(408) 970-9825; fax (408) 970-8864

Colorado

U.S. Department of Commerce
US&FCS District Office
World Trade Center Denver
1625 Broadway, Suite 680
Denver, Colorado 80202
(303) 844-3246; fax (303) 844-5651

U.S. Small Business Administration
U.S. Customhouse, Room 454
721 19th Street
Denver, Colorado 80202
(303) 844-3984

International Trade Office of Colorado
Governor's Office of Economic Development
World Trade Center Denver
1625 Broadway, Suite 680
Denver, Colorado 80202
(303) 892-3850

Colorado Department of Agriculture, Markets Division
700 Kipling
Lakewood, Colorado 80215
(303) 239-4114

Colorado International Capital Corporation
1981 Blake Street
Denver, Colorado 80202
(303) 297-2605; Colorado toll-free (800) 877-2432

Rocky Mountain World Trade Center Association
World Trade Center Denver
1625 Broadway, Suite 680
Denver, Colorado 80202
(303) 592-5760

Greater Denver Chamber of Commerce
1445 Market Street
Denver, Colorado 80202
(303) 534-8500

Colorado Springs Chamber of Commerce
P.O. Drawer B
Colorado Springs, Colorado 80901
(719) 635-1551

International Business Association of the Rockies
10200 West 44th Avenue, Suite 304
Wheat Ridge, Colorado 80033
(303) 422-7905

Export Legal Assistance Network
(Federal Bar Association/U.S. Small Business
  Administration/U.S. Department of Commerce)
(303) 922-7687   Federal Bar Association
(303) 844-3984   Small Business Administration
(303) 844-3246   Department of Commerce

Note: The above network is an agreement that allows a small firm to receive an initial, free consultation with an attorney to discuss legal issues and concerns relating to international trade.

Connecticut

U.S. Department of Commerce
US&FCS District Office
Federal Building, Room 610-B
450 Main Street
Hartford, Connecticut 06103
(203) 240-3530; fax (203) 844-5651

U.S. Small Business Administration
33 Main Street
Hartford, Connecticut 06106
(203) 240-4670

International Division
Department of Economic Development
865 Brook Street
Hartford, Connecticut 06067-3405
(203) 258-4256

Delaware

U.S. Department of Commerce
US&FCS District Office
  See listing for US&FCS, Philadelphia, Pennsylvania

U.S. Small Business Administration
920 King Street, Room 412
Wilmington, Delaware 19801
(302) 573-6295

Delaware Development Office
Box 1401
Dover, Delaware 19903
(302) 736-4271; fax (302) 736-5749

Delaware Department of Agriculture
2320 South DuPont Highway
Dover, Delaware 19901
(302) 736-4811; fax (302) 697-6287

Delaware State Chamber of Commerce
One Commerce Center, Suite 200
Wilmington, Delaware 19801
(302) 655-7221

Delaware-Eastern Pennsylvanla Export Council
475 Allendale Road, Suite 202
King of Prussia, Pennsylvania 19406
(215) 962-4980; fax (215) 951-7959

World Trade Center Institute (Delaware)
Dupont Building, Suite 1022
Wilmington, Delaware 19899
(302) 656-7905; fax (302) 656-2145

District of Columbia

U.S. Department of Commerce
US&FCS Branch Office
    See listing for US&FCS, Gaithersburg, Maryland

World Trade Center, Washington, D.C.
1101 King Street, Suite 700
Alexandria, Virginia 22314
(703) 684-6630

Office of International Business
Government of the District of Columbia
1250 Eye Street, N.W., Suite 1003
Washington, DC 20005
(202) 727-1576

Washington/Baltimore Regional Association
1129 20th Street, N.W., Suite 202
Washington, DC 20036
(202) 861-0400

Florida

U.S. Department of Commerce
US&FCS District Office
Federal Building, Suite 224
51 S.W. First Avenue
Miami, Florida 33130
(305) 536-5267; fax (305) 536-4765

U.S. Department of Commerce
US&FCS Branch Office
c/o Clearwater Chamber of Commerce
128 North Osceola Avenue
Clearwater, Florida 34615
(813) 461-0011; fax (813) 449-2889

U.S. Department of Commerce
US&FCS Branch Office
c/o University of Central Florida
RM 346, CEBA II
Orlando, Florida 32816
(407) 648-6235

U.S. Department of Commerce
US&FCS Branch Office
Rm 401, Collins Building
107 West Gaines Street
Tallahassee, Florida 32304
(904) 488-6469; fax (904) 487-1407

U.S. Small Business Administration
7825 Bay Meadows Way, Suite 100-B
Jacksonville, Florida 32256-7504
(904) 443-1900; fax (904) 443-1980

U.S. Small Business Administration
1320 South Dixie Highway, Suite 501
Coral Gables, Florida 33146
(305) 536-5521; fax (305) 536-5058

U.S. Small Business Administration
501 East Polk Street, Suite 104
Tampa, Florida 33602
(813) 228-2594; fax (813) 228-2111

Division of International Trade and Development
Florida Department of Commerce
Collins Building, Room 366
Tallahassee, Florida 32399-2000
(904) 488-6124; fax (904) 487-1407

Tampa Bay International Trade Council
P.O. Box 420
Tampa, Florida 33601
(813) 228-7777; fax (813) 223-7899

World Trade Center Miami
One World Trade Plaza, Suite 1800
80 S.W. 8th Street
Miami, Florida 33130
(305) 579-0064; fax (305) 536-7701

Office for Latin American Trade
Florida Department of Commerce
2701 LeJeune Road, Suite 330
Coral Gables, Florida 33134
(305) 442-6921; fax (305) 442-6931

Georgia

U.S. Department of Commerce
US&FCS District Office
Plaza Square North
4360 Chamblee Dunwoody Road, Suite 310
Atlanta, Georgia 30341
(404) 452-9101; fax (404) 452-9105

U.S. Department of Commerce
US&FCS District Office
Room A-107
120 Barnard Street
Savannah, Georgia 31401
(912) 944-4204; fax (912) 944-4241

U.S. Small Business Administration
1720 Peachtree Road, N.W., 6th Floor
Atlanta, Georgia 30309
(404) 347-4749; fax (404) 347-4745

U.S. Small Business Administration
52 North Main Street, Room 225
Statesboro, Georgia 30458
(912) 489-8719

Department of Industry, Trade and Tourism
Suite 1100
285 Peachtree Center Avenue
Atlanta, Georgia 30303
(404) 656-3545; fax (404) 656-3567

International Trade Division
Division of Marketing
Department of Agriculture
19 Martin Luther King, Jr., Drive, Room 330
Atlanta, Georgia 30334
(404) 656-3740; fax (404) 656-9380

Hawaii

U.S. Department of Commerce
US&FCS District Office
40 Ala Moana Boulevard
P.O. Box 50026
Honolulu, Hawaii 96850
(808) 541-1782; fax (808) 541-3435

U.S. Small Business Administration
2213 Federal Building
300 Ala Moana Boulevard, Box 50207
Honolulu, Hawaii 96850
(808) 541-2987

Department of Business, Economic Development,
    & Tourism
Business Development and Marketing Division
P.O. Box 2359
Honolulu, Hawaii 96804
(808) 548-7719

Chamber of Commerce of Hawaii
World Trade Association
735 Bishop Street
Honolulu, Hawaii 96813
(808) 531-4111

Economic Development Corporation of Honolulu
1001 Bishop Street, Suite 735
Honolulu, Hawaii 96813
(808) 545-4533

Also served by the Honolulu District Office:

American Samoa

Office of Development Planning
Territory of American Samoa
Pago Pago, American Samoa 96799
(684) 633-5155; fax (684) 633-4195

Guam

Department of Commerce
Territory of Guam
590 South Marine Drive
Tamuning, Guam 96911
(671) 646-5841; fax (671) 646-7242

Guam Chamber of Commerce
P.O. Box 283
Agana, Guam 96910
(671) 472-6311; fax (671) 472-6202

Commonwealth of the Northern Mariana Islands

Department of Commerce & Labor
Commonwealth of the Northern Mariana Islands
Saipan, MP 96950
(670) 322-8711; fax (670) 322-4008

Saipan Chamber of Commerce
P.O. Box 806
Saipan, MP 96950
(670) 234-6132; fax (670) 234-7151

Idaho

U.S. Department of Commerce
US&FCS Branch Office
2nd Floor, Joe R. Williams Building
700 West State Street
Boise, Idaho 83720
(202) 334-3857; fax (202) 334-2783

U.S. Small Business Administration
1020 Main Street, Suite 290
Boise, Idaho 83702
(208) 334-1696

Idaho Department of Commerce
International Business Division
700 West State Street, 2nd Floor
Boise, Idaho 83720
(208) 334-2470; fax (208) 334-2783

Department of Agriculture
International Marketing Division
2270 Old Penitentiary Road
P.O. Box 790
Boise, Idaho 83701
(208) 334-2227; fax (208) 334-2170

District Export Council
    See Boise US&FCS Branch Office listing

World Trade Committee
Boise Area Chamber of Commerce
P.O. Box 2368
Boise, Idaho 83701
(208) 344-5515

Illinois

U.S. Department of Commerce
US&FCS District Office
55 East Monroe Street, Room 1406
Chicago, Illinois 60603
(312) 353-4450; fax (312) 886-8025

U.S. Department of Commerce
US&FCS Branch Office
IIT – Rice Campus
201 East Loop Drive
Wheaton, Illinois 60187
(708) 353-4332

U.S. Department of Commerce
US&FCS Branch Office
P.O. Box 1747
515 North Court Street
Rockford, Illinois 61110-0247
(815) 363-4347; fax (815) 987-8122

U.S. Small Business Administration
Business Development Office
500 West Madison, Suite 1250
Chicago, Illinois 60606
(708) 353-4578

U.S. Small Business Administration/SCORE
500 West Madison, Suite 1250
Chicago, Illinois 60606
(312) 353-4528

U.S. Small Business Administration
511 West Capitol, Suite 302
Springfield, Illinois 62704
(217) 492-4416

International Business Division
Illinois Department of Commerce & Community Affairs
100 West Randolph Street, Suite 3-400
Chicago, Illinois 60601
(312) 814-7166

Illinois Department of Agriculture
1010 Jorie Boulevard, Room 20
Oak Brook, Illinois 60521
(708) 990-8256

Illinois Department of Agriculture
Division of Marketing and Promotion
State Fairgrounds
P.O. Box 19281
Springfield, Illinois 62794-9281
(217) 782-6675

Automotive Exporters Council
463 North Harlem Avenue
Oak Park, Illinois
(708) 524-1880

Carnets
U.S. Council for International Business
1930 Thoreau Drive, Suite 101
Schaumburg, Illinois 60173
(708) 490-9696

Central Illinois Exporters Association
302 East John Street, Suite 202
Champaign, Illinois 61820
(217) 333-1465

Chicago Association of Commerce and Industry
World Trade Division
200 North LaSalle Street
Chicago, Illinois 60616
(312) 580-6928

Chicago Convention and Tourism Bureau
McCormick Place on the Lake
Chicago, Illinois 60616
(312) 567-8500

Chicago Council on Foreign Relations
116 South Michigan Avenue, 10th Floor
Chicago, Illinois 60603
(312) 726-3860

Chicago Midwest Credit Management Associations
315 South Northwest Highway
Park Ridge, Illinois 60068
(708) 696-3000

City of Chicago
Economic Development Commission
1503 Merchandise Mart
Chicago, Illinois 60654
(312) 744-2622

City of Chicago
Department of Economic Development
International Division
24 East Congress Parkway, 7th Floor
Chicago, Illinois 60605
(312) 408-7485

Customs Brokers and Foreign Freight
    Forwarders Association of Chicago, Inc.
P.O. Box 66584/AMF O'Hare
Chicago, Illinois 60666
(708) 678-5400

Foreign Credit Insurance Association
19 South LaSalle Street, Suite 902
Chicago, Illinois 60603
(312) 641-1915

Foreign Trade Zones
U.S. Customs Service
Warehouse Desk
610 South Canal Street
Chicago, Illinois 60607
(312) 353-5822

Illinois District Export Council
55 East Monroe Street, Room 1406
Chicago, Illinois 60603
(312) 353-4450

Illinois Export Council
321 North Clark Street, Suite 550
Chicago, Illinois 60610
(312) 793-4982

Illinois Export Development Authority
321 North Clark Street, Suite 550
Chicago, Illinois 60610
(312) 793-4995

Illinois International Port District
3600 East 95th Street
Chicago, Illinois 60617
(312) 646-4400

Illinois Manufacturers' Association
209 West Jackson Boulevard, Suite 700
Chicago, Illinois 60606
(312) 922-6575

Illinois State Chamber of Commerce
International Trade Division
20 North Wacker Drive, Suite 1960
Chicago, Illinois 60606
(312) 372-7373

Illinois World Trade Center Association
321 North Clark Street, Suite 550
Chicago, Illinois 60610
(312) 793-4982

International Trade Association of Greater Chicago
P.O. Box 454
Elk Grove Village, Illinois 60009
(708) 980-4109

International Trade Club of Chicago
203 North Wabash, Suite 1102
Chicago, Illinois 60601
(312) 368-9197

International Visitors Center
520 North Michigan Avenue, Suite 522
Chicago, Illinois 60611
(312) 645-1836

Library of International Relations
77 South Wacker Drive
Chicago, Illinois 60606
(312) 567-5234

Mid-America International Agri-Trade Council (MIATCO)
820 Davis Street, Suite 212
Evanston, Illinois 60201
(708) 866-7300

Overseas Sales & Marketing Association of America, Inc.
P.O. Box 37
Lake Bluff, Illinois 60044
(708) 234-1760

World Trade Council of Northern Illinois
515 North Court Street
Rockford, Illinois 61103
(815) 987-8128

Indiana

U.S. Department of Commerce
US&FCS District Office
One North Capitol, Suite 520
Indianapolis, Indiana 46204-2227
(317) 226-6214; fax (317) 226-6139

U.S. Small Business Administration
429 North Pennsylvania Street, Suite 100
Indianapolis, Indiana 46204
(317) 226-7272

Indiana District Export Council
One North Capitol, Suite 520
Indianapolis, Indiana 46204-2227
(317) 226-6214; fax (317) 226-6139

Indiana Department of Commerce
International Trade Division
One North Capitol, Suite 700
Indianapolis, Indiana 46204-2248
(317) 232-3527

Indiana Chamber of Commerce
One North Capitol, Suite 200
Indianapolis, Indiana 46204-2248
(317) 264-3100

World Trade Committee
Fort Wayne Chamber of Commerce
826 Ewing Street
Fort Wayne, Indiana 46802
(219) 424-1435

World Trade Club of Indiana, Inc.
One North Capitol, Suite 200
Indianapolis, Indiana 46204-2248
(317) 264-3100

Tri-State World Trade Council
Old Post Office Place
100 N.W. 2nd Street, Suite 202
Evansville, Indiana 47708
(812) 425-8147

Michiana World Trade Club
P.O. Box 1715-A
South Bend, Indiana 46634
(219) 289-7323

Forum for International Professional Services
One North Capitol, Suite 200
Indianapolis, Indiana 46204-2248
(317) 264-3100

Indiana-ASEAN Council, Inc.
One American Square, Box 82017
Indianapolis, Indiana 46282
(317) 685-1341

Iowa

U.S. Department of Commerce
US&FCS District Office
817 Federal Building
210 Walnut Street
Des Moines, Iowa 50309
(515) 284-4222; fax (515) 284-4021

U.S. Department of Commerce
US&FCS Branch Office
424 First Avenue, N.E.
Cedar Rapids, Iowa 52401
(319) 362-8418; fax (319) 398-5228

U.S. Small Business Administration
373 Collins Road, N.E.
Cedar Rapids, Iowa 52402
(319) 393-8630; fax (319) 393-7585

U.S. Small Business Administration
749 Federal Building
210 Walnut Street
Des Moines, Iowa 50309
(515) 284-4422; fax (515) 284-4572

Iowa Department of Economic Development
Bureau of International Marketing
200 East Grand Boulevard
Des Moines, Iowa 50309
(515) 242-4743; fax (515) 242-4749

Iowa Department of Agriculture and Land Stewardship
International Trade Bureau
Wallace Building
Des Moines, Iowa 50319
(515) 281-5993; fax (515) 242-5015

Northeast Iowa Small Business Development Center
770 Town Clock Plaza
Dubuque, Iowa 52001
(319) 588-3350; fax (319) 557-1591

Siouxland International Trade Association
Sioux City Chamber of Commerce
101 Pierce Street
Sioux City, Iowa 51101
(712) 255-7903; fax (712) 258-7578

Iowa-Illinois International Trade Association
Davenport Chamber of Commerce
112 East Third Street
Davenport, Iowa 52801
(319) 322-1706; fax (319) 322-2251

International Trade Bureau
Cedar Rapids Area Chamber of Commerce
424 First Avenue, N.E.
Cedar Rapids, Iowa 52401
(319) 398-5317; fax (319) 398-5228

International Traders of Iowa
P.O. Box 897
Des Moines, Iowa 50309
(515) 245-5284; fax (515) 245-5286

Northeast Iowa International Trade Council
Regional Economic Development Center
Hawkeye Institute of Technology
1501 East Orange Street
Waterloo, Iowa 50704
(319) 296-2320; fax (319) 296-2874

Top of Iowa Trade Forum
Regional Economic Development Center
North Iowa Community College
500 College Drive
Mason City, Iowa 50401
(515) 421-4353; fax (515) 424-2011

Kansas

U.S. Department of Commerce
US&FCS Branch Office
151 North Volutsia
Wichita, Kansas 67214-4695
(316) 269-6160; fax (316) 262-5652

U.S. Small Business Administration
110 East Waterman Street
Wichita, Kansas 67202
(316) 269-6571

Kansas Department of Commerce
400 S.W. 8th, Suite 500
Topeka, Kansas 66603-3957
(913) 296-4027

International Trade Council
P.O. Box 1588
Manhattan, Kansas 66502
(913) 539-6799

Kansas District Export Council
c/o Sunflower Manufacturing Company
Box 628
Beloit, Kansas 67420
(913) 738-2261

World Trade Council of Wichita
Wichita State University
Barton School of Business, MBMT-IB
Campus Box 88
Wichita, Kansas 67208
(316) 689-3176

Kentucky

U.S. Department of Commerce
US&FCS District Office
U.S. Post Office & Courthouse Building, Room 636-B
601 West Broadway
Louisville, Kentucky 40202
(502) 582-5066; fax (502) 582-6573

U.S. Small Business Administration
600 Federal Place, Room 188
Louisville, Kentucky 40201
(502) 582-5971

Office of International Marketing
Kentucky Cabinet for Economic Development
Capitol Plaza Tower, 24th Floor
Frankfort, Kentucky 40601
(502) 564-2170

Louisville/Jefferson County Office
    for Economic Development
200 Brown & WIlliamson Tower
401 South Fourth Avenue
Louisville, Kentucky 40202
(502) 625-3051

Kentucky District Export Council
601 West Broadway, Room 636-B
Louisville, Kentucky 40202
(502) 582-5066

Kentuckiana World Commerce Council
P.O. Box 58456
Louisville, Kentucky 40258
(502) 583-5551

Bluegrass International Trade Association
P.O. Box 24074
Lexington, Kentucky 40524
(606) 272-6656

Northern Kentucky International Trade Association
7505 Sussex Drive
Florence, Kentucky 41042
(606) 283-1885; fax (606) 283-8178

Kentucky World Trade Center
410 West Vine Street, Suite 290
Lexington, Kentucky 40507
(606) 258-3139; fax (606) 233-0658

University of Louisville
School of Business
Louisville, Kentucky 40292

University of Kentucky
Patterson School of Diplomacy
Lexington, Kentucky 40506

Louisiana

U.S. Department of Commerce
US&FCS District Office
432 World Trade Center
2 Canal Street
New Orleans, Louisiana 70130
(504) 589-6546; fax (504) 586-2337

U.S. Small Business Administration
1661 Canal Street, Suite 2000
New Orleans, Louisiana 70114-2890
(504) 589-6685

Office of Commerce and Industry
Louisiana Department of Economic Development
P.O. Box 94185
Baton Rouge, Louisiana 70804-9185
(504) 342-9232; fax (504) 342-5389

Chamber of Commerce/
    New Orleans and the River Region
301 Camp Street
New Orleans, Louisiana 70130
(504) 527-6900

International Business Council of North Louisiana
c/o Shreveport Chamber of Commerce
P.O. Box 20074
Shreveport, Louisiana 71120
(318) 667-2510

International Trade Center
(Small Business Administration Office)
University of New Orleans – Lakefront Campus
New Orleans, Louisiana 70148
(504) 286-6978

World Trade Center of New Orleans
Executive Offices, Suite 2900
2 Canal Street
New Orleans, Louisiana 70130
(504) 529-1601; fax (504) 529-1691

Le Centre International de Lafayette
P.O. Box 4017-C
Lafayette, Louisiana 70502-4017
(318) 268-5474

Small Business Development Center
Northeast Louisiana University
Monroe, Louisiana 71209
(318) 342-1224

Maine

U.S. Department of Commerce
US&FCS Branch Office
77 Sewall Street
Augusta, Maine 04330
(207) 622-8249; fax (207) 626-9156

U.S. Small Business Administration
40 Western Avenue, Room 512
Augusta, Maine 04333
(207) 622-8378

State Development Office
State House, Station 59
Augusta, Maine 04333
(207) 289-2656

Maryland

U.S. Department of Commerce
US&FCS District Office
413 U.S. Customhouse
40 South Gay Street
Baltimore, Maryland 21202
(301) 962-3560; fax (301) 962-7813

U.S. Department of Commerce
US&FCS Branch Office
c/o National Institute for Standards and Technology
Building 411
Gaithersburg, Maryland 20899
(301) 962-3560; fax (301) 962-7813

U.S. Small Business Administration
Equitable Building
10 North Calvert Street
Baltimore, Maryland 21202
(301) 962-2235

Maryland International Division
World Trade Center
7th Floor
Baltimore, Maryland 21202
(301) 333-4295

Maryland Chamber and Economic Growth Associates
111 South Calvert Street, Suite 2220
Baltimore, Maryland 21202
(301) 837-6068

Maryland Chamber and Economic Growth Associates
275 West Street, Suite 400
Annapolis, Maryland 21401

Foundation for Manufacturing Excellence, Inc.
Catonsville Community College
800 South Rolling Road
Baltimore, Maryland 21228
(301) 455-4919

Eastern Baltimore Area Chamber of Commerce
2 Dunmanway
Suite 238 Dunkirk Building
Dundalk, Maryland 21222
(301) 282-9100

Greater Baltimore Committee
Legg Mason Tower
111 South Calvert Street, Suite 1500
Baltimore, Maryland 21202
(301) 727-2820

Office of Economic Development
Anne Arundel County
Arundel Center
Annapolis, Maryland 21401
(301) 280-1122

Office of Economic Development
Prince George's County
9200 Basil Court, Suite 200
Landover, Maryland 20785
(301) 386-5600

Baltimore County Economic Development Commission
400 Washington Avenue
Courthouse Mezzanine
Towson, Maryland 21204
(301) 887-8000

Office of Economic Development
Montgomery County
Executive Office Building
101 Monroe Street, Suite 1500
Rockville, Maryland 20850
(301) 762-6325

Howard County Office of Economic Development
3430 Court House Drive
Ellicott City, Maryland 21043
(301) 313-2900

World Trade Center Institute
401 East Pratt Street, Suite 1355
Baltimore, Maryland 21202
(301) 516-0022

Montgomery County High-Tech Council, Inc.
51 Monroe Street, Suite 1701
Rockville, Maryland 20850
(301) 762-6325

Maryland Small Business Development Center
(Central Maryland)
1414 Key Highway
Baltimore, Maryland 21230
(301) 234-0505

International Visitors Center
The World Trade Center, Suite 1353
Baltimore, Maryland 21202
(301) 837-7150

Washington/Baltimore Regional Association
1129 20th Street, N.W., Suite 202
Washington, DC 20036
(202) 861-0400

Massachusetts

U.S. Department of Commerce
US&FCS District Office
World Trade Center, Suite 307
Boston, Massachusetts 02110-2071
(617) 565-8563; fax (617) 565-8530

U.S. Small Business Administration
155 Federal Street, 9th Floor
Boston, Massachusetts 02110
(617) 451-2047

U.S. Small Business Administration
1550 Main Street
Springfield, Massachusetts 01103
(413) 785-0268

Massachusetts Department of Commerce & Development
Office of Economic Affairs
100 Cambridge Street, 13th Floor
Boston, Massachusetts 02202
(617) 727-3206

Office of International Trade
100 Cambridge Street, Suite 902
Boston, Massachusetts 02202
(617) 367-1830

Massachusetts Department of Food and Agriculture
100 Cambridge Street
Boston, Massachusetts 02202
(617) 727-3018

Massachusetts Port Authority (MASSPORT)
Foreign Trade Unit
World Trade Center, Suite 321
Boston, Massachusetts 02210
(617) 439-5560

International Business Center of New England
World Trade Center, Suite 323
Boston, Massachusetts 02210
(617) 439-5280

Smaller Business Association of New England, Inc.
69 Hickory Drive
Waltham, Massachusetts 02254-9117
(617) 890-9070

Associated Industries of Massachusetts
441 Stuart Street, 5th Floor
Boston, Massachusetts 02116
(617) 262-1180

Metro South Chamber of Commerce
60 School Street
Brockton, Massachusetts 02401
(508) 586-0500

Central Berkshire Chamber of Commerce
60 West Street
Pittsfield, Massachusetts 01201
(413) 499-4000

Chamber of Commerce of the Attleboro Area
42 Union Street
Attleboro, Massachusetts 02703
(508) 222-0801

Fall River Area Chamber of Commerce
P.O. Box 1871
200 Pocasset Street
Fall River, Massachusetts 02722
(508) 676-8226

Greater Boston Chamber of Commerce
600 Atlantic Avenue
Boston, Massachusetts 02110
(617) 227-4500

North Central Massachusetts Chamber of Commerce
110 Erdman Way
Leominster, Massachusetts 01453
(508) 840-4300

Greater Gardner Chamber of Commerce
55 Lake Street
Gardner, Massachusetts 01440
(508) 632-1780

Greater Lawrence Chamber of Commerce
264 Essex Street
Lawrence, Massachusetts 01840
(508) 686-0900

Greater Springfield Chamber of Commerce
1350 Main Street, Third Floor
Springfield, Massachusetts 01103
(413) 787-1542

New Bedford Area Chamber of Commerce
P.O. Box G-827, 794 Purchase Street
New Bedford, Massachusetts 02742
(508) 999-5231

North Suburban Chamber of Commerce
7 Alfred Street
Woburn, Massachusetts 01801
(617) 933-3499

Metro West Chamber of Commerce
1671 Worcester Street, Suite 201
Framingham, Massachusetts 01701
(508) 879-5600

South Shore Chamber of Commerce
36 Miller Stile Road
Quincy, Massachusetts 02169
(617) 479-1111

Waltham/West Suburban Chamber of Commerce
500 Main Street
Waltham, Massachusetts 02154
(617) 894-4700

Watertown Chamber of Commerce
101 Walnut Street, P.O. Box 45
Watertown, Massachusetts 02272-0045
(617) 926-1017

Worcester Area Chamber of Commerce
33 Waldo Street
Worcester, Massachusetts 01608
(508) 753-2924

Michigan

U.S. Department of Commerce
US&FCS District Office
1140 McNamara Building
Detroit, Michigan 48226
(313) 226-3650; fax (313) 226-3657

U.S. Department of Commerce
US&FCS Branch Office
300 Monroe Avenue N.W., Room 406A
Grand Rapids, Michigan 49503
(616) 456-2411; fax (616) 456-2695

U.S. Small Business Administration
515 McNamara Building
Detroit, Michigan 48226
(313) 226-6075; fax (313) 226-4769

U.S. Small Business Administration
300 South Front
Marquette, Michigan 49855
(9O6) 225-1108; fax (906) 225-1109

Office of International Development
Michigan Department of Commerce
Law Building, 5th Floor
Lansing, Michigan 48909
(517) 373-6390; fax (517) 335-2521

Michigan Export Development Authority
Michigan Department of Commerce
Law Building, 5th Floor
Lansing, Michigan 48909
(517) 373-6390; fax (517) 335-2521

Michigan Department of Agriculture
Office of International Trade
P.O. Box 30017
Lansing, Michigan 48909
(517) 373-1054; fax (517) 335-2521

City of Detroit
Community & Economic Development Department
150 Michigan Avenue
Detroit, Michigan 48226
(313) 224-6533; fax (313) 224-4579

Detroit/Wayne County Port Authority
174 Clark Street
Detroit, Michigan 48209
(313) 841-6700; fax (313) 841-6705

Michigan State Chamber of Commerce
Small Business Programs
200 North Washington Square, Suite 400
Lansing, Michigan 48933
(517) 371-2100; fax (517) 371-7224

Ann Arbor Chamber of Commerce
211 East Huron, Suite 1
Ann Arbor, Michigan 48104
(313) 665-4433; fax (313) 995-7283

Greater Detroit Chamber of Commerce
600 West Lafayette Boulevard
Detroit, Michigan 48226
(313) 964-4000; (313) 964-0531

Downriver Community Conference
15100 Northline
Southgate, Michigan 48195
(313) 283-8933; fax (313) 281-3418

Flint Area Chamber of Commerce
708 Root
Flint, Michigan 49503
(313) 232-7101; fax (313) 233-7437

Greater Grand Rapids Chamber of Commerce
17 Fountain Street, N.W.
Grand Rapids, Michigan 49503
(616) 459-7221; fax (616) 771-0318

Kalamazoo Chamber of Commerce
128 North Kalamazoo Mall
Kalamazoo, Michigan 49007
(616) 381-4000; fax (616) 343-0430

Macomb County Chamber of Commerce
10 North Avenue, P.O. Box 855
Mt. Clemens, Michigan 48043
(313) 463-1528

Muskegon Area Chamber of Commerce
1065 Fourth Street
Muskegon, Michigan 49441
(616) 722-3751

Greater Port Huron-Marysville Chamber of Commerce
920 Pine Grove Avenue
Port Huron, Michigan 48060
(313) 985-7101

Greater Saginaw Chamber of Commerce
901 South Washington
Saginaw, Michigan 48606
(517) 752-7161; fax (517) 752-9055

Cornerstone Alliance
P.O. Box 428
Benton Harbor, Michigan 49023
(616) 925-0044; fax (616) 925-4471

Detroit Customhouse Brokers &
    Foreign Freight Forwarders Association
1237-45 First National Building
Detroit, Michigan 48226
(313) 961-4130

Michigan Manufacturers Association
124 East Kalamazoo
Lansing, Michigan 48933
(517) 372-5900; fax (517) 372-3322

Business & Institutional Furniture
    Manufacturers Association
2335 Burton, S.E.
Grand Rapids, Michigan 49506
(616) 243-1681; fax (616) 243-1011

Michigan District Export Council
c/o Arthur Anderson & Company
400 Renaissance Center, Suite 2500
Detroit, Michigan 48243
(313) 568-9210

Kalamazoo International Trade Council (KITCO)
128 North Kalamazoo Mall
Kalamazoo, Michigan 49007
(616) 382-5966

Central Business District Association
700 Penobscot Building
Detroit, Michigan 48226
(313) 961-1403; fax (313) 961-9547

President's Export Council
c/o ASC, Inc.
One Sunroof Center
Southgate, Michigan 48195
(313) 285-4911; fax (313) 246-0500

Port Huron Trade Center
511 Fort Street, Suite 530
Port Huron, Michigan 48060
(313) 982-3510

World Trade Center
150 West Jefferson Avenue
Detroit, Michigan 48226
(313) 965-6500; fax (313) 965-1525

International Business Centers
Michigan State University
6 Kellogg Center
East Lansing, Michigan 48824-1022
(517) 353-4336; fax (517) 336-1009

West Michigan World Trade Association
17 Fountain Street, N.W.
Grand Rapids, Michigan 49503
(616) 771-0319; fax (616) 771-0318

World Trade Club of Detroit
600 West Lafayette Boulevard
Detroit, Michigan 48226
(313) 964-4000; fax (313) 964-0531

Minnesota

U.S. Department of Commerce
US&FCS District Office
110 South 4th Street, Room 108
Minneapolis, Minnesota 55401-2227
(612) 348-1638; fax (612) 348-1650

U.S. Small Business Administration
100 North 6th Street, Suite 610C
Minneapolis, Minnesota 55403-1504
(612) 370-2324; fax (612) 370-2303

Minnesota Export Finance Authority
30 East 7th Street, Suite 1000
St. Paul, Minnesota 55101-4902
(612) 297-4659; fax (612) 296-3555

Minnesota Trade Office
30 East 7th Street, Suite 1000
St. Paul, Minnesota 55101-4902
(612) 297-4222; fax (612) 296-3555

Minnesota World Trade Center Corporation
30 East 7th Street, Suite 400
St. Paul, Minnesota 55101-4901
(612) 297-1580; fax (612) 297-4812

Minnesota World Trade Association
P.O. Box 24341
Apple Valley, Minnesota 55124
(612) 441-9261

Mississippi

U.S. Department of Commerce
US&FCS District Office
300 Woodrow Wilson Boulevard, Suite 328
Jackson, Mississippi 39213
(601) 965-4388; fax (601) 965-5386

U.S. Small Business Administration
101 West Capitol Street, Suite 400
Jackson, Mississippi 39201
(601) 965-4378

U.S. Small Business Administration
One Hancock Plaza, Suite 1001
Gulfport, Mississippi 39501
(601) 863-4449

Mississippi Department of Economic
  and Community Development
P.O. Box 849
Jackson, Mississippi 39205
(601) 359-3552

Mississippi Department of Agriculture and Commerce
P.O. Box 1609
Jackson, Mississippi 39205
(601) 961-4725

International Trade Club of Mississippi, Inc.
P.O. Box 16673
Jackson, Mississippi 39236
(601) 366-0331

Missouri

U.S. Department of Commerce
US&FCS District Office
7911 Forsyth Boulevard, Suite 610
St. Louis, Missouri 63105
(314) 425-3302; fax (314) 425-3381

U.S. Department of Commerce
US&FCS District Office
601 East 12th Street, Room 635
Kansas City, Missouri 64106
(816) 426-3141; fax (816) 426-3140

U.S. Small Business Administration
1103 Grand Avenue, 6th Floor
Kansas City, Missouri 64106
(816) 374-6760

U.S. Small Business Administration
620 South Glenstone, Suite 110
Springfield, Missouri 65802
(417) 864-7670

U.S. Small Business Administration
815 Olive Street, Second Floor
St. Louis, Missouri 63101
(314) 539-6600

Export Development Office
Missouri Department of Economic Development
P.O. Box 118
Jefferson City, Missouri 65102
(314) 751-4855

Missouri Department of Agriculture
International Marketing Division
P.O. Box 630
Jefferson City, Missouri 65102
(314) 751-5611

Missouri District Export Council
7911 Forsyth Boulevard, Suite 610
St. Louis, Missouri 63105
(314) 425-3306

Mid America District Export Council (MADEC)
601 East 121th Street, Room 635
Kansas City, Missouri 64106
(816) 426-3141

International Trade Club of Greater Kansas City
920 Main Street, Suite 600
Kansas City, Missouri 64105
(816) 221-1462

World Trade Club of St. Louis, Inc.
135 North Meramec Avenue, Fifth Floor
St. Louis, Missouri 63105
(314) 725-9605

Montana

U.S. Department of Commerce
US&FCS Branch Office
2nd Floor, Joe R. Williams Buildling
700 West State Street
Boise, Idaho 83720
(208) 334-3857; fax (208) 334-2783

U.S. Small Business Administration
301 South Park, Room 528
Helena, Montana 59626-0054
(406) 449-5381

U.S. Small Business Administration
2525 Fourth Avenue North, 2nd Floor
Billings, Montana 59101
(406) 657-6567

Department of Commerce
International Trade Division
1424 Ninth Avenue
Helena, Montana 59620-0401
(406) 444-3923

Nebraska

U.S. Department of Commerce
US&FCS District Office
11133 O Street
Omaha, Nebraska 68137
(402) 221-3664; fax (402) 221-3668

U.S. Small Business Administration
11145 Mill Valley Road
Omaha, Nebraska 68154
(402) 221-3604

International Division
Nebraska Department of Economic Development
P.O. Box 94666
301 Centennial Mall South
Lincoln, Nebraska 68509
(402) 471-3111

Omaha Chamber of Commerce
International Affairs
1301 Harney Street
Omaha, Nebraska 68102
(402) 346-5000

Midwest International Trade Association
P.O. Box 37402
Omaha, Nebraska 68137
(402) 221-3664

Nevada

U.S. Department of Commerce
US&FCS District Office
1755 East Plumb Lane, Room 152
Reno, Nevada 89502
(702) 784-5203; fax (702) 784-5343

U.S. Small Business Administration
301 East Stewart Street
Las Vegas, Nevada 89125
(702) 385-6611

U.S. Small Business Administration
50 South Virginia Street, Room 238
Reno, Nevada 89505
(702) 388-5268

Commission on Economic Development
Capitol Complex
Carson City, Nevada 89710
(702) 687-4325

Economic Development Authority of Western Nevada
5190 Neil Road, Suite 111
Reno, Nevada 89502
(702) 829-3700

Latin Chamber of Commerce
P.O. Box 7534
Las Vegas, Nevada 89125-2534
(702) 385-7367

Nevada Development Authority
3900 Paradise Road, Suite 155
Las Vegas, Nevada 89109
(702) 791-0000

Nevada District Export Council
1755 East Plumb Lane, Suite 152
Reno, Nevada 84502
(702) 784-5305

New Hampshire

U.S. Department of Commerce
US&FCS District Office
    See listing for US&FCS Boston, Massachusetts

U.S. Small Business Administration
55 Pleasant Street, Room 211
Concord, New Hampshire 03301
(603) 244-4041

New Hampshire Department of Resources
    & Economic Development
Office of Industrial Development
172 Pembroke Street, P.O. Box 856
Concord, New Hampshire 03301
(603) 271-2591

New Jersey

U.S. Department of Commerce
US&FCS District Office
3131 Princeton Pike
Building 6, Suite 100
Trenton, New Jersey 08648
(609) 989-2100; fax (609) 989-2395

U.S. Department of Commerce
US&FCS District Office
c/o Bergen Community College
368 Paramus Road
Paramus, New Jersey 07632
(201) 447-9624

U.S. Small Business Administration
60 Park Place, 4th Floor
Newark, New Jersey 07102
(201) 645-6065

World Trade Association of New Jersey
c/o Schering-Plough International
27 Commerce Drive
Cranford, New Jersey 07016
(908) 709-2632

New Jersey Division of International Trade
Department of Commerce & Economic Development
153 Halsey Street
Newark, New Jersey 07102
(201) 648-3518

New Jersey Small Business Development
    Center – International Trade (NJSBDC)
Rutgers, the State University
Graduate School of Management
180 University Avenue
Newark, New Jersey 07102
(201) 648-5950

Raritan Valley Community College
International Education Program
P.O. Box 3300
Somerville, New Jersey 08876
(908) 526-1200, ext. 312

New Mexico

U.S. Department of Commerce
US&FCS Branch Office
625 Silver, S.W., 3rd Floor
Albuquerque, New Mexico 87102
(505) 766-2070; fax (505) 766-1057

U.S. Small Business Administration
625 Silver, S.W., 3rd Floor
Albuquerque, New Mexico 87102
(505) 766-1879; fax (505) 766-1057

Trade Division
State of New Mexico
Economic Development and Tourism Department
1100 St. Francis Drive, Joseph M. Montoya Building
Santa Fe, New Mexico 87503
(505) 827-0307; fax (505) 827-0263

New Mexico Department of Agriculture
Marketing and Development Division
Box 30005, Dept. 5600
Las Cruces, New Mexico 88003
(505) 646-4929; fax (505) 646-3303

New Mexico Small Business
   Development Center Network
P.O. Box 4187
Santa Fe, New Mexico 87502-4187
(505) 438-1362; fax (505) 438-1237

New Mexico International Trade Council
P.O. Box 25381
Albuquerque, New Mexico 87125-5831
(505) 821-2318; fax (505) 821-2318

Greater Albuquerque Chamber of Commerce
International Trade Committee
P.O. Box 25100
Albuquerque, New Mexico 87125
(505) 764-3700; fax (505) 247-9140

Albuquerque Hispano Chamber of Commerce
International Trade Committee
1600 Lomas Street, N.W.
Albuquerque, New Mexico 87104
(505) 842-9003; fax (505) 764-9003

New York

U.S. Department of Commerce
US&FCS District Office
1312 Federal Building
111 West Huron Street
Buffalo, New York 14202
(716) 846-4191; fax (716) 846-5290

U.S. Department of Commerce
US&FCS Branch Office
111 East Avenue, Suite 220
Rochester, New York 14604
(716) 263-6480; fax (716) 325-6505

U.S. Department of Commerce
US&FCS District Office
Federal Office Building, Room 3718
26 Federal Plaza
New York, New York 10278
(212) 264-0600; fax (212) 264-1356

U.S. Department of Commerce
US&FCS Associate Office
216 C.E.D.C.
Jamestown Community College
Jamestown, New York 14701
(716) 665-6066

U.S. Small Business Administration
26 Federal Plaza, Room 3100
New York, New York 10278
(212) 264-4355

U.S. Small Business Administration
35 Pinelawn Road, Room 102E
Melville, New York 11747
(516) 454-0750

U.S. Small Business Administration
100 South Clinton Street, Room 1071
P.O. Box 7317
Syracuse, New York 13260-7317
(315) 423-5383

U.S. Small Business Administration
111 West Huron Street, Room 1311
Buffalo, New York 14202
(716) 846-4301

U.S. Small Business Administration
333 East Water Street
Elmira, New York 14901
(607) 734-8130

U.S. Small Business Administration
445 Broadway, Room 2368
Albany, New York 12207
(518) 472-6300

U.S. Small Business Administration
100 State Street, Room 601
Rochester, New York 14614
(716) 263-6700

International Division
New York State Department of Economic Development
1515 Broadway, 51st Floor
New York, New York 10036
(212) 827-6100

International Division
New York State Department of Economic Development
111 East Avenue, Suite 220
Rochester, New York 14604
(716) 325-1944

International Division
New York State Department of Economic Development
16 Hawley Street
Binghampton, New York 13901
(607) 773-7813

International Division
New York State Department of Commerce
333 East Washington Street
Syracuse, New York 13202
(315) 428-4097

Canada-United States Trade Center
State University of New York at Buffalo
130 Wilkeson Quadrangle
Buffalo, New York 14261
(716) 636-2299

Southern Tier World Commerce Association
c/o School of Management
State University of New York at Binghampton
P.O. Box 6000
Binghamton, New York 13902-6000
(607) 777-2342

American Association of Exporters and Importers
11 West 42nd Street
New York, New York 10036
(212) 944-2230

Foreign Credit Insurance Association
40 Rector Street, 51st Floor
New York, New York 10006
(212) 306-5000

National Association of Export Companies
747 Middle Neck Road
Great Neck, New York 11024
(516) 487-0700

World Trade Institute
One World Trade Center
New York, New York 10048
(212) 466-4044

Syracuse International Trade Council
Greater Syracuse Chamber of Commerce
572 South Salina Street
Syracuse, New York 13202
(315) 470-1883

U.S. Council of the International
    Chamber of Commerce
1212 Avenue of the Americas
New York, New York 10036
(212) 354-4480

Albany-Colonie Regional Chamber of Commerce
518 Broadway
Albany, New York 11207
(518) 434-1214

Greater Buffalo Area Chamber of Commerce
107 Delaware Avenue
Buffalo, New York 14202
(716) 852-7100

Long Island Association, Inc.
80 Hauppauge Road
Commack, New York 11725
(516) 499-4400

International Business Council of the
    Rochester Area Chamber of Commerce
55 St. Paul Street
Rochester, New York 14604
(716) 454-2220

New York Chamber of Commerce & Industry
One Battery Park Plaza
New York, New York 10009
(212) 493-7500

Buffalo World Trade Association
P.O. Box 39
Tonawanda, New York 14150
(716) 877-1452

Long Island Association, Inc., World Trade Club
Legislative & Economic Affairs
80 Hauppauge Road
Commack, New York 11725
(516) 499-4400

Mohawk Valley World Trade Council
P.O. Box 4126
Utica, New York 13540
(315) 826-3600

Tappan Zee International Trade Association
One Blue Hill Plaza, Suite 812
Pearl River, New York 10965-1575
(914) 735-7040

Westchester County Association, Inc.
World Trade Club of Westchester
235 Mamaroneck Avenue
White Plains, New York 10605
(914) 948-6444

World Trade Club of New York, Inc.
28 Vesey Street, Suite 230
New York, New York 10007
(212) 435-8335

Western New York International Trade Council
P.O. Box 1271
Buffalo, New York 14240
(716) 852-7160

Western New York Economic Development Corp.
Liberty Building, Suite 717
424 Main Street
Buffalo, New York 14202
(716) 856-8111

North Carolina

U.S. Department of Commerce
US&FCS District Office
324 West Market Street, Room 203
P.O. Box 1950
Greensboro, North Carolina 27402
(919) 333-5345; fax (919) 333-5158

U.S. Small Business Administration
222 South Church, Suite 300
Charlotte, North Carolina 28202
(704) 371-6563

North Carolina Department of Economic and
    Community Development – International Division
430 North Salisbury Street
Raleigh, North Carolina 27611
(919) 733-7193

North Carolina Department of Agriculture
P.O. Box 27647
Raleigh, North Carolina 27611
(919) 733-7912

North Carolina World Trade Association
P.O. Box 28271
Raleigh, North Carolina 27611
(919) 794-4327

Research Triangle World Trade Center
1007 Slater Road, Suite 200
Morrisville, North Carolina 27560
(919) 549-7467

North Carolina Port Authority Headquarters
North Carolina Maritime Building
2202 Burnett Boulevard, P.O. Box 9002
Wilmington, North Carolina 28402
(919) 763-1621; outside North Carolina (800) 334-0682

North Carolina Small Business and
    Technology Development Center
4509 Creedmoor Road, Suite 201
Raleigh, North Carolina 27612
(919) 733-4643

North Dakota

U.S. Department of Commerce
US&FCS District Office
    See listing for US&FCS Omaha, Nebraska

U.S. Small Business Administration
657 2nd Avenue, North, Room 218
Fargo, North Dakota 58108
(701) 237-5771

International Trade Division
North Dakota Department of Economic
    Development and Finance
1833 East Expressway
Bismarck, North Dakota 58504
(701) 224-2810

Fargo Chamber of Commerce
321 North 4th Street
Fargo, North Dakota 58108
(701) 237-5678

Ohio

U.S. Department of Commerce
US&FCS District Office
9504 Federal Building
550 Main Street
Cincinnati, Ohio 45202
(513) 684-2944; fax (513) 684-3200

U.S. Department of Commerce
US&FCS District Office
668 Euclid Avenue, Room 600
Cleveland, Ohio 44114
(216) 522-4750; fax (216) 522-2235

U.S. Small Business Administration
1240 East 9th Street, Room 317
Cleveland, Ohio 44199
(216) 552-4180

U.S. Small Business Administration
85 Marconi Boulevard
Columbus, Ohio 43215
(614) 469-6860

U.S. Small Business Administration
5028 Federal Office Building
550 Main Street, Room 5028
Cincinnati, Ohio 45202
(513) 684-2814

International Trade Development Office
37 North High Street
Columbus, Ohio 43215
(614) 221-1321

State of Ohio Department of Development
International Trade Division
77 South High Street
P.O. Box 1001
Columbus, Ohio 43266
(614) 466-5017

Greater Cincinnati Chamber of Commerce
Export Development and World Trade Association
441 Vine Street, 300 Carew Tower
Cincinnati, Ohio 45202
(513) 579-3122

Columbus Area Chamber of Commerce
Economic Development
37 North High Street
Columbus, Ohio 43215
(614) 221-1321

Dayton Area Chamber of Commerce
Chamber Plaza
5th and Main
Dayton, Ohio 45402

Columbus Council on World Affairs
Two Nationwide Plaza, Suite 705
Columbus, Ohio 43215
(614) 249-8450

Cleveland World Trade Association
Greater Cleveland Growth Association
200 Tower City Center
50 Public Square
Cleveland, Ohio 44113
(216) 621-3300

Dayton Council on World Affairs
Wright Brothers Branch
P.O. Box 9190
Dayton, Ohio 45409
(513) 229-2319

Miami Valley International Trade Association
P.O. Box 291945
Dayton, Ohio 45429
(513) 439-9465

International Business & Trade Association
    of Akron Regional Development Board
One Cascade Plaza, 8th Floor
Akron, Ohio 44308
(216) 376-5550

Toledo Area International Trade Association
Toledo Area Chamber of Commerce
218 Huron Street
Toledo, Ohio 43604
(419) 243-8191

Stark International Marketing
Greater Canton Chamber of Commerce
229 Wells Avenue, N.W.
Canton, Ohio 44703
(216) 456-9654

Youngstown Area Chamber of Commerce
200 Wick Building
Youngstown, Ohio 44503
(216) 744-2131

Oklahoma

U.S. Department of Commerce
US&FCS District Office
6601 Broadway Extension
Oklahoma City, Oklahoma 73116
(405) 231-5302; fax (405) 841-5245

U.S. Small Business Administration
200 N.W. 5th Street, Suite 670
Oklahoma City, Oklahoma 73102
(405) 231-4301

Oklahoma Department of Commerce
International Trade and Investment Division
6601 Broadway Extension
Oklahoma City, Oklahoma 73116
(405) 841-5220

Oklahoma Department of Agriculture
Market Development Division
2800 Lincoln Boulevard
Oklahoma City, Oklahoma 73105
(405) 521-3864

Oklahoma State Chamber of Commerce
4020 Lincoln Boulevard
Oklahoma City, Oklahoma 73105
(405) 424-4003

Oklahoma City Chamber of Commerce
Economic and Community Development
One Santa Fe Plaza
Oklahoma City, Oklahoma 73102
(405) 278-8900

Oklahoma District Export Council
6601 Broadway Extension
Oklahoma City, Oklahoma 73116
(405) 231-5302

Metropolitan Tulsa Chamber of Commerce
Economic Development Division
616 South Boston Avenue
Tulsa, Oklahoma 74119
(918) 585-1201

Oklahoma City International Trade Association
P.O. Box 1936
Oklahoma City, Oklahoma 73101
(405) 943-9590

Tulsa World Trade Association
616 South Boston Avenue
Tulsa, Oklahoma 74119
(918) 585-1201

Small Business Development Center
6420 S.E. 15th Street
Midwest City, Oklahoma 73110
(405) 733-7348

Center for International Trade Development
Oklahoma State University
Hall of Fame and Washington
Stillwater, Oklahoma 74078
(405) 744-7693

Oregon

U.S. Department of Commerce
US&FCS District Office
One World Trade Center
121 S.W. Salmon, Suite 242
Portland, Oregon 97204
(503) 326-3001; fax (503) 326-6351

U.S. Small Business Administration
International Trade Program
One World Trade Center
121 S.W. Salmon, Suite 210
Portland, Oregon 97204
(503) 274-7482

Department of Economic Development
International Trade Division
One World Trade Center
121 S.W. Salmon, Suite 300
Portland, Oregon 97204
(503) 229-5625

Oregon Department of Agriculture
One World Trade Center
121 S.W. Salmon, Suite 240
Portland, Oregon 97204
(503) 229-6734

International Trade Institute
One World Trade Center
121 S.W. Salmon, Suite 230
Portland, Oregon 97204
(503) 725-3246

World Trade Center Portland
One World Trade Center
121 S.W. Salmon, Suite 250
Portland, Oregon 97204
(503) 464-8888

Central Oregon International Trade Council
2600 N.W. College Way
Bend, Oregon 97701
(503) 385-5524

Mid-Willamette Valley Council of Governments
105 High Street, S.E.
Salem, Oregon 97301
(503) 588-6177

Pacific Northwest International Trade Association
200 S.W. Market, Suite 190
Portland, Oregon 97201
(503) 228-4361

Portland Chamber of Commerce
221 N.W. 2nd Avenue
Portland, Oregon 97209
(503) 228-9411

Southern Oregon International Trade Council
290 N.E. "C" Street
Grants Pass, Oregon 97526
(503) 474-0762

Willamette International Trade Center
1059 Willamette, Room 209
Eugene, Oregon 97401
(503) 686-0195

Pennsylvania

U.S. Department of Commerce
US&FCS District Office
475 Allendale Road, Suite 202
King of Prussia, Pennsylvania 19406
(215) 962-4980; fax (215) 951-7959

U.S. Department of Commerce
US&FCS District Office
2002 Federal Building
1000 Liberty Avenue
Pittsburgh, Pennsylvania 15222
(412) 644-2850; fax (412) 644-4875

Delaware-Eastern Pennsylvania District Export Council
475 Allendale Road, Suite 202
King of Prussia, Pennsylvania 19406
(215) 962-4980; fax (215) 951-7959

U.S. Small Business Administration
475 Allendale Road, Suite 201
King of Prussia, Pennsylvania 19406
(215) 962-3815; fax (215) 962-3795

U.S. Small Business Administration Branch Office
100 Chestnut Street, Suite 309
Harrisburg, Pennsylvania 17101
(717) 782-3840

U.S. Small Business Administration Branch Office
20 North Pennsylvania Avenue
Wilkes-Barre, Pennsylvania 18701
(717) 826-6495

U.S. Small Business Administration District Office
960 Pennsylvania Avenue, 5th Floor
Pittsburgh, Pennsylvania 15222
(412) 644-2780

Pennsylvania Department of Commerce
Bureau of International Development
433 Forum Building
Harrisburg, Pennsylvania 17120
(717) 783-5107

Pennsylvaia Department of Agriculture
   Bureau of Markets
2301 North Cameron Street
Harrisburg, Pennsylvania 17110
(717) 783-3181; fax (717) 234-4560

Economic Development Council
   of Northwestern Pennsylvania
1151 Oak Street
Pittston, Pennsylvania 18640
(717) 655-5581; fax (717) 654-5137

Technology Development and Education Corporation
4516 Henry Street
Pittsburgh, Pennsylvania 15213
(412) 687-2700

Western Pennsylvania District Export Council
1000 Liberty Avenue, Room 2002
Pittsburgh, Pennsylvania 15222
(412) 644-2850

American Society of International Executives, Inc.
15 Sentry Parkway, Suite One
Blue Bell, Pennsylvania 19422
(215) 540-2295; fax (215) 540-2290

Berks County Chamber of Commerce
P.O. Box 1698
645 Penn Street
Reading, Pennsylvania 19603
(215) 376-6766; fax (215) 376-6769

Delaware County Chamber of Commerce
602 East Baltimore Pike
Media, Pennsylvania 19063
(215) 565-3677; fax (215) 565-1606

Delaware River Port Authority
World Trade Division
Bridge Plaza
Camden, New Jersey 08101
(215) 925-8780, ext. 2264; fax (609) 964-8106

International Business Forum
1520 Locust Street
Philadelphia, PA 19102
(215) 732-3250; fax (215) 732-3258

Lancaster Chamber of Commerce and Industry
Southern Market Center
100 South Queen Street, P.O. Box 1558
Lancaster, Pennsylvania 17603-1558
(717) 397-3531; fax (717) 293-3159

Lehigh University Small Business Development Center
International Trade Development Program
30 Broadway
Bethlehem, Pennsylvania 18015
(215) 758-4630; fax (215) 758-5205

Montgomery County Department of Commerce
3 Stoney Creek Office Center
151 West Marshall Road
Norristown, Pennsylvania 19401
(215) 278-5950; fax (215) 278-5944

Northern Tier Regional Planning
   and Development Commission
507 Main Street
Towanda, Pennsylvania 18848
(717) 265-9103; fax (717) 265-7585

Pennsylvania State University Small
 Business Development Center
Export Development Program
 of South Central Pennsylvania
Middletown, Pennsylvania 17057
(717) 948-6069; fax (717) 249-4468

Greater Philadelphia Chamber of Commerce
1346 Chestnut Street, Suite 800
Philadelphia, Pennsylvania 19107
(215) 545-1234; fax (215) 875-6700

Philadelphia Industrial Development Corp.
123 South Broad Street, 22nd Floor
Philadelphia. Pennsylvania 19109
(215) 875-3508; fax (215) 790-1537

University of Scranton Small
 Business Development Center
415 North Washington Avenue
Scranton, Pennsylvania 18510
(717) 961-7577; fax (717) 961-4053

SEDA-Council of Governments
Timberhaven Road, #1
Lewisburg, Pennsylvania 17838
(717) 524-4491; fax (717) 524-9190

Wharton Export Network
Wharton School
University of Pennsylvania
3733 Spruce Street, 413 Vance Hall
Philadelphia, Pennsylvania 19104
(215) 898-4187; fax (215) 898-1299

Wilkes College Small Business Development Center
Hollenbeck Hall
192 South Franklin Street
Wilkes-Barre, Pennsylvania 18766

Clarion University of Pennsylvania
Small Business Development Center
Dana Still Building
Clarion, Pennsylvania
(814) 226-2060; fax (814) 226-2636

Duquesne University
Small Business Development Center
Rockwell Hall, Room 10
600 Forbes Avenue
Pittsburgh, Pennsylvania 15282
(412) 434-6233; fax (412) 434-5072

Gannon University
Small Business Development Center
University Square
Erie, Pennsylvania 16541
(814) 871-7714; fax (814) 871-7383

Greater Pittsburgh World Trade Association
3 Gateway Center, 14th Floor
Pittsburgh, Pennsylvania 15222
(412) 392-4500; fax (415) 392-4520

Indiana University of Pennsylvania
Small Business Development Center
202 McElhaney Hall
Indiana, Pennsylvania 15705
(412) 357-2929; fax (412) 357-5743

North Central Pennsylvania Regional Planning
 and Development Commission
P.O. Box 488
Ridgway, Pennsylvania 15853
(814) 722-6901; fax (814) 722-1552

SMC/Pennsylvania Small Business
1400 South Braddock Avenue
Pittsburgh, Pennsylvania 15218
(412) 371-1500; fax (412) 371-0460

Southern Alleghenies Commission
541 58th Street
Altoona, Pennsylvania 16602
(814) 252-3595; fax (814) 949-6505

St. Francis College
Small Business Development Center
Schwab, Suite A-2
Loretto, Pennsylvania 15940
(814) 472-3200; fax (814) 472-3154

St. Vincent College
Small Business Development Center
Latrobe, Pennsylvania 15650
(412) 537-4572; fax (412) 537-4554

Southwestern Pennsylvania
 Economic Development District
12300 Perry Highway
Wexford, Pennsylvania 15090
(412) 935-6122; fax (412) 935-6888

Greater Willow Grove Chamber of Commerce
603 North Easton Road, P.O. Box 100
Willow Grove, Pennsylvania 19090
(215) 657-2227; fax (215) 657-8564

Erie Area Chamber of Commerce
1006 State Street
Erie, Pennsylvania 16501
fax (814) 459-0241

Women's International Trade Association
P.O. Box 40004
Philadelphia, Pennsylvania 19106
(215) 922-6610; fax (215) 922-0784

World Trade Association of Philadelphia
P.O. Box 58640
Philadelphia, Pennsylvania 19110
(215) 988-0711

York Area Chamber of Commerce
13 East Market Street
York, Pennsylvania 17401
(717) 848-4000; fax (717) 843-8837

Puerto Rico/U.S. Virgin Islands

U.S. Department of Commerce
US&FCS District Office
U.S. Federal Building, Suite G-55
150 Carlos Chardon Avenue
Hato Rey, Puerto Rico 00918-1738
(809) 766-5555

U.S. Small Business Administration
U.S. Federal Building, Suite 691
150 Carlos Chardon Avenue
Hato Rey, Puerto Rico 00918-1729
(809) 766-5572

Puerto Rico Department of Commerce
Box 4275
San Juan, Puerto Rico 00936
(809) 721-3290

Puerto Rico Economic Development Administration
GP.O. Box 2350
San Juan, Puerto Rico 00936
(809) 758-4747

Puerto Rico Chamber of Commerce
Box 3789
San Juan, Puerto Rico 00904
(809) 721-6060

Puerto Rico Manufacturers Association
Box 2410
Hato Rey, Puerto Rico 00919
(809) 759-9445

Puerto/Rico/Virgin Islands District Export Council
U.S. Federal Building, Suite G-55
150 Carlos Chardon Avenue
Hato Rey, Puerto Rico 00918-1738
(809) 766-5555

Virgin Islands Department of Economic
   Development & Agriculture
Commissioner of Commerce
P.O. Box 6400
St. Thomas, Virgin Islands 00801
(809) 774-8784

Rhode Island

U.S. Department of Commerce
US&FCS Branch Office
7 Jackson Walkway
Providence, Rhode Island 02903
(401) 528-5104; fax (401) 528-5067

U.S. Small Business Administration
380 Westminster Mall
Providence, Rhode Island 02903
(401) 528-4562

Department of Economic Development
7 Jackson Walkway
Providence, Rhode Island 02903
(401) 277-2601

South Carolina

U.S. Department of Commerce
US&FCS District Office
1835 Assembly Street, Suite 172
Columbia, South Carolina 29201
(803) 765-5345; fax (803) 253-3614

U.S Department of Commerce
US&FCS Branch Office
JC Long Building
9 Liberty Street
Charleston, South Carolina 29424
(803) 724-4361

South Carolina District Export Council
1835 Assembly Street, Suite 172
Columbia, South Carolina 29201
(803) 765-5345; fax (803) 253-3614

U.S. Small Business Administration
Strom Thurmond Federal Building, Suite 172
1835 Assembly Street, Room 358
Columbia, South Carolina 29202
(803) 765-5376

International Division
South Carolina State Development Board
P.O. Box 927
Columbia, South Carolina 29202
(803) 737-0400; fax (803) 737-0481

South Carolina State Ports Authority
P.O. Box 817
Charleston, South Carolina 29402
(803) 577-8100; fax (803) 577-8616

Jobs-Economic Development Authority
1201 Main Street, Suite 1750
Columbia, South Carolina 29201
(803) 737-0079; fax (803) 737-0016

Charleston-Trident Chamber of Commerce
P.O. Box 975
Charleston, South Carolina 29402
(803) 577-2510; fax (803) 723-4853

Greater Greenville Chamber of Commerce
P.O. Box 10048
Greenville, South Carolina 29603
(803) 242-1050; fax (803) 282-8549

Greater Columbia Chamber of Commerce
P.O. Box 1360
Columbia, South Carolina 29202
(803) 733-1110; fax (803) 733-1149

Small Business Development Center
College of Business
University of South Carolina
Columbia, South Carolina 29208
(803) 777-5118; fax (803) 777-4403

Low Country International Trade Association
P.O. Box 159
Charleston, South Carolina 29402
(803) 724-3566; fax (803) 724-3400

Midlands International Trade Association
P.O. Box 1481
Columbia, South Carolina 29202
(803) 822-5039; fax (803) 822-5147

Pee Dee International Trade Association (Florence)
P.O. Box 669
Hartsville, South Carolina 29550
(803) 383-4507, ext. 42; fax (803) 332-8003

Western South Carolina International Trade Association
P.O. Box 2081
Greenville, South Carolina 29602-2081
(803) 574-9540; fax (803) 574-9566

South Dakota

U.S. Department of Commerce
US&FCS District Office
    See listing for US&FCS Omaha, Nebraska

U.S. Small Business Administration
101 South Main Avenue, Suite 101
Sioux Falls, South Dakota 57102
(605) 336-2980

South Dakota Governor's Office
    of Economic Development
Export, Trade, & Marketing Division
Capitol Lake Plaza
Pierre, South Dakota 57501
(605) 773-5032

Rapid City Area Chamber of Commerce
P.O. Box 747
Rapid City, South Dakota 57709
(605) 343-1774

Sioux Falls Chamber of Commerce
127 East 10th Street
Sioux Falls, South Dakota 57101
(605) 336-1620

Tennessee

U.S. Department of Commerce
US&FCS District Office
Parkway Towers, Suite 1114
404 James Robertson Parkway
Nashville, Tennessee 37219-1505
(615) 736-5161

U.S. Department of Commerce
US&FCS Branch Office
Falls Building, Suite 200
22 North Front Street
Memphis, Tennessee 38103
(901) 544-4137

U.S. Department of Commerce
US&FCS Branch Office
301 East Church Avenue
Knoxville, Tennessee 37915
(615) 549-9268

U.S. Small Business Administration
50 Vantage Way, Suite 201
Nashville, Tennessee 37228-1500
(615) 736-5881

Tennessee Export Office
Department of Economic & Community Development
7th Floor, Rachel Jackson Building
Nashville, Tennessee 37219
(615) 741-5870

Tennessee Department of Agriculture
Ellington Agricultural Center
P.O. Box 40627, Melrose Station
Nashville, Tennessee 37294
(615) 360-0160

Tennessee Small Business Development Center
International Trade Center
Memphis, Tennessee 38152
(901) 678-4174

Tennessee Export Council
Suite 114, Parkway Towers
404 James Robertson Parkway
Nashville, Tennessee 37219-1505
(615) 736-7771

World Trade Center – Chattanooga
1001 Market Street
Chattanooga, Tennessee 37402
(615) 752-4316

Chattanooga World Trade Council
1001 Market Street
Chattanooga, Tennessee 37402
(615) 752-4302

East Tennessee International Commerce Council
P.O. Box 2688
Knoxville, Tennessee 37901
(615) 637-4550

Memphis World Trade Club
P.O. Box 3577
Memphis, Tennessee 38173-0577
(901) 345-5420

World Affairs Council of Memphis
577 University
Memphis, Tennessee 38112
(901) 523-6764

Mid-South Exporters' Roundtable
P.O. Box 3521
Memphis, Tennessee 38173
(901) 523-4420

Middle Tennessee World Trade Council
P.O. Box 198073
Nashville, Tennessee 37219-8073
(615) 736-6223

Texas

U.S. Department of Commerce
US&FCS District Office
1100 Commerce Street, Room 7A5
Dallas, Texas 75242
(214) 767-0542; fax (214) 767-8240

U.S. Department of Commerce
US&FCS District Office
2625 Federal Building
515 Rusk Street
Houston, Texas 77002
(713) 229-2578; fax (713) 229-2203

U.S. Department of Commerce
US&FCS Branch Office
P.O. Box 12728
816 Congress Avenue
Austin, Texas 78701
(512) 482-5939; fax (512) 320-9674

U.S. Small Business Administration
300 East 8th Street, Room 520
Austin, Texas 78701
(512) 482-5288

U.S. Small Business Administration
7400 Blanco, Suite 20
San Antonio, Texas 78216
(512) 229-4551

U.S. Small Business Administration
400 Mann Street, Suite 403
Corpus Christi, Texas 78401
(512) 888-3301

U.S. Small Business Administration
1100 Commerce Street, Room 3C36
Dallas, Texas 75242
(214) 767-0496

U.S. Small Business Administration
819 Taylor Street, Room 8A32
Ft. Worth, Texas 76102
(817) 334-5613

U.S. Small Business Administration
222 East Van Buren Street, Room 500
Harlingen, Texas 78550
(512) 427-8533

U.S. Small Business Administration
505 East Traves, Room 103
Marshall, Texas 75670
(903) 935-5257

U.S. Customs Service
P.O. Box 61050
DFW Airport, Texas 75261
(214) 574-2170

Texas Department of Agriculture
Export Services Division
P.O. Box 12847, Capitol Station
Austin, Texas 78711
(512) 463-7624

Texas Department of Commerce
Office of International Trade
P.O. Box 12728, Capitol Station
816 Congress
Austin, Texas 78711
(512) 472-5059

Texas Department of Commerce
Export Finance
P.O. Box 12728, Capitol Station
816 Congress
Austin, Texas 78711
(512) 320-9662

South Texas District Export Council
515 Rusk Street, Room 2625
Houston, Texas 77002
(713) 229-2578

North Texas District Export Council
1100 Commerce Street, Room 7A5
Dallas, Texas 75242
(214) 767-0496

City of Dallas Office of International Affairs
City Hall 5EN
Dallas, Texas 75201
(214) 670-3319

Foreign Credit Insurance Association
600 Travis
Suite 2860
Houston, Texas 77002
(713) 227-0987

Dallas/Fort Worth Airport Board
P.O. Box DFW
DFW Airport, Texas 75261
(214) 574-3079

Export Assistance Center
Greater Austin Chamber of Commerce
P.O. Box 1967
111 Congress, Suite 10
Austin, Texas 78767
(512) 322-5695

International Committee
P.O. Box 1967
Austin, Texas 78767
(512) 322-5695

Austin World Affairs Council
P.O. Box 5912
Austin, Texas 78763
(512) 469-0158

Port of Beaumont
P.O. Drawer 2297
Beaumont, Texas 77704
(409) 835-5367

Brownsville Economic Development Council
1600 East Elizabeth
Brownsville, Texas 78520
(512) 541-1183

Brownsville Minority Business Development Center
2100 Boca Chica Tower, Suite 301
Brownsville, Texas 78521-2265
(512) 546-3400

Brownsville Navigation District
P.O. Box 3070
Brownsville, Texas 78523-3070
(512) 831-4592

Cameron County Private Industry Council
285 Kings Highway
Brownsville, Texas 78521
(512) 542-4351

Texas Information and Procurement Service
601 Jefferson, Suite 2330
Houston, Texas 77002
(713) 752-8477

Port of Corpus Christi Authority
P.O. Box 1541
Corpus Christi, Texas 78403
(512) 882-5633

Corpus Christi Area Economic Development Corp. and
    Corpus Christi Small Business Development Center
1201 North Shoreline, P.O. Box 640
Corpus Christi, Texas 78403-0640
(512) 883-5571

Council for South Texas Economic Progress (COSTEP)
1701 West Business Highway 83
Texas Commerce Bank, Suite 600
McAllen, Texas 78501
(512) 682-1201

Greater Dallas Chamber of Commerce
1201 Elm Street, Suite 2000
Dallas, Texas 75270
(214) 746-6739

Fort Worth Chamber of Commerce
777 Taylor, Suite 900
Fort Worth, Texas 76102
(817) 336-2491

Port of Houston Authority
111 East Loop North
Houston, Texas 77029
(713) 670-2400

International Small Business Development Center
P.O. Box 58299
Dallas, Texas 75258
(214) 653-1777

International Trade Association of Dallas/Fort Worth
P.O. Box 58035
Dallas, Texas 75258
(214) 748-3777

International Trade Resource Center
P.O. Box 581249
Dallas, Texas 75258
(214) 653-1113

McAllen Minority Business Development Center
1701 West Business Highway 83, Suite 1023
McAllen, Texas 78501
(512) 687-5224

North Harris County College
Small Business Development Center
20000 Kingwood Drive
Kingwood, Texas 77339
(713) 359-1624

Port of Port Arthur
Box 1428
Port Arthur, Texas 77641
(409) 983-2011

San Antonio World Trade Center
118 Broadway, Suite 600
P.O. Box 1628
San Antonio, Texas 78205
(512) 978-7601

San Antonio World Trade Association
118 Broadway, Suite 640
San Antonio, Texas 78205
(512) 229-9036

International Trade Center
Greater San Antonio Chamber of Commerce
P.O. Box 1628
San Antonio, Texas 78296
(512) 229-2113

Greater Houston Partnership, World Trade Division
1100 Milam Building, 25th Floor
Houston, Texas 77002
(713) 658-2408

U.S. Chamber of Commerce
4835 LBJ Freeway, Suite 750
Dallas, Texas 75244
(214) 387-0404

Dallas Council on World Affairs
P.O. Box 58232
Dallas, Texas 75258
(214) 748-5663

Utah

U.S. Department of Commerce
US&FCS District Office
324 South State Street, Suite 105
Salt Lake City, Utah 84111
(801) 524-5116; fax (801) 524-5886

U.S. Small Business Administration
125 South State Street, Room 2237
Salt Lake City, Utah 84138
(314) 524-5800

Utah Economic & Industrial Development Division
324 South State Street, Suite 201
Salt Lake City, Utah 84111
(801) 538-8700

Salt Lake Area Chamber of Commerce
Export Development Committee
175 East 400 South, 6th Floor
Salt Lake City, Utah 84111
(801) 364-3631

World Trade Association of Utah
324 South State Street, Suite 105
Salt Lake City, Utah 84111
(801) 524-5116

Salt Lake County Inland Port
2001 South State Street, Suite S-2100
Salt Lake City, Utah 84109
(801) 468-3246; fax (801) 468-3684

Vermont

U.S. Department of Commerce
US&FCS District Office
   See listing for US&FCS Boston, Massachusetts

U.S. Small Business Administration
87 State Street, Room 204
Montpelier, Vermont 05602
(802) 229-0538

Agency of Development & Community Affairs
Pavillion Office Building
109 State Street
Montpelier, Vermont 05602
(802) 828-3221

Virginia

U.S. Department of Commerce
US&FCS District Office
Suite 8010
400 North 8th Street
Richmond, Virginia 23240
(804) 771-2246; fax (804) 771-2390

U.S. Small Business Administration
P.O. Box 10126
400 North 8th Street
Richmond, Virginia 23240
(804) 771-2765

Virginia Department of Economic Development
2 James Center
P.O. Box 798
Richmond, Virginia 23206-0798
(804) 371-8100

Virginia Department of Agriculture
Office of International Marketing
1100 Bank Street, Suite 915
Richmond, Virginia 23219
(804) 786-3953

Virginia Port Authority
600 World Trade Center
Norfolk, Virginia 23510
(804) 771-2765

Virginia Chamber of Commerce
9 South Fifth Street
Richmond, Virginia 23219
(804) 644-1607

Virginia District Export Council
P.O. Box 10190
Richmond, Virginia 23240
(804) 771-2246

International Trade Association of Northern Virginia
P.O. Box 2982
Reston, Virginia 22090

Piedmont World Trade Council
P.O. Box 1374
Lynchburg, Virginia 24505
(804) 528-7511

Washington

U.S. Department of Commerce
US&FCS District Office
3131 Elliott Avenue, Suite 290
Seattle, Washington 98121
(206) 553-5615; fax (206) 553-7253

U.S. Department of Commerce
US&FCS Branch Office
Room 625
West 808 Spokane Falls Boulevard
Spokane, Washington 99201
(509) 456-2922; fax (509) 458-2224

U.S. Small Business Administration
915 Second Avenue, Room 1792
Seattle, Washington 98174
(206) 553-8405; fax (206) 553-8635

U.S. Small Business Administration
Farm Credit Building, 10th Floor
Spokane, Washington 99204
(509) 353-2424; fax (509) 353-2829

Washington State Department of Trade
   and Economic Development
2001 6th Avenue, Suite 2600
Seattle, Washington 98121
(206) 464-7143; fax (206) 464-7222

Washington State Department of Agriculture
406 General Administration Building
Olympia, Washington 98504
(206) 753-5046

Export Assistance Center of Washington
2001 Sixth Avenue, Suite 1700
Seattle, Washington 98121
(206) 464-7123

Washington State International Trade Fair
1020 First Interstate Center
Seattle, Washington 98104
(206) 682-6900; fax (206) 682-6190

Trade Development Alliance of Greater Seattle
One Union Square, 12th Floor
Seattle, Washington 98101
(206) 389-7301; fax (206) 389-7288

Inland Northwest World Trade Council
P.O. Box 1124
Spokane, Washington 99210
(509) 456-3243; fax (509) 458-2224

Spokane International Coordinating Council
City Hall, Room 650
West 808 Spokane Falls Boulevard
Spokane, Washington 99201
(509) 456-3243

Washington Council on International Trade
Suite 350, Fourth and Vine Building
Seattle, Washington 98121
(206) 443-3826; fax (206) 443-3828

World Affairs Council
515 Madison Street, Suite 501
Seattle, Washington 98104
(206) 682-6986

World Trade Club of Seattle
P.O. Box 21488
Seattle, Washington 98111
(206) 624-9586

World Trade Center, Tacoma
3600 Port of Tacoma Road
Tacoma, Washington 98424
(206) 383-9474; fax (206) 926-0384

International Trade Institute
North Seattle Community College
9600 College Way North
Seattle, Washington 98103
(206) 527-3732; fax (206) 527-3734

West Virginia

U.S. Department of Commerce
US&FCS District Office
405 Capitol Street, Suite 809
Charleston, West Virginia 25301
(304) 347-5123; fax (304) 347-5408

U.S. Small Business Administration
District Office
P.O. Box 1608
Clarksburg, West Virginia 26302-1608
(304) 623-5631; fax (304) 623-0023

U.S. Small Business Administration
Branch Office
550 Eagan Street
Charleston, West Virginia 25301
(304) 347-5220; fax (304) 347-5350

Governor's Office of Community
  & Industrial Development
International Development Division
Room 517, Building #6
1900 Washington Street, East
Charleston, West Virginia 25305
(304) 348-2234; fax (304) 348-0449

Institute for International Trade Development
Marshall University
1050 Fourth Avenue
Huntington, West Virginia 25755-2131
(304) 696-6271; fax (304) 696-6880

West Virginia Chamber of Commerce
P.O. Box 2789
Charleston, West Virginia 25330
(304) 342-1115; fax (304) 342-1130

West Virginia Export Council
P.O. Box 26
Charleston, West Virginia 25321
(304) 347-5123; fax (304) 347-5408

West Virginia Manufacturers Association
405 Capitol Street, Suite 503
Charleston, West Virginia 25301
(304) 342-2123; fax (304) 342-4552

Wisconsin

U.S. Department of Commerce
US&FCS District Office
Room 596
517 East Wisconsin Avenue
Milwaukee, Wisconsin 53202
(414) 297-3473; fax (414) 297-3470

U.S. Small Business Administration
212 East Washington Avenue, Room 213
Madison, Wisconsin 53703
(608) 264-5261

U.S. Small Business Administration
500 South Barstow Street, Room 17
Eau Claire, Wisconsin 54701
(715) 834-9012

U.S. Small Business Administration
310 West Wisconsin Avenue, Room 400
Milwaukee, Wisconsin 53203
(414) 291-3941

Wisconsin Department of Development
123 West Washington Avenue
Madison, Wisconsin 53702
(608) 266-1767

Small Business Development Center
602 State Street
Madison, Wisconsin 53703
(608) 263-7766

Milwaukwee Association of Commerce
756 North Milwaukee Street
Milwaukee, Wisconsin 53202
(414) 273-3000

Central Wisconsin World Trade Association
P.O. Box 803
Stevens Point, Wisconsin 54481
(715) 346-2728

Northeastern Wisconsin World Trade Association
213 Nicolet Boulevard
Neenah, Wisconsin 54956
(414) 722-7758

Madison World Trade Association
P.O. Box 7900
Madison, Wisconsin 53707
(608) 222-3484

Milwaukee World Trade Association
756 North Milwaukee Street
Milwaukee, Wisconsin 53202
(414) 273-3000

Western Wisconsin World Trade Association
P.O. Box 1425
Eau Claire, Wisconsin 54702
(715) 232-2311

South Central Wisconsin World Trade Association
Small Business Development Center
University of Wisconsin – Whitewater
2000 Carlson Hall
Whitewater, Wisconsin 53190
(414) 472-3217

Wyoming

U.S. Department of Commerce
US&FCS District Office
   See listing for US&FCS Denver, Colorado

U.S. Small Business Administration
100 East "B" Street, Room 4001
Casper, Wyoming 82602
(307) 261-5761

Department of Commerce
Division of Economic and Community Development
Herschler Building, 2nd Floor West
Cheyenne, Wyoming 82002

Department of Commerce
International Trade Office
Herschler Building, 2nd Floor West
Cheyenne, Wyoming 82002

U.S. and overseas contacts for major foreign markets

Algeria

American Embassy Commercial Section
4 Chemin Cheikh Bachir El Ibrahimi
Algiers, Algeria
c/o U.S. Department of State (Algiers)
Washington, DC 20521-6030
Tel: 213-2-60-18-63
Telex: 66047
Fax: 213-2-60-18-63

Argentina

American Embassy Commercial Section
4300 Columbia, 1425
Buenos Aires, Argentina
APO Miami 34034
Tel: 54-1-773-1063
Telex: 18156 USICA AR
Fax: 54-1-775-6040

Embassy of Argentina Commercial Section
1667 K Street, N.W., Suite 610
Washington, DC 20006
Tel: 202-939-6400
Telex: 89-2537 EMBARG WSH

Australia

American Consulate General – Sydney
    Commercial Section
36th Floor, T&G Tower, Hyde Park Square
Park and Elizabeth Streets
Sydney 2000, N.S.W., Australia
APO AP 96554
Tel: 61-2-261-9200
Telex: 74223 FCSSYD
Fax: 61-2-261-8148

American Consulate General – Melbourne
    Commercial Section
553 St. Kilda Road
South Melbourne, Victoria 3004, Australia
APO AP 96551
Tel: 61-3-526-5900
Telex: 30982 AMERCON
Fax: 61-3-510-4660

American Consulate General – Perth
    Commercial Section
246 St. George's Terrace
Perth, WA 6000, Australia
Tel: 61-9-221-1177
Fax: 61-9-325-3569

American Chamber of Commerce in Australia
60 Margaret Street
Sydney, N.S.W., 2000, Australia
Tel: 61-2-221-3055
Telex: 72729

Embassy of Australia Commercial Section
1601 Massachusetts Avenue, N.W.
Washington, DC 20036
Tel: 202-797-3201

Austria

American Embassy Commercial Section
Boltzmanngasse 16
A-1091, Vienna, Austria
APO AE 09108-0001
Tel: 43-222-31-55-11
Telex: 114634
Fax: 43-222-34-12-61

Barbados

American Embassy Commercial Section
Broad Street
Bridgetown, Barbados
Box B, FPO AA 34054
Tel: 809-436-4950
Telex: 2259
Fax: 809-426-2275

Belgium

American Embassy Commercial Section
27 Boulevard du Regent
B-1000 Brussels
APO AE 09724
Tel: 32-2-513-3830
Telex: 846-21336
Fax: 32-2-512-6653

American Chamber of Commerce in Belgium
Rue de la Fusee 100
1130 Brussels, Belgium
Tel: 02-720-9130
Telex: 62788

Embassy of Belgium Commercial Section
3330 Garfield Street, N.W.
Washington, DC 20008
Tel: 202-333-6900
Telex: 89 566 AMBEL WSH

Brazil

American Embassy Commercial Section
Avenida das Nacoes, Lote 3
Brasilia, Brazil
APO AA 34030
Tel: 55-61-321-7272
Telex: 061-1091
Fax: 55-61-225-3981

American Consulate General – Rio de Janeiro
    Commercial Section
Avenida Presidente Wilson, 147
Rio de Janeiro, Brazil
APO AA 34030
Tel: 55-21-292-7117
Telex: AMCONSUL 021-21466
Fax: 55-21-240-9738

American Consulate General – Sao Paulo
    Commercial Section
Rua Padre Joao Manoel, 933
Caixa Postal 8063
Sao Paulo, Brazil
APO AA 34030
Tel: 55-11-853-2011
Telex: 011-22183
Fax: 55-11-853-2744

American Chamber of Commerce in Brazil – Sao Paulo
Caixa Postal 1980
01051, Sao Paulo, SP – Brazil
Tel: 55-11-212-3132
Telex: 1132311 CASE BR

American Chamber of Commerce in Brazil –
    Rio de Janeiro
20.040 Rio de Janiero, RJ – Brazil
Tel: 55-21-203-2477
Telex: 2123539 RJRT BR
Cable: REYNOTABA

American Chamber of Commerce in Brazil – Salvador
c/o TABARAMA – Tobacos do Brazil Ltda.
Caixa Postal 508
40.000 Salvador, Bahia – Brazil
Tel: 241-1844

Embassy of Brazil Commercial Section
3006 Massachusetts Avenue, N.W.
Washington, DC 20008
Tel: 202-745-2700
Telex: 440371 BRASMB 89430 BRASMB

Cameroon

American Embassy Commercial Section
Rue Nachtigal
Yaounde, Cameroon
c/o U.S. Department of State (Yaounde)
Washington, DC 20521-2520
Tel: 237-23-40-14

American Consulate General – Douala
    Commercial Section
21 Avenue du General De Gaulle
Douala, Cameroon
c/o U.S. Department of State (Douala)
Washington, DC 20521-2530
Tel: 237-42-34-34
Fax: 237-427-790

Canada

American Embassy Commercial Section
100 Wellington Street
Ottawa, Ontario
Canada, K1P5T1
P.O. Box 5000
Ogdensburg, NY 13669-0430
Tel: 613-238-5335
Telex: 0533582
Fax: 613-233-8511

American Consulate General – Montreal
    Commercial Section
Suite 1122, South Tower
Place Desjardins
Montreal, Quebec
Canada, H5B1G1
P.O. Box 847
Champlain, NY 12919-0847
Tel: 514-398-9695
Telex: 05-268751
Fax: 514-398-0711

American Consulate General – Toronto
    Commercial Section
360 University Avenue
Toronto, Ontario
Canada, M5G1S4
P.O. Box 135
Lewiston, NY 15092-0135
Tel: 416-595-5413
Telex: 065-24132
Fax: 416-595-5419

American Consulate General – Vancouver
    Commercial Section
1075 West Georgia Street, 21st Floor
Vancouver, British Columbia
Canada, V6E4E9
P.O. Box 5002
Point Roberts, WA 98281-5002
Tel: 604-685-3382
Telex: 04-55673
Fax: 604-685-5285

Embassy of Canada Commercial Section
1746 Massachusetts Avenue, N.W.
Washington, DC 20036
Tel: 202-785-1400
Telex: 8 9664 DOMCAN A WSH

Chile

American Embassy Commercial Section
Edificio Codina, Agustinas 1343
Santiago, Chile
APO AA 34033
Tel: 56-2671-0133
Telex: 40062-ICA-CL
Fax: 56-2-697-2051

American Chamber of Commerce in Chile
Pedro de Valdivia 291
Santiago, Chile
Tel: 220063
Telex: 645129 CMDLC

Embassy of Chile Commercial Section
1732 Massachusetts Avenue, N.W.
Washington, DC 20036
Tel: 202-785-1746
Telex: 89-2663 EMBACHILE WSH

China, People's Republic of

American Embassy Commercial Section
Guang Hua Lu 17
Beijing, China
FPO AP 96521
Tel: 86-1-532-3831 x490
Telex: AMEMB CN 22701
Fax: 86-1-532-3297

American Consulate General –
Guangzou Commercial Section
Dong Fang Hotel
Box 100, FPO AP 96522
Tel: 86-20-677-842
Fax: 86-20-666-409

American Consulate General –
Shanghai Commercial Section
1469 Huai Hai Middle Road
Box 200
FPO AP 96522
Tel: 86-21-433-2492
Fax: 86-21-433-1576

American Consulate General –
Shenyang Commercial Section
40 Lane 4, Section 5
Sanjing St., Heping District
Box 45
FPO AP 96522-0002
Tel: 86-24-222-000
Telex: 80011 AMCS CN
Fax: 86-24-290-074

American Chamber of Commerce in China
Jian Guo Hotel
Jian Guo Men Wai
Beijing, People's Republic of China
Tel: 86-1-59-5261
Telex: 20446 MHTBJ CN

Embassy of the People's Republic of China
Commercial Section
2300 Connecticut Avenue, N.W.
Washington, DC 20008
Tel: 202-328-2520

Colombia

American Embassy Commercial Section
Calla 38, No. 8-61
Bogota, Colombia
APO AA 34038
Tel: 57-1-232-6550
Telex: 44843
Fax: 57-1-285-7945

American Chamber of Commerce in Colombia – Bogota
Trv. 18, No. 78-80
Apartado Aereo 75240
Bogota, Colombia
Tel: 57-1-234-7921/241-8437

American Chamber of Commerce in Colombia – Cali
Apartado Aereo 101
Cali, Valle, Colombia
Tel: 689-506, 689-409
Telex: 55442

Embassy of Colombia Commercial Section
2118 Leroy Place, N.W.
Washington, DC 20008
Tel: 202-387-8338
Telex: 197 624 COLE UT

Costa Rica

American Embassy Commercial Section
Pavas
San Jose, Costa Rica
APO AA 34020
Tel: 506-20-3939
Fax: 506-31-47-83

Cote d'Ivoire

American Embassy Commercial Section
5 Rue Jesse Owens
Abidjan, Cote d'Ivoire
c/o U.S. Department of State
Washington, DC 20521-2010
Tel: 225-21-46-16
Fax: 225-22-32-59

Czechoslovakia

American Embassy Commercial Section
Trziste 15
12548 Prague, Czechoslovakia
APO AE 09213 (PRG)
Tel: 42-2-53-6641
Telex: 21196
Fax: 42-2-532-457

Denmark

American Embassy Commercial Section
Dag Hammarskjold Alie 24
2100 Copenhagen, Denmark
APO AE 09716
Tel: 45-31-42-31-44
Telex: 22216
Fax: 45-1-42-01-75

Embassy of Denmark Commercial Section
3200 Whitehaven Street, N.W.
Washington, DC 20008
Tel: 202-234-4300
Telex: 089525 DEN EMB WSH
      64444 DEN EMB WSH

Dominican Republic

American Embassy Commercial Section
Calle Cesar Nicolas Penson con Calle Leopoldo Navarro
Santo Domingo, Dominican Republic
APO AA 34041-0008
Tel: 809-541-2171
Telex: 3460013
Fax: 809-688-4838

American Chamber of Commerce
  in the Dominican Republic
P.O. Box 1221
Santo Domingo, Dominican Republic
Tel: 809-563-3151
Telex: 0034 TATEM DR

Embassy of the Dominican Republic Commercial Section
1715 22nd Street, N.W.
Washington, DC 20007
Tel: 202-332-6280
Telex: 44-0031 DOR EMB

Ecuador

American Embassy Ecuador
120 Avenida Patria
Quito, Ecuador
APO AA 34039
Tel: 593-2-561-404
Telex: 02-2329 USICAQ ED
Fax: 593-2-504-550

American Consulate General –
  Guayaquil Commercial Section
9 de Octubre y Garcia Moreno
Guayaquil, Ecuador
APO AA 34039
Tel: 593-4-323-570
Telex: 04-3452 USICAG ED
Fax: 593-4-324-558

American Chamber of Commerce in Ecuador
P.O. Box 9103 Suc. Almagro
Quito, Ecuador
Tel: 593-2-523-152

American Chamber of Commerce in Ecuador
Escobedo 1402 y Chile
P.O. Box 4767
Guayaquil, Ecuador
Tel: 593-4-529-855

Embassy of Ecuador Commercial Section
2535 15th Street, N.W.
Washington, DC 20009
Tel: 202-234-7200
Telex: 440129 ECUAI

Egypt

American Embassy Commercial Section
5 Sharia Latin America
Cairo, Republic of Eqypt
FPO AE 09835
Tel: 20-2-354-1583
Telex: 93773 AMEMB
Fax: 20-2-355-8368

American Consulate General –
  Alexandria Commercial Section
110 Avenue Horreya
Alexandria, Republic of Egypt
FPO AE 09835
Tel: 20-3-482-1911
Fax: 20-3-482-9199

American Chamber of Commerce in Egypt
Cairo Marriott Hotel, Suite 1537
P.O. Box 33 Zamalek
Cairo, Egypt
Tel: 20-2-340-8888
Telex: 20870

Embassy of Egypt Commercial Section
2715 Connecticut Avenue, N.W.
Washington, DC 20008
Tel: 202-265-9111
Telex: 89-2481 COMRAU WSH
      64-251 COMRAU WSH

Finland

American Embassy Commercial Section
Itained Puistotie 14A
SF-00140 Helsinki, Finland
APO AE 09723
Tel: 358-0-171-821
Telex: 125541
Fax: 358-0-635-332

France

American Embassy Commercial Section
2 Avenue Gabriel
75382 Paris Cedex 08
Paris, France
APO AE 09777
Tel: 33-1-42-96-1202
Telex: 650-221
Fax: 33-1-4266-4827

American Consulate General –
  Marseille Commercial Section
No. 9 Rue Armeny 13006
13006 Marseilles, France
Tel: 33-91-54-92-00
Telex: 430597

American Consulate General –
  Strasbourg Commercial Section
15 Avenue D'Alsace
67082 Strasbourg Cedex
Strasbourg, France
APO New York 09777
Tel: 33-88-35-31-04
Telex: 870907

American Chamber of Commerce in France
21 Avenue George V
F-75008 Paris, France
Tel: 33-1-47237028
Fax: 33-1-47201862

Embassy of France Commercial Section
4101 Reservoir Road, N.W.
Washington, DC 20007
Tel: 202-944-6000
Telex: 248320 FRCC UR

Germany

American Embassy Commercial Section
Delchmannsaue
5300 Bonn 2, Germany
APO AE 09080
Tel: 49-228-339-2895
Telex: 885-452
Fax: 49-228-334-649

American Embassy Office – Berlin Commercial Section
Neustaedtische Kirchstrasse 4-5
D-1080 Berlin, Germany
APO AE 09235
Tel: 49-30-819-7888
Fax: 37-2-229-2167

U.S. Commercial Office – Dusseldorf
Emmanuel-Leutze-Strasse 1B
4000 Dusseldorf 11, Germany
Tel: 49-211-596-798
Fax: 49-211-594-897

American Consulate General – Frankfurt am Main
  Commercial Section
Siesmayerstrasse 21
6000 Frankfurt, Germany
APO AE 09213
Tel: 49-69-7535-2453
Telex: 412589 USCON-D
Fax: 49-69-748204

American Consulate General –
  Hamburg Commercial Section
Alsterufer 27/28
2000 Hamburg 36, Germany
APO AE 09215
Tel: 49-40-4117-304
Telex: 213777
Fax: 49-40-410-6958

American Consulate General –
  Munich Commercial Section
Koeniginstrasse 5
8000 Muenchen 22, Germany
APO AE 09108
Tel: 49-89-2888-748
Telex: 5-22697 ACGM D
Fax: 49-89-285-261

American Consulate General –
  Stuttgart Commercial Section
Urbanstrasse 7
7000 Stuttgart, Germany
APO AE 09154
Tel: 49-711-246-513
Telex: 07-22945
Fax: 49-711-234-350

American Chamber of Commerce in Germany
Rossmarkt 12, Postfach 21 23
D-6000 Frankfurt 1, Germany
Tel: 49-69-283-401
Fax: 49-69-285-632

Embassy of the Federal Republic of Germany
4645 Reservoir Road, N.W.
Washington, DC 20007
Tel: 202-298-4000
Telex: 8 9481 DIPLOGERMA WSH

Greece

American Embassy Commercial Section
91 Vasillis Sophias Boulevard
10160 Athens, Greece
APO AE 09842
Tel; 30-1-723-9705
Fax: 30-1-723-9705

Guatemala

American Embassy Commercial Section
7-01 Avenida de la Reforma, Zone 10
Guatemala City, Guatemala
APO AE 34024
Tel: 502-2-34-84-79
Fax: 502-2-31-73-73

Honduras

American Embassy Commercial Section
Avenida La Paz
Tegucigalpa, Honduras
APO AE 34022
Tel: 504-32-3120
Fax: 504-32-0027

Hong Kong

American Consulate General – Commercial Section
26 Garden Road
Hong Kong
FPO AP 96522
Tel: 852-521-1467
Telex: 63141 USDOC HX
Fax: 852-845-9800

American Chamber of Commerce in Hong Kong
1030 Swire Road, Central P.O. Box 355
Hong Kong
Tel: 852-526-0165
Fax: 852-810-1289

Hong Kong Office/British Embassy
3100 Massachusetts Avenue, N.W.
Washington, DC 20008
Tel: 202-898-4591
Telex: 440484 HK WSH UY

Hungary

American Embassy Commercial Section
Bajza Utca 31
H-1062 Budapest, Hungary
APO AE 09213 (BUD)
Tel: 36-1-122-8600
Telex: 227136
Fax: 36-1-142-2529

India

American Embassy Commercial Section
Shanti Path, Chanahyapuri
110021 New Delhi, India
c/o U.S. Department of State (New Delhi)
Washington, DC 20521-9000
Tel: 91-11-600-651
Telex: USCS IN 031-4589
Fax: 91-11-687-2391

American Consulate General –
   Bombay Commercial Section
Lincoln House
78 Bhulabhai Desai Road
Bombay 400026, India
c/o U.S. Department of State (Bombay)
Washington, DC 20521-6240
Tel: 91-022-822-3611/8
Telex: 011-6525 ACON IN
Fax: 91-22-822-0350

American Consulate General –
   Calcutta Commercial Section
5/1 Ho Chi Minh Sarani
Calcutta 700071, India
c/o U.S. Department of State (Calcutta)
Washington, DC 20521-6250
Tel: 91-033-44-3611/6
Telex: 021-2483
Fax: 91-033-283-823

American Consulate General –
   Madras Commercial Section
Mount Road – 6
Madras 600006, India
c/o U.S. Department of State (Madras)
Washington, DC 20521-6260
Tel: 91-44-477-542
Fax: 91-44-825-0240

Embassy of India Commercial Section
2107 Massachusetts Avenue, N.W.
Washington, DC 20008
Tel: 202-939-7000

Indonesia

American Embassy Commercial Section
Medan Merdeka Selatan 5
Jakarta, Indonesia
APO AP 96520
Tel: 62-21-360-360
Telex: 44218 AMEMB JKT
Fax: 62-21-360-644

American Consulate – Medan Commercial Section
Jalan Imam Bonjol 13
Medan, Indonesia
APO AP 96520
Tel: 62-61-322-200
Telex: 51764

American Consulate – Surabaya Commercial Section
Jalan Raya Dr. Sutomo 33
Surabaya, Indonesia
APO AP 96520
Tel: 62-31-67100
Telex: 031-334

American Chamber of Commerce in Indonesia
The Landmark Centre, 22nd Floor
Jalan Jendral Sudirman I
Jakarta, Indonesia
Tel: 62-21-578-0656

Embassy of Indonesia Commercial Section
2020 Massachusetts Avenue, N.W.
Washington, DC 20036
Tel: 202-775-5200

Ireland

American Embassy Commercial Section
42 Elgin Road
Ballsbridge
Dublin, Ireland
c/o U.S. Department of State (Dublin)
Washington, DC 20521-5290
Tel: 353-1-687-122
Telex: 25240
Fax: 353-1-608-469

American Chamber of Commerce in Ireland
20 College Green
Dublin 2, Ireland
Tel: 353-1-79-37-33
Telex: 31187 VCIL

Embassy of Ireland Commercial Section
2234 Massachusetts Avenue, N.W.
Washington, DC 20008
Tel: 202-462-3939
Telex: 64160 HIBERNIA 64160
        440419 HIBERNIA 440419

Israel

American Embassy Commercial Section
71 Hayarkon Street
Tel Aviv, Israel
APO AE 09830
Tel: 972-3-654-338
Telex: 33376
Fax: 972-3-658-033

American Chamber of Commerce in Israel
35 Shaul Hamelech Boulevard
P.O. Box 33174
Tel Aviv, Israel
Tel: 972-3-252-341
Telex: 32129
Fax: 972-3-251-272

Embassy of Israel Commercial Section
3514 International Drive, N.W.
Washington, DC 20008
Tel: 202-364-5500

Italy

American Embassy Commercial Section
Via Veneto 119/A
00187 Rome, Italy
APO AE 09624
Tel: 39-6-4674-2202
Telex: 622322 AMBRMA
Fax: 39-6-4674-2113

American Consulate General –
   Milan Commercial Section
Via Principe Amedeo, 2/10
20121 Milan, Italy
Box M, APO AE 09624
Tel: 39-2-498-2241
Telex: 330208
Fax: 39-2-481-4161

American Chamber of Commerce in Italy
Via Cantu 1
20123 Milan, Italy
Tel: 39-2-869-0661
Telex: 352128 AMCHAM I
Fax: 39-2-805-7737

Embassy of Italy Commercial Section
1601 Fuller Street, N.W.
Washington, DC 20009
Tel: 202-328-5500
Telex: 90-4076 ITALY EMB WSH

Jamaica

American Embassy Commercial Section
2 Oxford Road, 3rd Floor
Kingston, Jamaica
c/o U.S. Department of State (Kingston)
Washington, DC 20521-3210
Tel: 809-929-4850
Fax: 809-929-3637

Japan

American Embassy Commercial Section
10-5 Akasaka, 1-chome
Minato-ku (107)
Tokyo, Japan
APO AP 96337
Tel: 81-3-3224-5050
Telex: 2422118
Fax: 81-3-3589-4235

American Consulate General –
   Osaka Commercial Section*
11-15, Nishitenma 2-chome
Kita-ku
Osaka (530), Japan
APO AP 96337
Tel: 81-6-315-5953
Fax: 81-6-361-5978

* Includes American merchandise display.

American Consulate – Fukuoka Commercial Section
5-26 Ohori 2-chome
Chuo-ku
Fukuoka (810), Japan
Box 10
FPO AP 96322
Tel: 81-92-751-9331
Telex: 725679
Fax: 81-92-71-3922

American Chamber of Commerce in Japan – Tokyo
Fukide Building, No.2
4-1-21 Toranomon
Minato-ku
Tokyo (105), Japan
Tel: 81-3-433-5381
Fax: 81-3-436-1446

American Chamber of Commerce in Japan – Okinawa
P.O. Box 235
Okinawa City (904), Japan
Tel: 81-989-352-684
Telex: J79873 NANSEI OK
Cable: AMCHAM OKINAWA

American Electronics Association
Nambu Building, 3F, 3-3, Kiochio
Chiyoda-ku
Tokyo (105), Japan
Tel: 81-3-237-7195
Fax: 81-3-237-1237

Semiconductor Industry Association, Japan Office
Nambu Building, 3F, 3-3, Kiochio
Chiyoda-ku
Tokyo (105), Japan
Tel: 81-3-237-7683
Fax: 81-3-237-1237

U.S. Automotive Parts Industry, Japan Office
Towa Horidomecho Building, 3F, 2-1-1
Nihonbashi-Horidomecho
Chuo-ku
Tokyo (103), Japan
Tel: 81-3-663-8484
Fax: 81-3-663-8483

Japan External Trade Organization (JETRO)
2-2-5 Toranomon
Minato-ku
Tokyo (105), Japan
Tel: 81-3-582-5511

Embassy of Japan Commercial Section
2520 Massachusetts Avenue, N.W.
Washington, DC 20008
Tel: 202-939-6700
Telex: 89 540

Kenya

American Embassy Commercial Section
Moi Haile Selassie Avenue
Nairobi, Kenya
APO AA 09831
Tel: 254-2-334-141
Telex: 22964
Fax: 254-2-340-838

Korea

American Embassy Commercial Section
82 Sejong-Ro, Chongro-ku
Seoul, Korea
APO AP 96205
Tel: 82-2-732-2601
Fax: 82-2-739-1628

Kuwait

American Embassy Commercial Section
P.O. Box 77 SAFAT
Kuwait
APO AE 09880
Tel: 965-242-4151
Fax: 965-240-7368

Embassy of Kuwait Commercial Section
2940 Tilden Street, N.W.
Washington, DC 20008
Tel: 202-966-0702
Telex: 64142 KUWAIT WSH

Malaysia

American Embassy Commercial Section
AIA Building 376 Jalan Tun Razah
P.O. Box 10035
50700 Kuala Lumpur, Malaysia
c/o U.S. Department of State (Kuala Lumpur)
Washington, DC 20521-4210
Tel: 60-248-9011
Telex: FCSKL MA 32956
Fax: 60-3-242-1866

American Business Council of Malaysia
15 01, 15th Floor, Amoda, Lajan Imbi
55100 Kuala Lumpur, Malaysia
Tel: 60-3-243-7682

Embassy of Malaysia Commercial Section
2401 Massachusetts Avenue, N.W.
Washington, DC 20008
Tel: 202-328-2700
Telex: 440119 MAEM UI or 61435 MALAYEM 61435

Mexico

American Embassy Commercial Section
Paseo de la Reforma 305
Mexico City 06500, Mexico
P.O. Box 3087
Laredo, TX 78044-3087
Tel: 52-5-211-0042
Telex: 017-73-091 or 017-75-685
Fax: 52-5-207-8938

American Consulate General –
    Guadalajara Commercial Section
Progresso 175
Guadalajara, Jal., Mexico
P.O. Box 3088
Laredo, TX 78044-3088
Tel: 52-3-625-2998
Telex: 068-2-860
Fax: 52-36-26-6549

American Consulate General –
    Monterrey Commercial Section
Avenida Constitucion
411 Poniente, 64000
Monterrey, N.L., Mexico
P.O. Box 3098
Laredo, TX 78044-3098
Tel: 52-83-45-2120
Telex: 0382853
Fax: 52-83-41-5172

American Chamber of Commerce of Mexico –
    Mexico City
Lucerna 78-4
Mexico 6, D.F., Mexico
Tel: 905-566-0866

American Chamber of Commerce in Mexico –
    Guadalajara
Avenida 16 de Septiembre 730-1209
Guadalajara, Jalisco, Mexico
Tel: 52-36-146-300

American Chamber of Commerce in Mexico – Monterrey
Picacho 760, Despachos 4 y 6
Colonia Obispado
Monterrey, N.L., Mexico
Tel: 52-82-848-4749

Embassy of Mexico Commercial Section
1911 Pennsylvania Avenue, N.W.
Washington, DC 20006
Tel: 202-728-1600
Telex: 90 4307 OCCMEX

Morocco

American Consulate General
Commercial Section – Casablanca
8 Boulevard Moulay Youssef
Casablanca, Morocco
APO AE 09718
Tel: 212-26-45-50
Fax: 212-22-02-59

American Embassy Commercial Section
2 Avenue de Marrakech
Rabat, Morocco
APO AE 09718
Tel: 212-7-622-65
Telex: 31005
Fax: 212-7-656-61

Netherlands

American Embassy Commercial Section
Lange Voorhout 102
The Hague, the Netherlands
APO AE 09715
Tel: 31-70-310-9417
Telex: (044) 31016
Fax: 31-70-363-29-85

American Consulate General –
Amsterdam Commercial Section
Museumplein 19
Amsterdam, the Netherlands
APO AE 09715
Tel: 31-20-664-8111
Telex: 044-16176 CGUSA NL
Fax: 31-20-675-28-56

The American Chamber of Commerce in the Netherlands
Carnegieplein 5
2517 KJ The Hague, the Netherlands
Tel: 31-70-65-98-08
Fax: 31-70-64-69-92

Embassy of the Netherlands Commercial Section
4200 Linnean Avenue, N.W.
Washington, DC 20008
Tel: 202-244-5300

New Zealand

American Consulate General
Auckland Commercial Section
4th Floor, Yorkshire General Building
Auckland, New Zealand
FPO AP 96531
Tel: 64-9-303-2038
Fax: 64-9-366-0870

American Embassy Commercial Section
29 Fitzherbert Terrace
Thorndon
Wellington, New Zealand
FPO AP 96531
Tel: 64-4-722-068
Telex: NZ 3305
Fax: 64-4-781-701

The American Chamber of Commerce in New Zealand
P.O. Box 3408
Wellington, New Zealand
Tel: 64-4-727-549

Embassy of New Zealand Commercial Section
37 Observatory Circle, N.W.
Washington, DC 20008
Tel: 202-328-4800
Telex: 8 9526 TOTARA WSH

Nigeria

American Embassy Commercial Section
2 Eleke Crescent
P.O. Box 554
Lagos, Nigeria
c/o U.S. Department of State (Lagos)
Washington, DC 20521-8300
Tel: 234-1-616-477
Telex: 21670 USEMBLA NG
Fax: 234-1-619-856

American Consulate General –
Kaduna Commercial Section
2 Maska Road
P.O. Box 170
Kaduna, Nigeria
c/o U.S. Department of State (Kaduna)
Washington, DC 20521-2260
Tel: 234-62-201070

Embassy of Nigeria Commercial Section
2201 M Street, N.W.
Washington, DC 20037
Tel: 202-822-1500
Telex: 89 2311 NIGERIAN WSH

Norway

American Embassy Commercial Section
Drammensveien 18
Oslo 2, Norway
APO AE 09707
Tel: 47-2-44-85-50
Telex: 18470
Fax: 47-2-55-88-03

Embassy of Norway Commercial Section
2720 34th Street, N.W.
Washington, DC 20008
Tel: 333-6000
Telex: 89-2374 NORAMB WSH

Pakistan

American Consulate General – Karachi, Pakistan
8 Abdullah Harroon Road
Karachi, Pakistan
APO AE 09814
Tel: 92-21-518-180
Telex: 82-02-611
Fax: 92-21-511-381

American Embassy Econ/Commercial Section
Diplomatic Enclave, Ramna 5
P.O. Box 1048
Islamabad, Pakistan
Tel: 92-51-826-161
Telex: 952-05-864

American Consulate General –
Lahore Commercial Section
50 Zafar Ali Road
Gulberg 5
Lahore, Pakistan
APO AE 09812
Tel: 92-42-871-406

American Chamber of Commerce in Pakistan
3rd Floor, Shaheen Commercial Complex
G.P.O. 1322
M.R. Kayani Road
Karachi, Pakistan
Tel: 92-21-526-436

Embassy of Pakistan Commercial Section
2315 Massachusetts Avenue, N.W.
Washington, DC 20008
Tel: 202-939-6200
Telex: 89-2348 PARAP WSH

Panama

American Embassy Commercial Section
Avenida Balboa y Calle 38
Apartado 6959
Panama 5, Republic of Panama
Box E
APO AA 34002
Tel: 507-27-1777
Fax: 507-27-1713

American Chamber of Commerce & Industry of Panama
Apartado 168, Estafeta Balboa
Panama 1, Republic of Panama
Tel: 507-693-881

Embassy of Panama Commercial Section
2862 McGill Terrace, N.W.
Washington, DC 20008
Tel: 202-483-1407

Peru

American Embassy Commercial Section
P.O. Box 1995
Lima 100 Peru
APO AA 34031
Tel: 51-14-33-0555
Telex: 25028PE USCOMATT
Fax: 51-14-33-4687

American Chamber of Commerce in Peru
Avenida Ricardo Palma 836, Miraflores
Lima 18, Peru
Tel: 51-14-47-9349
Telex: 21165 BANKAMER PE

Embassy of Peru Commercial Section
1700 Massachusetts Avenue, N.W.
Washington, DC 20036
Tel: 202-833-9860
Telex: 197675 LEPRU UT

Philippines

American Embassy Commercial Section
395 Buendia Avenue
Extension Makati
Manila, the Philippines
APO AP 96440
Tel: 63-2-818-6674
Telex: 66887 COSEC PN
Fax: 63-2-818-2684

American Chamber of Commerce in the Philippines
P.O. Box 1578, MCC
Manila, the Philippines
Tel: 63-2-818-7911
Fax: 63-2-816-6359

Embassy of the Philippines Commercial Section
1617 Massachusetts Avenue, N.W.
Washington, DC 20036
Tel: 202-483-1414
Telex: 44 0059 AMBPHIL

Poland

American Embassy Commercial Section
Ulica Wiejska 20
Warsaw, Poland
APO AE 09213 (WAW)
Tel: 48-22-21-45-15
Telex: 813934
Fax: 48-22-21-63-27

Portugal

American Embassy Commercial Section
Avenida das Forcas Armadas
1600 Lisbon, Portugal
APO AE 09726
Tel: 351-1-726-6600
Telex: 12528 AMEMB
Fax: 351-1-726-8914

American Chamber of Commerce in Portugal
Rue de D. Estafania 155, 5 Esq.
Lisbon 1000, Portugal
Tel: 351-1-572-561
Telex: 42356 AMCHAM P

Embassy of Portugal Commercial Section
1914 Connecticut Avenue, N.W.
Washington, DC 20008
Tel: 202-328-8610
Telex: 64399 PORT EMB P

Romania

American Embassy Commercial Section
Strada Tudor Arghezi 7-9
Bucharest, Romania
APO AE 09213 (BUCH)
Tel: 40-0-10-40-40
Telex: 11416
Fax: 40-0-11-84-47

Saudi Arabia

American Embassy Commercial Section
Collector Road M, Riyadh Diplomatic Quarter
Riyadh, Saudi Arabia
APO AE 09803
Tel: 966-1-488-3800
Telex: 406866 AMEMB SJ
Fax: 966-1-488-3237

American Consulate General –
   Dhahran Commercial Section
Between Aramco Headquarters and
   Dhahran International Airport
P.O. Box 81, Dhahran Airport
Dhahran, Saudi Arabia
APO AE 09808
Tel: 966-3-8913200
Telex: 601925 AMCON SJ
Fax: 966-3-891-8332

American Consulate General –
   Jeddah Commercial Section
Palestine Road, Ruwais
P.O. Box 149
Jeddah, Saudi Arabia
APO AE 09811
Tel: 966-2-667-0040
Telex: 401459 AMEMB SJ
Fax: 966-2-665-8106

American Businessmen's Association – Eastern Province
c/o ARAMCO
PO Box 1255
Dharain, Saudi Arabia 31311
Tel: 966-3-875-3138
Fax: 966-3-876-1018

The American Businessmen of Jeddah, Saudi Arabia
P.O. Box 4553
Jeddah, Saudi Arabia
Tel: 966-2-682-2201
Fax: 966-2-651-6260

Embassy of Saudi Arabia Commercial Section
601 New Hampshire Avenue, N.W.
Washington, DC 20037
Tel: 202-337-4088

Singapore

American Embassy Commercial Section
One Colombo Court #05-12
Singapore 0617
FPO AP 96534
Tel: 65-338-9722
Fax: 65-338-5010

American Business Council of Singapore
354 Orchard Road, #10-12 Shaw House
Singapore 0923
Tel: 65-235-0077
Fax: 65-732-5917

Embassy of Singapore Commercial Section
1824 R Street, N.W.
Washington, DC 20009
Tel: 202-667-7555
Telex: 440024 SING EMB

South Africa

American Consulate General –
   Johannesburg Commercial Section
Kine Center, 11th Floor
Commissioner and Kruis Streets
P.O. Box 2155
Johannesburg, South Africa
Tel: 27-11-331-3937
Telex: 8-3780
Fax: 27-11-331-6178

American Chamber of Commerce in South Africa
P.O. Box 62280
Johannesburg, South Africa
Tel: 27-11-788-0265

Embassy of South Africa Commercial Section
3051 Massachusetts Avenue, N.W.
Washington, DC 20016
Tel: 202-232-4400

Spain

American Embassy Commercial Section
Serrano 75
Madrid, Spain
APO AE 09642
Tel: 34-1-577-4000
Telex: 27763
Fax: 34-1-575-8655

American Consulate General –
   Barcelona Commercial Section
Via Layetana
Barcelona, Spain
Box 5
APO AE 09642
Tel: 34-3-319-9550
Telex: 52672
Fax: 34-3-319-5621

American Chamber of Commerce in Spain
Avenida Diagonal 477, Box 8
Barcelona 36, Spain
Tel: 34-3-319-9550
Fax: 34-3-321-8197

Embassy of Spain Commercial Section
2700 15th Street, N.W.
Washington, DC 20009
Tel: 202-265-8600
Telex: 89 2747 SPAIN WSH

Sweden

American Embassy Commercial Section
Strandvagen 101
c/o U.S. Department of State (Stockholm)
Washington, DC 20521-5750
Tel: 46-8-783-5346
Telex: 12060
Fax: 46-8-660-9181

Embassy of Sweden Commercial Section
600 New Hampshire Avenue, N.W.
Washington, DC 20037
Tel: 202-944-5600
Telex: 89 2724 SVENSK WSH

Switzerland

American Embassy Commercial Section
Jubilaeumstrasse 93
3005 Bern, Switzerland
c/o U.S. Department of State (Bern)
Washington, DC 20521-5110
Tel: 41-31-437-341
Telex: (845) 912603
Fax: 41-31-437336

Swiss American Chamber of Commerce
Talacker 41
8001 Zurich, Switzerland
Tel: 41-1-211-2454
Fax: 41-1-211-9572

Embassy of Switzerland Commercial Section
2900 Cathedral Avenue, N.W.
Washington, DC 20008
Tel: 202-745-7900
Telex: 64180 AMSWIS

Thailand

American Embassy Commercial Section
95 Wireless Road
Bangkok, Thailand
APO AP 96546
Tel: 66-2-253-4920
Fax: 66-2-255-9215

American Chamber of Commerce in Thailand
7th Floor, Kian Gwan Building
140 Wireless Road
PO Box 11-1095
Bangkok, Thailand
Tel: 66-2-251-9266
Fax: 66-2-255-2454

Embassy of Thailand Commercial Section
2300 Kalorama Road, N.W.
Washington, DC 20008
Tel: 202-467-6790
Telex: 248 275 TTHAI UR

Trinidad and Tobago

American Embassy Commercial Section
15 Queen's Park West
P.O. Box 752
Port-of-Spain, Trinidad and Tobago
c/o U.S. Department of State (Port-of-Spain)
Washington, DC 20521-3410
Tel: 809-622-6371
Telex: 22230 AMEMB POS
Fax: 809-622-9583

Embassy of Trinidad and Tobago Commercial Section
1708 Massachusetts Avenue, N.W.
Washington, DC 20036
Tel: 202-467-6490
Telex: 64321 TRINOFF

Turkey

American Embassy Commercial Section
110 Ataturk Boulevard
Ankara, Turkey
APO AE 09822
Tel: 90-4-167-0949
Telex: 43144 USIA TR
Fax: 90-4-167-1366

American Consulate General –
    Istanbal Commercial Section
104-108 Mesrutiyet Caddesi
Tepebasl
Istanbul, Turkey
APO AE 09827
Tel: 90-1-151-1651
Telex: 24306 USIC TR
Fax: 90-1-152-2417

Embassy of Turkey Commercial Section
2523 Massachusetts Avenue, N.W.
Washington, DC 20008
Tel: 202-483-5366
Telex: 904143 TURKFIN

Union of Soviet Socialist Republics

U.S. Commercial Office – Moscow
Ulitsa Chaykovskogo 15
Moscow, U.S.S.R.
APO AE 09721
Tel: 7-096-255-4848
Telex: 413-205 USCO SU
Fax: 7-095-230-2101

U.S.S.R. Trade Representative in the U.S.A.
2001 Connecticut Avenue, N.W.
Washington, DC 20008
Tel: 202-234-8304

United Arab Emirates

American Embassy Commercial Section
Blue Tower Building, 8th Floor
Shaikh Khalifa Bin Zayed Street
Abu Dhabi, U.A.E.
c/o U.S. Department of State (Abu Dhabi)
Washington, DC 20521-6010
Tel: 971-2-345545
Telex: 22229 AMEMBY EM
Fax: 971-2-331-374

American Consulate General – Dubai
   Commercial Section
Dubai International Trade Center
P.O. Box 9343
Dubai, U.A.E.
c/o U.S. Department of State (Dubai)
Washington, DC 20521-6020
Tel: 971-4-378-584
Telex: 98346031 BACCUS EM
Fax: 971-4-375-121

Embassy of the United Arab Emirates
   Commercial Section
600 New Hampshire Avenue, N.W., Suite 740
Washington, DC 20037
Tel: 202-338-6500

United Kingdom

American Embassy Commercial Section
24/31 Grosvenor Square
London W. 1A 1AE, England
Box 40
FPO AE 09498
Tel: 44-71-499-9000
Telex: 266777
Fax: 44-71-491-4022

American Chamber of Commerce in the United Kingdom
75 Brook Street
London WIY 2EB, England
Tel: 44-71-493-0381
Telex: 23675 AMCHAM
Fax: 44-71-493-2394

Embassy of Great Britain Commercial Section
3100 Massachusetts Avenue, N.W.
Washington, DC 20008
Tel: 202-462-1340
Telex: 892384 WSH
        892380 WSH

Venezuela

American Embassy Commercial Section
Avenida Francisco de Mirandola and
   Avenida Principal de la Floresta
P.O. Box 62291
Caracas 1060 A, Venezuela
APO AA 34047
Tel: 58-2-285-3111
Telex: 25501 AMEMB VE
Fax: 58-2-285-0336

Venezuelan-American Chamber of Commerce
   and Industry
Torre Credival, Piso 10
2da Avenida de Campo Alegre, Apartado 5181
Caracas 1010A, Venezuela
Tel: 58-2-32-49-76
Fax: 58-2-32-07-64

Embassy of Venezuela Commercial Section
1099 30th Street, N.W.
Washington, DC 20007
Tel: 202-342-2214

Yugoslavia

American Embassy Commercial Section
Kneza Milosa 50
Belgrade, Yugoslavia
APO AE 09213-5070
Tel: 38-11-645-655
Telex: 11529
Fax: 38-11-645-096

American Consulate General –
   Zagreb Commercial Section
Brace Kavurica 2
Zagreb, Yugoslavia
APO AE 09213-5080
Tel: 38-41-444-800
Telex: 21180
Fax: 38-41-440-235

Taiwan*

American Chamber of Commerce in Taiwan
Rm 1012, Chia Hsin Building Annex
96 Chung Shan Road, Section 2
P.O. Box 17-277
Taipei, Taiwan
Tel: 886-2-551-2515
Fax: 886-2-542-3376

American Institute in Taiwan (AIT – WashDC)
1700 North Moore Street
17th Floor
Arlington, VA 22209
Tel: 703-525-8474

American Institute in Taiwan (AIT – Taipei)
American Trade Center
Room 3207, International Trade Building
Taipei World Trade Center
333 Keelung Road Section 1
Taipei 10548, Taiwan
Tel: 886-2-720-1550
Telex: 23890 USTRADE
Fax: 886-2-757-7162

Coordination Council for North American Affairs
Economic Division
4301 Connecticut Avenue, N.W.
Suite 420
Washington, DC 20008
Tel: 202-686-6400
Telex: 440292 SINOECO

*Although the United States does not maintain official relations with Taiwan (Republic of China), unofficial commercial relations are maintained through the American Institute in Taiwan and the Coordination Council for North American Affairs.

Selected bibliography

The following publications are additional sources of information recommended to American exporters by U.S. Department of Commerce district offices.

AgExporter – Monthly magazine published by U.S. Department of Agriculture's Foreign Agricultural Service (FAS). Available from Trade Assistance and Planning Office, Foreign Agricultural Service, U.S. Department of Agriculture, Washington, DC 20250; telephone 703-756-6001. Annual subscription cost: $14.

AID Procurement Information Bulletin – Advertises notices of intended procurement of AID-financed commodities. Available from USAID's Office of Small and Disadvantaged Business Utilization/Minority Resource Center, Washington, DC 20523-1414; telephone 703-875-1551. Subscription cost: free.

American Export Register – Published annually, this is a two-volume directory of 38,000 U.S. exporters. Available from Thomas International Publishing Company, Inc., One Penn Plaza, New York, NY 10119; telephone 212-290-7343. Cost: $120.

(Annual) National Trade Estimate Report on Foreign Trade Barriers – U.S. Trade Representative (USTR), 600 17th Street, N.W., Washington, DC 20506; telephone 202-395-3230. Cost: free.

Background Notes – Prepared by the Department of State to provide economic and trade information on major trading partners. Available by set or by subscription from Superintendent of Documents, U.S. Government Printing Office, Washington, DC 20402; telephone 202-783-3238. Price of the set is $58 (GPO: 844-000-91214-7); if binder is desired, $4.75 extra. Annual subscription cost: $18 (GPO: 844-002-00000-9).

Bureau of the Census Foreign Trade Report: Annual U.S. Exports, Harmonized Schedule B Commodity by Country, FT 447 – Available from Superintendent of Documents, U.S. Government Printing Office, Washington, DC 20402; telephone 202-783-3238.

Bureau of the Census Foreign Trade Report: Monthly Exports and Imports – SITC Commodity by Country, FT 925. Available from Superintendent of Documents, U.S. Government Printing Office, Washington, DC 20402; telephone 202-783-3238. Annual subscription cost: $139 (GPO: 703-091-00000-8).

Business America – Biweekly publication of the U.S. Department of Commerce. Available from Superintendent of Documents, U.S. Government Printing Office, Washington, DC 20402; telephone 202-783-3238. Annual subscription cost: $49 (GPO: 703-011-00000-4).

Commerce Business Daily – Available by subscription and on line (electronically). Subscription cost: first class, $260 annually or $130 for 6 months; second class, $208 annually or $104 for 6 months. (GPO:703-013-00000-7.) Contact Superintendent of Documents, U.S. Government Printing Office, Washington, DC 20402; telephone 202-783-3238.

Country Marketing Plans (CMPs) – Prepared annually by the commercial sections of the American embassies for the U.S. Department of Commerce's U.S. and Foreign Commercial Service, covering 67 individual countries. Available at a cost of $10 per report through the Commercial Information Management System (CIMS) and also through the National Trade Data Bank (NTDB) electronic data bases operated and managed by the U.S. Department of Commerce. Contact the local district office, or telephone 202-377-4767.

Do's and Taboos Around the World – By Roger E. Axtell. John Wiley & Sons, New York, 1990.

Do's and Taboos of Hosting International Visitors – By Roger E. Axtell. John Wiley & Sons, New York, 1990.

Export Administration Regulations – Available by subscription from the Superintendent of Documents, U.S. Government Printing Office, Washington, DC 20401; telephone 202-275-2091. Subscription forms may be obtained from the nearest Department of Commerce district office or from the Office of Export Licensing, Exporter Counseling Division, Room 1099D, U.S. Department of Commerce, Washington DC 20230; telephone 202-377-4811.

The Exporter – Monthly magazine. Write to 6 West 37th Street, New York, NY 10018; telephone 212-563-2772. Annual subscription cost: $95.

Exporters Directory/U.S. Buying Guide – Journal of Commerce, 110 Wall Street, New York, NY 10005; telephone 212-425-1616.

Exporter's Encyclopedia – Annual handbook covering more than 220 world markets. Available from Dun's Marketing Services, 3 Sylvan Way, Parsippany, NJ 07054-3896; telephone 800-526-0651 or 201-605-6749. Annual cost: $535.

Exporting: From Start to Finance – By L. Fargo Wells and Karin B. Dulat. Liberty House, Blue Ridge Summit, PA 17214-9988; telephone 800-822-8158. Cost: $39.95.

Exportise – A 250-page source book. The Small Business Foundation of America, 20 Park Plaza, Suite 438, Boston, MA 02116; telephone 617-350-5096. Cost: $29.50.

Export Sales and Marketing Manual – By John R. Jagoe. Export USA Publications, 4141 Parklawn Avenue South, Minneapolis, MN 55435; telephone 800-876-0624. Updated quarterly. Cost: $295.

Export Shipping Manual – A three-volume looseleaf reference, updated weekly. Available from Bureau of National Affairs, Inc., Distribution Center, Keywest Avenue, Rockville, MD 20850; telephone 800-372-1033 or 202-452-4200. Cost: $524.

Export Today – Bimonthly magazine. P.O. Box 28189, Washington, DC 20038; telephone 202-737-1060.

Financing and Insuring Exports: A User's Guide to Eximbank and FCIA Programs – Eximbank Public Affairs Office, 811 Vermont Avenue, N.W., Washington, DC 20571; telephone 800-424-5401. Cost: $50.

FINDEX: The Directory of Market Research Reports, Studies and Surveys – Contains more than 10,000 listings of reports, studies, and surveys. Available from Cambridge Information Group, 7200 Wisconsin Avenue, Bethesda, MD 20814; telephone 800-227-3052 or 301-961-6750. Cost (1991 edition): $325 (ISBN: 0-942189-03-5).

Foreign Agriculture – Annual factbook with agricultural profiles of 65 countries. Available from Trade Assistance and Planning Office, Foreign Agricultural Service, U.S. Department of Agriculture, Washington, DC 20250; telephone 703-756-6001. Cost: $12.

Foreign Economic Trends (FET) – Published by the U.S. Department of Commerce, each FET covers a single country. Available from Superintendent of Documents, U.S. Government Printing Office, Washington, DC 20402; telephone 202-783-3238. Annual subscription cost: $50 (GPO:803-006-00000-8).

F&S Index International (monthly) and **F&S Index Europe** (quarterly) – Provide two-line summaries of business and trade journal articles alphabetically and by SIC code. Predicasts, 10001 Cedar Avenue, Cleveland, OH 44106; telephone 800-321-6388. Subscription cost: $800 a year each.

Global Trade Magazine – Monthly. North American Publishing Company, 401 North Broad Street, Philadelphia, PA 19108; telephone 215-238-5300. Annual subscription cost: $45.

Glossary of International Terms – International Trade Institute, Inc., 5055 N. Main Street, Dayton, OH 45415; telephone 800-543-2453.

Going International – By Lennie Copeland and Lewis Griggs. Random House, 201 East 50th Street, New York, NY 10022; telephone 800-733-3000. Cost: $34.95.

Guide to Distributorship Agreements – Publication 441, ICC Publishing Corporation, 156 Fifth Avenue, Suite 820, New York, NY 10010; telephone 212-206-1150. Cost: $25.95.

Guide to Documentary Credit Operations – Publication 415, ICC Publishing Corporation, 156 Fifth Avenue, Suite 820, New York, NY 10010; telephone 212-206-1150. Cost: $18.95.

A Guide to Export Documentation – By Donald E. Ewert, International Trade Institute, 5055 N. Main Street, Dayton, OH 45415; telephone 800-543-2453. Cost: $44.50.

A Guide to International Shipping – By Donald E. Ewert, International Trade Institute, 5055 N. Main Street, Dayton, OH 45415; telephone 800-543-2453. Cost: $44.50.

A Guide to Selling Your Service Overseas – Northern California District Export Council (NORCALDEC), 450 Golden Gate Avenue, Box 36013, San Francisco, CA 94102. Cost: $17.

Incoterms 1990 – Publication 460, ICC Publishing Corporation, 156 Fifth Avenue, Suite 820, New York, NY 10010; telephone 212-206-1150. Cost: $23.95.

Industry Sector Analyses – Prepared annually by the commercial sections of American embassies for the U.S. Department of Commerce's U.S. and Foreign Commercial Service. Covers 67 individual countries. Available as printed articles at $10 per report through the Commercial Information Management System (CIMS) and also the National Trade Data Bank (NTDB) electronic data bases. Contact the local district office or branch; or telephone 202-377-4767.

International Trade Reporter: Current Reports – Weekly newsletter. Available from Bureau of National Affairs, Inc., Distribution Center, Key West Avenue, Rockville, MD 20850; telephone 800-372-1033. Annual subscription cost: $668.

Journal of Commerce – Daily newspaper. 110 Wall Street, New York, NY 10005; telephone 212-425-1616.

Key Officers of Foreign Service Posts – Available from the Superintendent of Documents, U.S. Government Printing Office, Washington, DC 20402-9371; telephone 202-783-3238. Issued three times per year. Annual cost: $5.

North American International Business Magazine – Monthly. Write to 401 Theodore Fremd Avenue, Rye, NY 10580; telephone 800-274-8187. Annual subscription cost: $59.97.

Overseas Business Reports – U.S. Department of Commerce. Provide background statistics and information on specific countries. Available from Superintendent of Documents, U.S. Government Printing Office, Washington, DC 20402; telephone 202-783-3238. Annual subscription cost: $14 (GPO: 803-007-00000-4).

Statesman's Year Book – Annual. St. Martin's Press, New York, NY.

Trade Policies and Opportunities for U.S. Farm Products – Covers 50 countries and the trading blocs of the European Community and the Gulf Cooperative Council. Available from Trade Assistance and Planning Office, Foreign Agricultural Service, U.S. Department of Agriculture, Washington, DC 20250; telephone 703-756-6001. Cost: free.

The Traveler's Guide to Asian Customs and Manners – By Kevin Chambers. Simon and Schuster, 1230 Avenue of the Americas, Dept. MBA, New York, NY 10020.

The Traveler's Guide to European Customs and Manners – By Nancy L. Braganti and Elizabeth Divine. Simon and Schuster, 1230 Avenue of the Americas, Dept. MBA, New York, NY 10020.

UN Statistical Yearbook – Economic and social data for 220 countries and territories. Available from UN Publications, Room DC2-0853, New York, NY 10017; telephone 212-963-8302. Cost: $85.

U.S. Industrial Outlook – Annual. Available from Superintendent of Documents, U.S. Government Printing Office, Washington, DC 20402; telephone 202-783-3238. Cost of the 1991 edition: $28 (GPO: 003-009-00586-8).

Worldcasts – An eight-volume annual series of 60,000 abstracted forecasts for products and markets outside the United States (150 countries), arranged by modified SIC codes in four product volumes and four regional volumes. Cost: complete annual set, $1,300; single volumes, $450 each; product set and regional set, $900 each. Contact Predicasts, 11001 Cedar Avenue, Cleveland, OH 44106; telephone 800-321-6388 or 216-795-3000.

World Class Negotiating: Dealmaking in the Global Marketplace – By Donald W. Hendon and Rebecca A. Hendon. John Wiley & Sons, New York, NY.

World Factbook – Produced annually by the Central Intelligence Agency. Available from Superintendent of Documents, U.S. Government Printing Office, Washington, DC 20402; telephone 202-783-3238. Cost: $23 (GPO:041-015-00169-8).

Notes